READERS' GUIDES TO ESSEN

CONSULTANT EDITOR: NICOLAS

Published

Thomas P. Adler	Tennesse[e] Hot Tin [Roof]/... Jacobean
Pascale Aebischer	
Lucie Armitt	George Eliot: *Adam Bede/The Mill on the Floss/Middlemarch*
Simon Avery	Thomas Hardy: *The Mayor of Casterbridge/Jude the Obscure*
Paul Baines	Daniel Defoe: *Robinson Crusoe/Moll Flanders*
Annika Bautz	Jane Austen: *Sense and Sensibility/Pride and Prejudice/Emma*
Matthew Beedham	The Novels of Kazuo Ishiguro
Richard Beynon	D. H. Lawrence: *The Rainbow/Women in Love*
Peter Boxall	Samuel Beckett: *Waiting for Godot/Endgame*
Claire Brennan	The Poetry of Sylvia Plath
Susan Bruce	Shakespeare: *King Lear*
Sandie Byrne	Jane Austen: *Mansfield Park*
Alison Chapman	Elizabeth Gaskell: *Mary Barton/North and South*
Peter Childs	The Fiction of Ian McEwan
Christine Clegg	Vladimir Nabokov: *Lolita*
John Coyle	James Joyce: *Ulysses/A Portrait of the Artist as a Young Man*
Martin Coyle	Shakespeare: *Richard II*
Sarah Dewar-Watson	Tragedy
Justin D. Edwards	Postcolonial Literature
Michael Faherty	The Poetry of W. B. Yeats
Sarah Gamble	The Fiction of Angela Carter
Jodi-Anne George	*Beowulf*
Jodi-Anne George	Chaucer: The General Prologue to *The Canterbury Tales*
Jane Goldman	Virginia Woolf: *To the Lighthouse/The Waves*
Huw Griffiths	Shakespeare: *Hamlet*
Vanessa Guignery	The Fiction of Julian Barnes
Louisa Hadley	The Fiction of A. S. Byatt
Sarah Haggarty and Jon Mee	William Blake: *Songs of Innocence and Experience*
Geoffrey Harvey	Thomas Hardy: *Tess of the d'Urbervilles*
Paul Hendon	The Poetry of W. H. Auden
Terry Hodgson	The Plays of Tom Stoppard for Stage, Radio, TV and Film
William Hughes	Bram Stoker: *Dracula*
Stuart Hutchinson	Mark Twain: *Tom Sawyer/Huckleberry Finn*
Stuart Hutchinson	Edith Wharton: *The House of Mirth/The Custom of the Country*
Betty Jay	E. M. Forster: *A Passage to India*
Aaron Kelly	Twentieth-Century Irish Literature
Elmer Kennedy-Andrews	Nathaniel Hawthorne: *The Scarlet Letter*
Elmer Kennedy-Andrews	The Poetry of Seamus Heaney
Daniel Lea	George Orwell: *Animal Farm/Nineteen Eighty-Four*
Rachel Lister	Alice Walker: *The Color Purple*
Sara Lodge	Charlotte Brontë: *Jane Eyre*
Philippa Lyon	Twentieth-Century War Poetry
Merja Makinen	The Novels of Jeanette Winterson
Matt McGuire	Contemporary Scottish Literature
Timothy Miln[er]	
Jago Morriso[n]	
Merritt Mose	

Carl Plasa	Tony Morrison: *Beloved*
Carl Plasa	Jean Rhys: *Wide Sargasso Sea*
Nicholas Potter	Shakespeare: *Antony and Cleopatra*
Nicholas Potter	Shakespeare: *Othello*
Nicholas Potter	Shakespeare's Late Plays: *Pericles/Cymbeline/The Winter's Tale/The Tempest*
Steven Price	The Plays, Screenplays and Films of David Mamet
Berthold Schoene-Harwood	Mary Shelley: *Frankenstein*
Nicholas Seager	The Rise of the Novel
Nick Selby	T. S. Eliot: *The Waste Land*
Nick Selby	Herman Melville: *Moby Dick*
Nick Selby	The Poetry of Walt Whitman
David Smale	Salman Rushdie: *Midnight's Children/The Satanic Verses*
Patsy Stoneman	Emily Brontë: *Wuthering Heights*
Susie Thomas	Hanif Kureishi
Nicolas Tredell	Joseph Conrad: *Heart of Darkness*
Nicolas Tredell	Charles Dickens: *Great Expectations*
Nicolas Tredell	William Faulkner: *The Sound and the Fury/As I Lay Dying*
Nicolas Tredell	F. Scott Fitzgerald: *The Great Gatsby*
Nicolas Tredell	Shakespeare: *A Midsummer Night's Dream*
Nicolas Tredell	Shakespeare: *Macbeth*
Nicolas Tredell	The Fiction of Martin Amis
Matthew Woodcock	Shakespeare: *Henry V*
Gillian Woods	Shakespeare: *Romeo and Juliet*
Angela Wright	Gothic Fiction

Forthcoming

Brian Baker	Science Fiction
Nick Bentley	Contemporary British Fiction
Sandie Byrne	The Poetry of Ted Hughes
Sarah Davison	Modernist Literature
Alan Gibbs	Jewish-American Literature since 1945
Keith Hughes	African-American Literature
Wendy Knepper	Caribbean Literature
Britta Martens	The Poetry of Robert Browning
Pat Pinsent and Clare Walsh	Children's Literature
Jane Poyner	The Fiction of J. M. Coetzee
Nicolas Tredell	Shakespeare: The Tragedies
Clare Wallace	Contemporary British Drama
Kate Watson	Crime and Detective Fiction
David Wheatley	Contemporary British Poetry
Martin Willis	Literature and Science
Andrew Wylie	The Plays of Harold Pinter

**Readers' Guides to Essential Criticism
Series Standing Order ISBN 978–1–403–90108–8**
(*outside North America only*)

You can receive future titles in this series as they are published by placing a standing order. Please contact your bookseller or, in the case of difficulty, write to us at the address below with your name and address, the title of the series and the ISBN quoted above.

Customer Services Department, Macmillan Distribution Ltd, Houndmills, Basingstoke, Hampshire, RG21 6XS, UK

Tragedy

SARAH DEWAR-WATSON

Consultant Editor: Nicolas Tredell

palgrave
macmillan

© Sarah Dewar-Watson 2014

All rights reserved. No reproduction, copy or transmission of this publication may be made without written permission.

No portion of this publication may be reproduced, copied or transmitted save with written permission or in accordance with the provisions of the Copyright, Designs and Patents Act 1988, or under the terms of any licence permitting limited copying issued by the Copyright Licensing Agency, Saffron House, 6–10 Kirby Street, London EC1N 8TS.

Any person who does any unauthorized act in relation to this publication may be liable to criminal prosecution and civil claims for damages.

The author has asserted her right to be identified as the author of this work in accordance with the Copyright, Designs and Patents Act 1988.

First published 2014 by
PALGRAVE MACMILLAN

Palgrave Macmillan in the UK is an imprint of Macmillan Publishers Limited, registered in England, company number 785998, of Houndmills, Basingstoke, Hampshire RG21 6XS.

Palgrave Macmillan in the US is a division of St Martin's Press LLC, 175 Fifth Avenue, New York, NY 10010.

Palgrave Macmillan is the global academic imprint of the above companies and has companies and representatives throughout the world.

Palgrave® and Macmillan® are registered trademarks in the United States, the United Kingdom, Europe and other countries.

ISBN 978–0–230–39260–1   hardback
ISBN 978–0–230–39258–8   paperback

This book is printed on paper suitable for recycling and made from fully managed and sustained forest sources. Logging, pulping and manufacturing processes are expected to conform to the environmental regulations of the country of origin.

A catalogue record for this book is available from the British Library.

A catalog record for this book is available from the Library of Congress.

Typeset by MPS Limited, Chennai, India.

Printed in China

WEST SUSSEX LIBRARY SERVICE	
201429139	
Askews & Holts	10-Jul-2014
809.9162	

For my mother

CONTENTS

Acknowledgements   xii

Introduction   1

Establishes that tragedy is a dynamic form which has attracted a wide range of thinkers from different disciplines. Examines the problem of attempting to define tragedy. Sketches out key questions posed by Raymond Williams and George Steiner about tragedy in the modern age.

CHAPTER ONE   7

The Gods

Examines the ritual origins of Greek tragedy in the festival of Dionysus. Looks at the foundational work of Gilbert Murray in identifying anthropological contexts for Greek tragedy. Notes that Murray's work has been superseded but interest in the ritual dimensions continues to inform the recent work of Rainer Friedrich, Simon Goldhill and others. Looks at René Girard's work on the *pharmakos* (or scapegoat). Discusses the importance of ritual motifs and structures outside Greek tragedy in Shakespeare and Yoruba drama. Introduces the paradox of Christian tragedy. Surveys recent criticism by Stephen Greenblatt and Robert N. Watson which suggests that the Reformation lent impetus to the emergence of early modern English tragedy.

CHAPTER TWO   26

The Chorus

Begins by reviewing the historical role of the chorus in Greek tragedy. Addresses the critical debate about the extent to which the chorus represents or embodies the audience's perspective. Considers the work of Jean-Pierre Vernant, who argues that the chorus is a projection of Athenian civic identity. Notes that other critics such as Helene Foley have stressed the 'otherness' of Attic choruses. Presents German aestheticist accounts of the chorus by, for example,

Schiller, Schlegel and Hegel. Engages with the problem of interpreting chorus in the modern age. Looks at ways in which the device of the chorus has been reconfigured in modern drama and the novel.

CHAPTER THREE   41

The Tragic Hero

Considers the centrality of the tragic hero in varying accounts of tragedy from the Greeks to the modern era. Focuses on A. C. Bradley's reading of tragedy as arising from the internal conflict of the protagonist. Compares Bernard Knox's account of the Sophoclean hero's isolation. Outlines work on early modern subjectivity by Dollimore and Belsey. Explores Padel's work on relationships between the tragic hero's interiority and physical self. Looks at constructions of 'nobility' in terms of both social rank and intensity of suffering. Recognises the role of the novel in promoting interest in the lives of bourgeois characters. Examines Miller's argument that suffering is democratised in the twentieth century through the work of Freud. Explicates the concept of *hamartia* (tragic guilt) and surveys arguments that the hero must play some part in his own downfall. Sees how critics have revised Bradley's reading of the fatal flaw as a character trait; Karl Jaspers and George Steiner see tragic guilt in existence itself.

CHAPTER FOUR   61

Tragic Women

Moves away from consideration of the 'hero' as a common gender noun to explore how the concept of tragic heroism might itself be gendered. Considers the prominent role played by female characters in tragedy and asks whether this is an expression of misogyny or a way of contesting it. Compares Froma Zeitlin and Linda Bamber's constructions of gender in tragedy in terms of Self/Other. Surveys feminist criticism of Shakespeare including Elaine Showalter's acclaimed account of Ophelia. Probes Nicole Loraux's argument that in the ancient Greek world, heroism is a male privilege. Juxtaposes this with critical work by Lisa Hopkins and Naomi Conn Liebler in which the term 'female hero' is preferred. Concludes with a detailed case study of Sophocles' *Antigone* as discussed by George Steiner, G. W. F. Hegel, Judith Butler and others.

CHAPTER FIVE 81
Tragic Dualities

Notes the centrality of conflict, in many different forms, as a recurring theme in many major accounts of tragedy. Cites the work of Jean-Pierre Vernant and Simon Goldhill on dialectical relationships between chorus and protagonist, city and individual. Identifies Sophocles' *Antigone* as a play that exemplifies important and recurring dialectics of male and female, private and public, human and divine. Revisits the dialectical relationship between Self and Other which was introduced in Chapter 4. Examines Edith Hall's suggestion that binary oppositions can be a mechanism for self-definition. Investigates Norman Rabkin's formulation of the principle of complementarity in Shakespeare's tragedies. Acknowledges the influence of nineteenth-century theories of conflict, particularly Darwin's work on evolution and Marx and Engel's account of social conflict as a process of history. Addresses Hegel's landmark account of *Antigone* as a play which stages the collision of equally justified rights. Concludes with Nietzsche's construction of tragedy as a synthesis of the Apollonian and the Dionysian.

CHAPTER SIX 96
Tragic Pleasure

Introduces the Aristotelian notion of tragic pleasure as an idea that embodies potential contradictions. Presents David Hume's account, which focuses on the fictional nature of tragedy. Considers Lionel Trilling's alternative view that tragedy helps us to develop immunity to suffering. Delineates the role of *catharsis* in Aristotle's definition of tragedy. Engages with problems of interpreting this term. Notes that critics have variously sought to explain this in terms of purgation, purification and, more recently, as 'intellectual clarification'. Investigates Boal's 'coercive system of tragedy' as one in which the spectator is purged of antisocial characteristics. Moves on to survey a wider category of emotional responses to tragedy and assesses the role of laughter in Jacobean tragedy. Looks at the staging of graphic scenes in the work of Sarah Kane and others which arouse powerful emotional responses and which deny the promise of consolation.

CHAPTER SEVEN   111
Tragedy and Form

Introduces the Aristotelian unities of Time, Place and Action. Notes that neoclassical commentators such as Sidney elaborate on the importance of unity in subsequent accounts. Assesses Schlegel's attack on French neoclassicists for their rigid concept of dramatic unity. Proceeds to look at tragedy in non-dramatic forms, for example, Milton's *Samson Agonistes* and the rise of the novel in the eighteenth and nineteenth centuries. Discusses Jeanette King's influential study of George Eliot, Henry James and Thomas Hardy as tragic novelists. Ends with Aldous Huxley's account which contrasts the 'chemically pure' form of tragedy with the more expansive form of the novel.

CHAPTER EIGHT   124
Modern Tragedy

Sets out George Steiner's view that the conditions of modernity are hostile to the production of tragedy. Contrasts this with Raymond Williams's view that these same conditions lend tragedy new meaning and relevance. Surveys the work of theorists such as Walter Benjamin, Max Horkheimer and Theodor Adorno which claim that twentieth-century culture as a whole is in decline. Investigates Nietzsche's claim that Euripides 'killed' tragedy. Engages with Steiner's assertion that modern culture can no longer refer to a 'higher order' of religion or mythology. Considers counter-arguments posed by Williams and Terry Eagleton that all suffering is potentially tragic. Closes by looking at Rita Felski's claim that it is more helpful to think not in terms of 'tragedy' but of 'the tragic'.

CHAPTER NINE   134
Postcolonial and Multiethnic Tragedy

Focuses on the reception of Greek tragedy in postcolonial contexts and the production of tragedy outside the Western world. Establishes the currency of postcolonial work on Shakespeare and relationships between ideas of race and gender that have been posited by Ania Loomba. Considers the reception of Greek tragedy in Ireland and the important work of Fiona Macintosh and Marianne McDonald in this area. Discusses adaptations of Greek tragedy in Africa by Athol Fugard and others. Explores Kevin Wetmore's model of Black Dionysus as a way of reading African tragedy intertextually. Concludes with a study of Yoruba tragedy as theorised by Wole Soyinka.

CONCLUSION 145
Recent and Future Directions

NOTES 150

BIBLIOGRAPHY 167

INDEX 175

ACKNOWLEDGEMENTS

I would like to express my warmest thanks to Sonya Barker and Nicolas Tredell at Palgrave Macmillan for all their support, guidance and encouragement throughout the development of this book. I would also like to thank Felicity Noble for her assistance during this process. I owe a debt of gratitude to the two external readers whose comments and suggestions have contributed significantly to the project as a whole. My thanks go also to Caroline Richards with whom it has been a pleasure to work in the final stages of editing. I would like to record my thanks to the staff at Western Bank Library at the University of Sheffield for all their assistance.

My family has helped and supported me in countless ways. I am grateful to Desiree Back for all her assistance. Above all, I would like to thank Andrew for all he has done during the writing of the book. Your anchor held.

Introduction

Tragedy is one of the oldest and most revered forms of literature in the Western world. The earliest extant tragedies date from Athens in the fifth century BC, and over the centuries tragedy has shown a tremendous capacity to reinvent itself for audiences at different times and in different places, often emerging at critical moments in the evolution of cultural, political and intellectual history. Critics in their numbers have recognised that tragedy is the form to which writers and their audiences turn again and again to explore the most important questions about human suffering in the most urgent and compelling way.

It is not only tragedy that is marked by its diversity; the field of critical literature is markedly diverse too. As a subject, tragedy has attracted the interest not only of literary scholars but of a wide range of thinkers from other fields: philosophy (especially aesthetics), anthropology, cultural history, gender studies, film studies, psychoanalysis and political theory to name but some. It is important to recognise that these responses to tragedy are not simply numerous and various, but that these different fields of enquiry richly inform one another. The field of tragic theory is essentially interdisciplinary, and, like tragedy itself, highly dynamic. As Arthur Miller acknowledges: 'There are whole libraries of books dealing with the nature of tragedy. That the subject is capable of interesting so many writers over the centuries is part proof that the idea of tragedy is constantly changing, and more, that it will never be finally defined.'[1]

The sheer diversity of Western tragedy poses a particular set of intellectual challenges for critics and theorists. Some critics have tried to find principles that are universal and transcendent. But it is very hard to say something that applies in equal measure (or even in any measure) to all tragedies. This is particularly true of definitions of tragedy: the more widely inclusive, the greater the risk of lapsing into redundancy of expression. As he picks through a series of possible definitions of tragedy, Terry Eagleton ruefully admits that 'The truth is that no definition of tragedy more elaborate than "very sad" has ever worked.'[2] Eagleton suggests we turn to Wittgenstein's philosophy of language for a possible solution to the problem of definition: 'In fact, tragedy would seem exemplary of Wittgenstein's "family resemblances," constituted as it is by a *combinatoire* of overlapping features rather than by a set of invariant forms or contents.'[3] In other words, we should think of tragedy in terms of the Venn diagram: there is a common set of characteristics but these can be configured in many different ways, and there is scope for leaving some of them out.

More recent generations of critics have tended not to think of tragedy in terms that are all-encompassing but instead have chosen to situate their readings of particular texts in relation to the specific cultural and historical contexts which give rise to their production and reception. In a reaction against A. C. Bradley's *Shakespearean Tragedy* (first published in 1904) – a classic work, but which now seems full of oversimplifications – Kenneth Muir refused to formulate a grand theory of Shakespearean tragedy. Instead of an overarching theme or pattern, he preferred to look at Shakespeare's plays sequentially, insisting on a sense of difference between the plays rather than their essential homogeneity: 'There is no such thing as Shakespearian Tragedy: there are only Shakespearian tragedies.'[4]

Of course there is no such thing as neutrality, and this statement too reveals its own critical bias. Muir's suggestion that Shakespeare's tragedies constitute a sequence implies its own theoretical position on the teleological development of Shakespeare's plays. In capitalising the term 'Shakespearian Tragedy', Muir is clearly poking fun at those who see the plays in monolithic terms. While Muir himself favours the plural 'tragedies' as an alternative to this monolithic singular, others have found it helpful to avoid the nominative 'tragedy' altogether and instead to think in terms of the more flexible, adjectival 'tragic'.[5] This is a point that receives further attention in Chapter 8.

Also in Chapter 8, we will see how many critics have asked whether 'tragedy' is a term – and indeed an art form – that has been, or should be, consigned to history. Has tragedy itself aged and decayed along with the amphitheatres of the ancient Greek world in which it was first staged? If we strip away the ritual functions of Attic tragedy, the dramatic devices of mask and chorus, and belief in the ancient Greek pantheon, what do we have left that we can recognisably describe as 'tragedy'?

It is a line of thought which led George Steiner in 1961 to proclaim the death of tragedy in an influential book of that name.[6] Somewhat paradoxically, Steiner's claim that tragedy has become outmoded and obsolete has been an important stimulus in generating a fruitful area of critical debate. Among the most crucial rebuttals of Steiner is Raymond Williams, whose book *Modern Tragedy* (1966), a Marxist account which was politically and intellectually radical at the time of writing, has now become a canonical work of criticism in its own right.[7]

But the Guide begins by looking at the roots of tragedy in the religious festivals of fifth-century BC Athens. Under the broad heading 'The Gods', Chapter 1 starts by tracing the religious contexts of Greek tragedy. Looking at the ritual origins of tragedy, the chapter also considers the importance of the motif of sacrifice as explored by René Girard.

The chapter introduces discussion of the Athenian *polis* (city-state) to which we will return in Chapter 2 ('The Chorus'). The chapter also considers the idea of Christian tragedy and asks whether this constitutes a contradiction in terms: some critics have argued that the redemptive ideology of Christian faith is essentially at odds with the tragic worldview, thus rendering tragedy obsolete in a Christian age. Recently, new historicist critics such as Michael Neill, Robert N. Watson and Stephen Greenblatt have sought to locate the rise of English Renaissance tragedy in relation to cultural conditions in the wake of the Reformation. We see how Protestant iconoclasm existed in tension with an apparent cultural nostalgia for old funerary rituals and ways of 'speaking with the dead'.

Chapter 2 begins, once again, with Jean-Pierre Vernant who influentially established a sociopolitical reading of Chorus as the voice of the Athenian citizen body. This has formed a touchpoint for contemporary critics such as Simon Goldhill, Froma Zeitlin and Edith Hall who have all been interested in Athenian discourses about identity and otherness. The central section of this chapter focuses on major nineteenth-century German theorists, and subsequent critical responses to them, particularly August Wilhelm von Schlegel's identification of the chorus as 'ideal spectator'. Schlegel's contemporary, Friedrich Schiller, describes the chorus as a non-naturalistic device by which tragedy separates itself from the world of reality: 'a living wall'. The chapter closes by drawing on recent work by Helene Foley and others which explores how the chorus has been reimagined and reconfigured outside Attic tragedy.

Chapter 3, 'The Tragic Hero', considers approaches to the concept of the tragic protagonist. In the first part of the chapter, we look at the way that many accounts of tragedy have centralised the figure of the tragic hero. Here we examine the concepts of selfhood and tragic agency, particularly in the work of Catherine Belsey and Jonathan Dollimore. Through the device of the soliloquy, Renaissance dramatists began to move away from the typology of medieval drama and to explore the idea of interiority. Also in this chapter, we examine the implications of Aristotle's claim that the tragic hero must be 'greater' than us. While it is not clear whether Aristotle means 'morally greater' or 'socially greater', later critics such as Sidney came to see tragedy as being almost by definition concerned with the fortunes of kings and emperors. In the twentieth century, Arthur Miller decisively moves away from this and declares a new democratic basis for tragedy: 'the common man is as apt a subject for tragedy in its highest sense as kings were'. The final part of the chapter considers critical views which have sought to emphasise not the protagonist's social rank, but his moral and/or psychological constitution (e.g., Bernard Knox in relation to Greek tragedy and A. C. Bradley in relation to Shakespearean tragedy). Each of these critics has been interested in extending the Aristotelian notion of *hamartia* in the context of character-based study. In such a reading, tragedy is about the particular limitations (and indeed excesses) of the individual, rather than about external agency in the form of the gods or fate. We also consider philosophical treatments of *hamartia* and tragic guilt in the work of Karl Jaspers, Søren Kierkegaard and G. W. F. Hegel.

Chapter 4, 'Tragic Women', begins by reviewing critical studies of the relationship between gender and genre. Linda Bamber has suggested that Shakespearean tragedy is characteristically male-dominated, while it is in the realm of comedy that female characters come to the fore. Meanwhile feminist critics such as Dympna Callaghan focus on the absence of women from Shakespearean drama: although the plays include female characters, these are not 'women' since the roles were played by boy actors. In the second part of the chapter, we consider the concept of heroism, and to what extent this concept can potentially be extended to female characters in tragedy. Critics such as Nicole Loraux have sought to constitute female tragic suffering as distinct from that of the male protagonist. She argues that tragedy frequently articulates ideas of female passivity in relation to images of sacrifice, suicide and martyrdom. Other critics such as Lisa Hopkins and Naomi Conn Liebler have sought to interrogate the notion of tragic heroism from a feminist point of view: if the very notion of heroism ultimately derives from a masculine, martial context, what does the term mean when applied to female suffering that is often – even typically – experienced in a domestic sphere? The final part of the chapter gives extended attention to readings of Sophocles' *Antigone*, which has provided a strong and influential paradigm for concepts of female tragic heroism. Steiner gives a landmark account of cultural and theoretical responses to the play and its central character.

Chapter 5, 'Tragic Dualities', looks at how tragedy is often discussed in terms of a matrix of binary oppositions: *polis/oikos*, public/private, male/female, amongst others. The central part of the chapter looks at important constructions of social, ethical and biological conflict by writers such as Darwin and Marx. While several practitioners and critics have been interested in tragedy as an artistic response to particular moments of social crisis, this chapter explores the way that tragedy has itself been influenced by the discourses of dialectic in science and political theory. This section also explores in detail Hegel's reading of tragedy as existing in 'the collision of equally justified powers' and examines critical responses to this ethical reading of tragedy. The final part of the chapter addresses Nietzsche's formulation of tragedy as a synthesis of the Apollonian and the Dionysian, and offers a careful explication of these complex terms.

Chapter 6, 'Tragic Pleasure', begins with David Hume's essay on tragedy which sets out the basic paradox: why does tragedy give pleasure? This very question forms the basis of a monograph by A. D. Nuttall, which explores Freudian and Nietzschean readings of tragedy. The chapter retraces the question of tragic pleasure to the Aristotelian notion of *catharsis*. Aristotle uses this medical loanword to describe the effect of tragedy on the spectator. While he uses specialised language, he is at the same time highly elliptical, and this has allowed a wealth of interpretative literature to spring up in an attempt to gloss and explicate what Aristotle may have meant. There has been particular controversy as to whether the term can more accurately be understood in terms of 'purgation' or 'purification'. In this chapter, we look at some of the earliest commentary work on the idea of *catharsis* amongst Renaissance critics, and bring these readings up to date with the work of contemporary philosophers such as Jonathan Lear and Martha Nussbaum. The last section of this chapter looks at critical work on the so-called tragic emotions, including pity, fear and horror, ranging from Nicholas Brooke's study of the grotesque in Jacobean tragedy to recent studies of the Theatre of Extremes.

Chapter 7, 'Tragedy and Form', considers debates about dramatic unity, and offers a particular focus on the critical culture of neoclassicism in seventeenth-century France. The idea of dramatic unity dates back to Aristotle's *Poetics*. Aristotelian theory was greatly expanded upon in Renaissance Italy, and systematised by Lodovico Castelvetro into the form that is now familiar to us. Although certain English critics (notably Philip Sidney) tried to insist on the importance of unity, English dramatists (particularly Shakespeare) largely did not adhere to the unities. On the Continent, however, there were more stringent attempts to enforce dramatic unity. Corneille was at the centre of a notable controversy concerning his play *Le Cid* (1637), which was deemed to be in breach of several key neoclassical precepts. This led him to advocate a more flexible approach to dramatic unity, a position which was strongly supported in England by John Dryden. In the second part of the chapter, we consider versions of tragedy as a non-dramatic form. The term 'tragedy' originates in a theatrical context, that of Attic drama of the fifth century BC. But even as early as Aristotle, points of contact between tragedy and non-dramatic literature have been recognised: Aristotle himself cites Homer's *Iliad* as the precursor of Attic tragedy. With the rise of the novel, tragedy offered a rich source of material and several major novelists such as Thomas Hardy and George Eliot experimented with ways of adapting tragic paradigms to suit prose narrative.

Chapter 8, 'Modern Tragedy', returns to the Hegelian and Marxist readings of tragedy that were introduced in Chapter 5. Here we look at the work by members of the Frankfurt School, who argued that technological innovations and mass culture fundamentally debased tragedy and art as a whole. This idea is echoed by Brecht, who argues that the political and aesthetic power of tragedy has diminished in response to conservative ideologies of the twentieth century. In an extension of these ideas, Steiner attributes the 'death of tragedy' to rationalism and society's secularisation. *Contra* Steiner, Williams argues that the ideological uncertainties of modern culture offer the potential for tragedy to become revitalised as a form. More recently, Terry Eagleton's polemical study has extended Williams's argument. Eagleton reviews tragic theory and pronounces it a 'theory in ruins'. But he argues that, far from killing tragedy, modernity has revitalised it by equipping it with a new and urgent sense of existential and ideological tensions. Rita Felski's thought-provoking essay collection argues for an understanding of tragedy as a 'mode' rather than a 'genre'. This provides a way of looking at tragedy that allows us to recognise its essential heterogeneity.

Chapter 9, 'Postcolonial and Multiethnic Tragedy', considers the extensive and developing literature on cross-cultural receptions of Greek tragedy in the Anglophone world and looks at the work of African, Afro-Caribbean and Irish writers. Hardwick and Gillespie's collection shows how Greek tragedy was once an expression of European colonial and cultural authority, but is now being appropriated in different cultures across the world to express resistance to a colonial past. In the next section, we look at the Irish reception of Greek tragedy, in particular at the comparative work of Fiona Macintosh. In the following section, we consider recent African reworkings of Greek tragedy, particularly Athol Fugard's *The Island*. While noting the specific topical and political contexts for each of these modern reworkings, we also note important points of contact in the reception of Greek tragedy in Ireland and in Africa. In the final part of the chapter, we return to the point at which we began, and consider Wole Soyinka's work on Yoruba drama and ritual.

Thus this Guide travels widely across ideologies, methodologies, historical periods, geographical spaces, ethnicities, languages and cultures. Our nine main chapters will help us to navigate material that is drawn from a diverse array of sources. Greek tragedy – a major touchstone in German ethical philosophy and aesthetics – and Shakespeare receive the most extensive coverage, partly to reflect the volume of criticism published in these areas. However, critical work on Seneca, Racine, Sarah Kane, Thomas Hardy, Arthur Miller, Wole Soyinka and many others is also represented. Within this broad spectrum of material, the reader should remain alert to the many points of cross-reference which this Guide suggests.

By beginning and ending with the subject of ritual, this Guide is not positing a teleological narrative of tragedy, but rather a framework in which to understand and grapple with the interconnectedness of some of the main theoretical preoccupations and ideas. With this in mind, let us turn to the first chapter and begin by looking at accounts of tragedy's ritual origins.

CHAPTER ONE

The Gods

Ritual and sacrifice

The precise origins of Attic tragedy – and thereby Western tragedy as a whole – have been heavily contested. The term 'tragedy' is etymologically derived from the Greek words *tragos* ('goat') and *oidia* ('song'), and this etymology has led to speculation that the performance of tragedy may originally have been associated with the sacrifice of a goat.[1] In the *Poetics*, Aristotle refers to the origins of tragedy 'in the improvisations of the leaders of the dithyramb', a hymn which was sung in honour of Dionysus.[2]

From these observations, a number of scholars have sought to locate the origins of Greek tragedy in sacrificial and ritual contexts. Among the first to do so was Gilbert Murray, one of a group of Cambridge academics who put forward an anthropological account of tragedy in which the tragic hero was figured as a substitute for the dying Dionysus.[3] Writing in 1912, Murray claimed that Greek tragedy celebrates Dionysus as a vegetation god, 'who represents the cyclic death and rebirth of the Earth and the World'.[4] Murray suggests that tragedy and comedy represent different moments in the life cycle of the god, so that comedy leads to his marriage feast and tragedy to his death and its lamentation. Murray identifies the formal elements of Greek tragedy enumerated by Aristotle, such as *peripeteia* (reversal of fortune) and *anagnorisis* (recognition), as originating in ritual practice. For example, Murray describes the ancient Dionysian mysteries as involving a *peripeteia* which, he says, marked 'a change from sorrow to joy, from darkness and sights of inexplicable terror to light and the discovery of the reborn God'.[5] Murray expounds this theory in relation to three plays by Euripides, the *Bacchae*, *Hippolytus* and the *Andromache*.

Murray's theory of the ritual origins of tragedy was comprehensively discredited by A. W. Pickard-Cambridge.[6] He argues that Murray's theory does not even apply to the three plays which he takes as test cases for his argument; 'nor, in fact, does it apply to any other play. There is not a single extant play in which the epiphany is the epiphany of the god or hero who has been slain.'[7] Enumerating the many inconsistencies in Murray's argument, Pickard-Cambridge goes on:

> ■ The kernel of tragedy, according to the theory, is the death and resurrection or epiphany of a slain daimon. Yet there is not one single tragedy in which the epiphany is that of the daimon or hero who has been slain, nor have we the faintest indication anywhere of any tragedy in which a slain character is resuscitated, with the possible exception of the *Alcestis* ... Is it possible to come to any other conclusion than that the theory simply does not fit the facts?[8] □

In their recent book on Shakespeare and ritual, Linda Woodbridge and Edward Berry have suggested that Murray and his fellow scholars of the Cambridge school were 'overenthusiastic, mistaken about many details, naïve about the relation between rite and literature, reductive in tracing all dramas (even all myths) to a single archaic ritual whose existence they failed to prove, led astray by Frazer's dubious anthropology'.[9]

In his own recent assault on the 'reductionist' position of the Cambridge school, Rainer Friedrich argues:

> ■ It turned the history of drama into the eternal recurrence of the same ritual pattern, with the same protagonist, Dionysos, in numerous disguises (as Prometheus, Oidipous, Agamemnon, Orestes, Antigone, Medeia, Hippolytos, Macbeth, King Lear, Hamlet, Dr Faustus, Puntila, etc.); it thereby distorted the plays and their meanings, and gave rise to the silly hocus-pocus of modern ritual productions of ancient, Elizabethan, and modern plays.[10] □

Friedrich notes that Murray's anthropological reading of tragedy was influential in a theatre movement in the 1960s and 1970s which adopted the slogan 'back to ritual'. This was part of an attempt to recover the ritual roots not only of Greek tragedy but of drama as a whole.[11] For further discussion of these objections, see Wole Soyinka's discussion of pseudo-ritual performance later in this chapter.

The question of the ritual origins of tragedy is inextricably linked with questions about the role of Dionysus, god of ancient Greek theatre, and the extent to which tragedy is rooted in Dionysiac ritual. The figure and the mythology of Dionysus will be discussed in more detail in Chapter 5, 'Tragic Dualities'. But Dionysus is also an important figure in critical work on the civic and ritual contexts for the performance of Greek tragedy, contexts which are seen to play a crucial role in constructing meaning in the plays themselves. As Charles Segal has observed, 'Dionysus' role in the origins of drama is one of the most controversial questions in the history of Greek literature.'[12] In recent years, attention has clustered around the ancient Greek question, 'What does tragedy have to do with Dionysus?' – a quotation which has reverberated in the titles of several key articles and essay collections in the field.[13]

In a seminal article, Simon Goldhill has given an account of the preliminary rituals at the City Dionysia, which preceded the dramatic contest.[14] It is important for Goldhill's argument that these rituals took place within the theatre; the theatre thus sets up an ideological juxtaposition between the 'preplay ceremonies' and the tragedies which followed. Goldhill's study notes a tension between the assertive confidence of these pre-play ceremonies and the interrogative character of tragedy itself which often probes and at times appears even to subvert the language of political order. Goldhill argues that the dialectic between the plays and the pre-play ceremonies complicates any attempt to retrieve simple didactic messages from the texts of Greek tragedy. The plays aim to 'make difficult the assumption of the values of the civic discourse'.[15] Goldhill concludes by pondering the maxim 'nothing to do with Dionysus', and argues that it is in the interplay between norms and transgression that the Dionysiac essence of the festival is realised and expressed.

Countering Goldhill, several important critics have suggested that Dionysus played only a comparatively marginal role in the performance of Greek tragedy and the celebration of the Great Dionysia as a whole. Oliver Taplin has gone so far as to claim that 'there is nothing intrinsically Dionysiac about Greek tragedy', a position which Scott Scullion has also shared.[16] Vernant sees the Dionysiac not as part of tragedy's past or its essence and instead emphasises tragedy as an aesthetic rather than religious phenomenon. Vernant argues that it is precisely in breaking away from and transcending its ritual origins that tragedy is possible. This position recalls Brecht's observation in *A Short Organum for Theatre* (1948): 'Theatre may be said to be derived from ritual but that is only to say that it becomes theatre once the two have separated.'[17]

Like Vernant and Brecht, Rainer Friedrich suggests that tragedy may indeed have its deep roots in the performance of ritual, but that we should recognise that it has undergone a process of evolution. According to Friedrich, Murray's argument is flawed because it presupposes too close a connection between the origins of tragedy and what it becomes as a mature form. Friedrich suggests that as tragedy grew from its ritual origins, there was a transitional form of drama which he calls 'youthful tragedy'.[18] In a refraction of Vernant's argument, Friedrich suggests that it is when tragedy turns its back on the Dionysian and broadens out to contemplate other subjects besides the Dionysian that it becomes a more mature form of 'literary drama'.[19]

Critical interest in ritual is not simply confined to the attempt to create a narrative of origins. As Pat Easterling points out, it is possible to recognise that tragedy draws on ritual themes and motifs without subscribing to the view that tragedy has grown out of ritual or that ritual shapes the basic structures of tragedy.[20] Easterling reminds us that sacrifice is not the only ritual which is regularly referred to in tragedy, but there are many others including supplication, oath taking, rites of hospitality and so on. Woodbridge and Berry note that ritual is a broad category: 'it has come to be understood as a referring to a mixed bag of phenomena – scapegoating, misrule, fertility, rites of passage – positioned at a crossroads where magic meets ceremony and literature meets anthropology'.[21]

Louis Gernet was the first scholar to link tragedy and the Athenian ritual of the *pharmakos*, an idea which has been influentially elaborated on by Walter Burkert.[22] This was a ritual form of exclusion which was practised in ancient Greek cities at times of crisis such as famine, plague or drought. Accounts from the sixth century describe how a victim was selected and offered a feast, before being paraded round the city and finally stoned as he was expelled from the city. Records of this kind of ritual at the Thargelia festival in Athens suggest that two victims were chosen, according to Burkert, for 'their particular loathsomeness'.[23] Burkert suggests that this ritual was designed to confer a sense of stability on a community in crisis:

> ■ To expel a trouble-maker is an elementary group reflex; perhaps in the most distant background there is also the situation of the pack surrounded by beasts of prey: only if one member, preferably a marginal, weak, or sick member, falls victim to the beasts can the others escape. The outcast is then also the saviour to whom all are most deeply indebted.[24] □

Among the most important theorists to develop this idea is René Girard, who argues that tragedy is analogous to the ritual sacrifice of a scapegoat.[25] It should be noted that Girard explicitly distances himself from the position of the Cambridge School in certain key respects: he does not support the idea that tragedy is a purely ritualistic phenomenon. Whereas Cambridge School scholars stress the importance of natural and seasonal cycles in their reading of the ritualistic origins of Greek tragedy, Girard emphasises sacrificial killing and ritual expulsion as *social* functions. He observes: 'there is nothing in nature that could encourage or even suggest such an atrocious sort of ritual killing as the death of the pharmakos'.[26]

Girard draws attention to the fine line between violence (as a criminal activity) and sacrifice as a form of sanctioned violence. Also reflecting on the role of sacrifice in creating a stable social order, Charles Segal argues: 'Sacrifice validates the world order by affirming the hierarchical relation of god–man–beast … [It] makes manifest the implicit logic of the world order. It separates gods from men and men from beasts, but also opens a way of access from men to gods.'[27] Girard, meanwhile, suggests that there is 'hardly any form of violence that cannot be described in terms of sacrifice – as Greek tragedy clearly reveals'.[28] Girard argues that through sacrifice, society is able to harness, redirect and legitimise violent impulses that are in its midst. In his interpretation, both the act of sacrifice, and its alternative, in the form of ritual expulsion, allow the community to focus its aggressive energy on a chosen victim in order to purify itself. He observes, 'When unappeased, violence seeks and always finds a surrogate victim.'[29] He gives the example of Euripides' Medea, whose anger towards Jason is displaced in the murder of her children:

> ■ Because the object of her hatred is out of reach, Medea substitutes her own children ... Medea, like Ajax, reminds us of a fundamental truth about violence; if left unappeased, violence will accumulate until it overflows its confines and floods the surrounding area. The role of sacrifice is to stem this rising tide of indiscriminate substitutions and redirect violence into 'proper' channels.[30] □

Girard suggests that the legacy of human sacrifice lived on in the ritual expulsion of the *pharmakos*. As an illustration of this ritual legacy in Greek tragedy, Girard takes the example of Oedipus. Contaminated by the dual *miasma* (pollution) of incest and parricide, Oedipus is exiled at the end of Sophocles' play in order to save the city from the plague which is afflicting it. Drawing an analogy with the *pharmakos* ritual, Girard argues:

> ■ Like Oedipus, the victim is considered a polluted object, whose living presence contaminates everything that comes into contact with it and whose death purges the community of its ills ... That is why the pharmakos was paraded about the city. He was used as a kind of sponge to sop up impurities, and afterward he was expelled from the community or killed in a ceremony that involved the entire populace.[31] □

Some theorists working in this area have suggested that the ritual victim is an innocent scapegoat who pays the price of another's guilt, but Girard disputes this interpretation. He writes:

> ■ As I see it, the relationship between the potential victim and the actual victim cannot be defined in terms of innocence or guilt. There is no question of 'expiation.' Rather, society is seeking to deflect upon a relatively indifferent victim, a 'sacrificeable' victim, the violence that would otherwise be vented on its own members, the people it most desires to protect.[32] □

It is Girard's insistence that the sacrificial victim is not a figure of absolute purity that opens up the application of his theory to tragedy since in tragedy, the characters who die are rarely (if ever) wholly innocent. (For further discussion of the relationship between tragic guilt and innocence, see Chapter 3.) Here, Girard draws an analogy with the ambivalent status of the *pharmakos*:

> ■ On the one hand he is a woebegone figure, an object of scorn who is also weighed down with guilt; a butt for all sorts of gibes, insults, and of course, outbursts of violence. On the other hand, we find him surrounded by a quasi-religious aura of veneration; he has become a sort of cult object. This duality reflects the metamorphosis the ritual victim is designed to effect; the victim draws to itself all the violence infecting the original victim and through its own death transforms this baneful violence into beneficial violence, into harmony and abundance.[33] □

Girard stresses that the sacrificial victim must be representative of the community which is engaged in the ritual sacrifice: to achieve this representative status, the victim must be both separate from the community and at the same time similar to its members. When this boundary is breached, there arises what Girard terms 'a sacrificial crisis', a term which refers to the disappearance of sacrificial rites. Girard sees the 'sacrificial crisis' as accompanying a dissolution of boundaries between pure and impure violence which in turn, he says, leads to the spread of reciprocal violence in the community.

In one notable Girardian reading of tragedy, Jan Kott characterises the role of Pentheus in Euripides' *Bacchae* as that of scapegoat. Kott notes the importance of the way in which the scapegoat is 'made into the image of the One to whom he is sacrificed'.[34] Kott makes extended comparisons between images of sacrifice and eating in the *Bacchae*, and aspects of Christian theology and ritual, particularly the celebration of the Eucharist and the Easter liturgy. For further discussion of Kott's account of *King Lear*, see the section on Christian tragedy which follows later in the chapter.

Following Girard, the French deconstructionist Jacques Derrida has also written influentially on the subject of the *pharmakos* in his essay, 'Plato's Pharmacy'.[35] Derrida argues that with the expulsion of the *pharmakos*:

> ■ The city's body *proper* thus reconstitutes its unity, closes around the security of its inner courts, gives back to itself the word that links it with itself within the confines of the agora, by violently excluding from its territory the representative of an external threat or aggression. That representative represents the otherness of the evil that comes to affect or infect the inside by unpredictably breaking into it. Yet the representative is

nonetheless *constituted*, regularly granted its place by the community, chosen, kept, fed, etc., in the very heart of the inside. These parasites were as a matter of course domesticated by the living organism that housed them at its expense.[36] ☐

This observation, that the city is initially host to and provider for the *pharmakos* which is eventually to be expelled, leads Derrida to consider the paradoxes which the figure embodies, and the liminal position which the *pharmakos* represents:

■ The ceremony of the *pharmakos* is thus played out on the boundary line between inside and outside, which it has as its function ceaselessly to trace and retrace ... The origin of difference and division, the *pharmakos* represents evil both introjected and projected. Beneficial insofar as he cures – and for that, venerated and cared for – harmful insofar as he incarnates the powers of evil – and for that, feared and treated with caution. Alarming and calming. Sacred and accursed.[37] ☐

Although most work on the relationship between tragedy and ritual has focused on the Greek context, there has been important work in the field of Shakespeare studies too. In an early study of its kind, John Holloway identifies scapegoating as a recurring pattern in Shakespeare. He argues that the tragic hero occupies a role which 'takes him from being the cynosure of his society to being estranged from it, and takes him, through a process of increasing alienation, to a point at which what happens to him suggests the expulsion of a scapegoat, or the sacrifice of a victim, or both'.[38]

In an extension of this idea, in *Shakespeare's Festive Tragedy: The Ritual Foundations of Genre*, Naomi Conn Liebler proposes a set of analogous relationships between 'festive comedy' (a term influentially coined by C. L. Barber) and what Liebler, correspondingly, refers to as 'festive tragedy'.[39] She argues:

■ 'Festive' means something more socially complex than 'merry'. The Latin root, *festum* ('feast') incorporates the sacramental, patterned, and entirely serious functions and meaning of ritual as communal activity ... 'Festive' thus carried a great deal of meaning available to tragedy. It recognizes that, like comedy, tragedy consecrates and celebrates something. That something varies insignificantly from play to play.[40] ☐

Liebler notes that theorists disagree as to what constitutes ritual. Among key elements, she suggests, are repetition and a sense that the ritual imparts legitimacy to what is being enacted. Rituals do not just mark key moments in the social order, they are the crux of the social order. She argues that Shakespeare's plays dramatise and comment on the absence and failure of ritual at moments when such rituals would be beneficial to the community. Drawing on Girardian theory, Liebler proposes that in Shakespeare, 'the community's drive to survive its crisis emerges as an urgent need to kill its hero-scapegoat'.[41] As other critics besides Liebler have recognised, the deposition scene in *Richard II* is an inverted coronation rite. In Liebler's reading of this scene, ritual is deconstructed in order to suggest the possibility of reconstruction. Richard's humiliation does not have the redressive features of ritual. 'The carnivalization of Richard ... prepares him, as Girard notes, for the role of pharmarkos, for it is only as his own double, not as his kingly self, that he can take on the sacrificial function of scapegoat.'[42] Liebler suggests that the play traces an important moment in the secularisation and emptying out of rituals associated with the English monarchy. 'Rituals evacuated of meaning cannot work,' Liebler comments: 'By attending to the changes during Richard's reign in the way ritual was variously honored, aborted, subverted, debased and ignored, *Richard II* dramatizes the inescapable cost of secularizing a ritual-centred political ecology.'[43]

In an account of *Romeo and Juliet*, Liebler takes up Derrida's argument that the *pharmakos* must embody paradox. Liebler suggests that Romeo and Juliet violate the proper performance of ritual, first by marrying in secret, and second, by staging false funeral rites for Juliet. In violating the proper social requirements, they become pollutants. Yet they also embody traits valued by the community: this dual identity, Liebler argues, is what makes them *pharmakoi*.

In his account of the ritual context for the performance of Yoruba tragedy, to which we will return in Chapter 9, Wole Soyinka writes:

■ The three deities that concern us here are Ogun, Obatala and Sango. They are represented in drama by the passage-rites of hero-gods, a projection of man's conflict with forces which challenge his efforts to harmonise with his environment, physical, social and psychic. The drama of the hero-god is a convenient expression; gods they are unquestionably, but their symbolic roles are identified by man as the role of an intermediary quester, an explorer into territories of 'essence-ideal' around whose edges man fearfully skirts. Finally, as a prefiguration of conscious being which is nevertheless a product of the conscious creativity of man, they enhance man's existence within the cyclic consciousness of time. These emerge as the principal features of the drama of the gods; it is within their framework that traditional society poses its social questions or formulates its moralities.[44] □

In the same work, Soyinka attacks Western performances of tragedy which have tried artificially to retrieve a sense of ritual origin and to impose this anachronistically on modern productions. Soyinka launches a polemical attack on those directors who 'retain the basic attitude that traditional drama is some kind of village craft which can be plonked down on any stall just like artifacts in any international airport boutique'. He continues:

> ■ Such presentations have been largely responsible for the multitude of false concepts surrounding the drama of the gods; that, and their subjection to anthropological punditry where they are reduced, *in extremis*, to behavioural manifestations in primitive society. The burden on a producer is one of knowledge, understanding, and of sympathetic imagination. Whatever deity is involved demands an intelligent communication of what is, indeed, pure essence.[45] □

Christian tragedy

In *Modern Tragedy*, Williams declares that, 'In one sense all drama after the Renaissance is secular, and the only fully religious tragedy we have is the Greek.'[46]

Georg Lukács argues that the divine order has no role to play in tragedy at all, asserting that, 'Only when the tragedy is over, when the dramatic meaning has become transcendent, do gods and demons appear on the stage; it is only in the drama of grace that the *tabula rasa* of the higher world is filled once more with superior and subordinate figures.'[47] Susan Sontag argues not that atheism and agnosticism have displaced Christian tragedy, but rather that such a thing never existed:

> ■ As everyone knows, there was no Christian tragedy, strictly speaking, because the content of Christian values – for it is a question of what values, however implacably held; not any will do – is inimical to the pessimistic vision of tragedy. ... In the world envisaged by Judaism and Christianity, there are no free-standing arbitrary events. All events are part of the plan of a just, good, providential deity; every crucifixion must be topped by a resurrection. Every disaster or calamity must be seen either as leading to a greater good or else as just and adequate punishment fully merited by the sufferer. This moral adequacy of the world asserted by Christianity is precisely what tragedy denies. Tragedy says there are disasters which are not fully merited, that there is ultimate injustice in the world.[48] □

For Sontag, the fundamental optimism of different religious traditions stands in the way of the rebirth of tragedy in a Christian age. Camus famously asserts that tragedy tends to arise at times of theological or epistemological crisis: 'It seems in fact that tragedy is born in the West each time that the pendulum of civilization is halfway between a sacred society and a society built around man.'[49] He thus sees the development of tragedy not in linear but in cyclical terms. In the final section of this chapter, we will be discussing the religious and cultural crisis of the English Reformation as a particular stimulus to the production of tragedy. Here Camus considers the view that Christianity fundamentally displaces the need for, and the possibility of, tragedy in the modern world:

> ■ Christianity plunges the whole of the universe, man and the world, into the divine order. There is thus no tension between the world and the religious principle, but, at the most, ignorance, together with the difficulty of freeing man from the flesh, of renouncing our passions in order to embrace spiritual truth. Perhaps there has been only one Christian tragedy in history. It was celebrated on Golgotha during one imperceptible instant, at the moment of the 'My God, my God, why hast thou forsaken me?' This fleeting doubt, and this doubt alone, consecrated the ambiguity of a tragic situation. Afterwards the divinity of Christ was never again called in doubt. The mass, which gives a daily consecration to this divinity, is the real form which religious theatre takes in the West. It is not invention, but repetition.[50] □

Like Sontag, some critics have seen the term 'Christian tragedy' as paradoxical because Christianity posits a view of death that is fundamentally optimistic. The Greeks believed in an afterlife in Hades, but this was regarded with a sense of dread, rather than hope. Greek tragedy does not address the promise of an afterlife for the hero. Death is typically presented as the climax of the tragedy. Several tragedies (most notably *Antigone*, a play which we will discuss at length in Chapter 4) address issues concerning the burial of the dead, but these concerns are worldly. In the *Antigone*, there is a much greater emphasis on what happens to the body than to the soul; and indeed in Sophocles' play, there is far greater emphasis on the moral and religious responsibilities which death places on the living, than on the issue of death per se.

In contrast, in Christian tradition, death is not regarded as the end, but is instead invested with hope of salvation and the promise of everlasting life in heaven. For Christians, Christ's death on the cross fundamentally changed the nature of death, so that in every image of death also lies the possibility of redemption. As the final section of this chapter will show, there are some major differences between Catholic and Protestant eschatology (particularly in relation to the doctrine of Purgatory, for example); these tensions in belief and cultural practice have served to animate the production of English tragedy in the sixteenth and early seventeenth century. Before exploring this major doctrinal shift in more detail, let us first sketch out the problem of Christian tragedy in its wider sense, and the conceptual difficulties that it poses.

As William Elton remarks in his study of *King Lear*, the term 'Christian tragedy' can mean a variety of things: it can recognise ways in which a text draws on biblical source material, characters and analogies, or it can imply that a text suggests a providential narrative at work.[51] In its most general sense, it can simply refer to tragedy which is produced in a Christian era. The term 'Christian tragedy' does not therefore imply a fixed theology or a fixed agenda. The implications of this term are best uncovered by means of comparison with the pagan tragedy of the ancient world.

Greek tragedy discloses a polytheistic system in which the gods are amoral. The Greeks believed that if the gods were offended by human *hubris* (often translated as 'arrogance') divine *nemesis* (retribution) would follow. The suffering inflicted on a transgressor might not necessarily appear proportionate to his crime. But the power of the gods exceeded all human claims to justice.

In Christianity, this view of divinity is radically altered. In Christian theology, God is regarded as wholly benevolent and Christ as a source of consolation in times of suffering. Reflecting on these constructions of Christian faith, Clifford Leech says that the tragic experience is not compatible 'with any form of religious belief that assumes the existence of a personal and kindly God'.[52] In Greek tragedy, the gods inflict pain and suffering on mortals, whereas in Christianity, God sustains the faithful through their suffering, and through Christ's death on the cross, took it upon Himself to share that suffering. As Steiner has observed, in this theology, 'The fall of man, pivotal to absolute tragedy, is a *felix culpa* ['happy fault'], a necessary prologue to salvation.'[53]

Milton's *Samson Agonistes* interestingly straddles the divisions which some critics have sought to put in place between Old and New Testament approaches to tragedy. The poem – which Milton calls a tragedy in the prose preface – dramatises an Old Testament story, taken from the Book of Judges, but written from a Christian perspective. The narrative is thus hybrid in form, an Old Testament story as interpreted through the lens of the New. As John Shawcross has pointed out, the poem does not fit with conventional definitions of tragedy because it does not trace a fall from greatness: when the play begins, the once mighty Samson is already held captive by the Philistines and so his fall, in a sense, is already in the past.[54] Indeed, Shawcross points out that Samson is not of noble birth, which is itself highly unusual for conceptions of tragedy in the seventeenth century. Furthermore, many readings of the play have seen Samson's destruction of the temple as regenerative. Although Samson dies, he is finally able to strike against his enemies, prompted by 'rousing motions' (line 1382) from God.[55] If the ending is regenerative, in what sense can the play be understood as tragedy at all?

Shawcross suggests that the play presents a view of Christian tragedy which turns on the idea that the play is not primarily about Samson's death, but about the world he leaves behind. This is a position which interestingly diminishes the role of the protagonist: for further discussion of critical views about the centrality of the tragic hero, see Chapter 3. The tragedy, Shawcross says, is that the Chorus does not learn anything from Samson's death. Shawcross draws a parallel between the death of Samson and the death of Christ: 'The martyrdom of Christ is not a tragedy; the continued "evil" of humankind is.'[56] For Shawcross, the movement towards spiritual regeneration in the play does not qualify its status as tragedy: even though Samson overcomes adversity, this only serves to emphasise Samson's earlier loss of fidelity to God.

Some critics have sought to invoke apparent tensions between the Old Testament and the New: the Old Testament places a greater emphasis on God's vengeance, whereas the New Testament places emphasis on forgiveness. For this reason, some critics have argued that the Old Testament is more compatible with the notion of tragedy than the New. Laurence Michel, for example, suggests that the Old Testament's emphasis on God's inscrutability is closer to the mood of Greek tragedy.[57] Yet in the following passage, Kierkegaard challenges the compatibility of tragedy with a Judaic worldview:

> ■ One might well conclude that the people who developed profound tragedy were the Jews. Thus, when they say of Jehovah that he is a jealous God who visits the sins of the fathers on the children unto the third and the fourth generations, or one hears those terrible imprecations in the Old Testament, one might feel tempted to look here for the material of tragedy. But Judaism is too ethically developed for this. Jehovah's curses, terrible as they are, are nevertheless also righteous punishment. Such was not the case in Greece, there the wrath of the gods has no ethical character, but aesthetic ambiguity.[58] □

Here Kierkegaard is drawing a clear distinction between the God of the Old Testament, who is wrathful but just, and the anger of the Greek gods, which is merely destructive and has no foundation in morality. For Kierkegaard, therefore, tragedy can only be concerned with divine anger which is arbitrarily destructive, and not with divine anger that imparts ethical consequences and a moral structure to the world.

Greek gods were anthropomorphic; this meant they could readily be presented as characters in tragedy, as we see with the appearance of Dionysus in Euripides' *Bacchae* or Artemis and Aphrodite in *Hippolytus*, also by Euripides. In the Middle Ages, the Christian God could be represented as a character in drama, for example in the York mystery plays. But liturgical drama was suppressed at the Reformation, and in the second half of the sixteenth century it was no longer possible to represent God on stage. Thus when Shakespeare represents divinity in his plays, it is in the form of pagan gods rather than Christian: Jupiter in *Cymbeline* (V.iv) and the oracle of Apollo in *The Winter's Tale* (III.ii). Yet the plays themselves are peppered with references to Christian sacraments such as baptism and confession. Recognising the tensions between the pagan surface of Shakespeare's plays and the biblical influences which are inscribed in them, J. C. Maxwell has called *King Lear* 'a Christian play about a pagan world'.[59] (There will be further discussion of *King Lear* as a Christian tragedy later in this section.) Likewise Raymond Williams reflects a sense of the hybrid nature of the drama of the period in his observation that 'Elizabethan drama is thoroughly secular in its immediate practice, but undoubtedly retains a Christian consciousness'.[60]

Given these difficulties, several critics have argued that tragedy is not possible in a Christian age. As we will see in more detail in Chapter 8, Steiner contends that tragedy needs to engage in its audience a framework of shared beliefs, a sense of a higher metaphysical order, to endow suffering with a sense of meaning. In a largely secular (some would say post-Christian) age, some have felt that dramatists and audiences are no longer able to draw on a divine frame of reference for human suffering. As Eugene O'Neill remarks in his working notes during the composition of *Mourning Becomes Electra* (1931), a reworking of Aeschylus' *Oresteia*, it is 'a hell of a problem, [to write] a modern tragic interpretation of classic fate without benefit of gods'.[61]

Lucien Goldmann sees God as an essential element in tragedy. He insists that tragedy cannot be understood in solely human terms, so that a hero's downfall results from some internal psychological flaw (see Chapter 3). Rather, he claims that 'tragedy is the representation of a universe dominated by a conflict of values'.[62] The tragic universe is one of absolutes; there are no degrees of right and wrong. In this uncompromising vision, 'Though he is *always present* this God remains a *hidden god*, a god who is *always absent*. This is the key to tragedy.'[63]

W. H. Auden takes the view that Greek tragedy and Christian tragedy reflect on suffering with a sense of anguish that is both shared, and at the same time, radically different. As he observes, 'Greek tragedy is the tragedy of necessity; i.e. the feeling aroused in the spectator is "What a pity it had to be this way"; Christian tragedy is the tragedy of possibility, "What a pity it was this way when it might have been otherwise."'[64] By this, Auden acknowledges that Christianity always entertains the possibility of conversion away from sin or error. For further discussion of the concepts of sin and tragic guilt, see Chapter 3.

Karl Jaspers embeds his discussion of the problem of Christian tragedy in the context of tragic knowledge. According to Jaspers, the

Christian does not merely endure suffering, he knowingly chooses it because this is his route to salvation. Jaspers says:

> ■ Seen from this point of view, Christian salvation opposes tragic knowledge. The chance of being saved destroys the tragic sense of being trapped without chance of escape. Therefore no genuinely Christian tragedy can exist. For in Christian plays, the mystery of redemption is the basis and framework of the plot, and the tension of tragic knowledge has been released from the outset with the experience of man's perfection and salvation through grace.[65] □

Enrica Zanin tries to dismantle the paradox of Christian tragedy and to suggest ways in which early modern dramatists negotiated the tensions inherent in this concept.[66] In summarising the problem, Zanin argues that in Greek tragedy, a character such as Oedipus can be simultaneously both guilty and innocent, since he committed the crimes of incest and parricide unwittingly and unwillingly. This duality of guilt and innocence is not possible in a Christian context. Sin damages the relationship between man and God, but there is a necessary emphasis on God's innocence in all matters of human suffering. Of particular interest is Zanin's discussion of Corneille's *Œdipe* (performed 1659), a play which he characterises as a study of martyrdom. Oedipe, he argues, freely accepts God's punishment and willingly sacrifices himself for his people: Zanin observes that this denouement 'reverses all tragic values into Christian hopes'.[67] The essay concludes by noting that the ethical ambiguities of Greek tragedy are replaced by a strong moral didacticism in classical French tragedy. According to Zanin, the ancient conception of the tragic lives on in the Christian era through the image of a protagonist who is blind to the possibilities of God's grace. For further discussion of the relationship between tragic *hamartia* and the Christian idea of sin, see Chapter 3.

The concept of Christian tragedy has been powerfully explored in relation to Shakespeare, and much of the most intense controversy has focused on *King Lear*. In the twentieth century, there was a strong interpretative trend to see the play as a Christian allegory, in which Cordelia and Kent stand as Christian symbols. Indeed in *Shakespearean Tragedy*, first published in 1904, Bradley suggests that *King Lear* could be called *The Redemption of King Lear*.[68]

Others have taken a bleaker view. In a seminal reading of the play that is not only atheist but also nihilist, Jan Kott suggests that the play anticipates the absurdist drama of Samuel Beckett. Kott argues that *King Lear* displays a 'philosophical cruelty' that is at odds with dramatic realism.[69] He argues that in the play, 'the tragic element has been superseded by the grotesque. The grotesque is more cruel than tragedy.'[70] For Kott, the grotesque is not an alternative to the tragic: 'The grotesque exists in a tragic world.'[71] In the tragic world, Kott suggests, man's freedom has been constrained by a variety of external forces: 'In the tragic world this compulsory situation has been imposed in turn by the Gods, Fate, the Christian God, Nature, and History that has been endowed with reason and inevitability.'[72] Each of these forces (to which Kott refers collectively as 'the absolute') is, in its own way, potentially overwhelming; yet the absence of the absolute in the postmodern world does not create a new vision of freedom but rather a new vision of man's guilt:

> ■ If Nature was the absolute, man was unnatural. If man was natural, the absolute was represented by Grace, without which there was no salvation. In the world of the grotesque, downfall cannot be justified by, or blamed on, the absolute. The absolute is not endowed with any ultimate reasons; it is stronger, and that is all. The absolute is absurd.[73] □

Kott suggests that dramatists have attempted to find a substitute for the absolute which he argues has been displaced from the drama of the modern age: 'Various kinds of impersonal and hostile mechanisms have taken the place of God, Nature and History found in the old tragedy ... But this absurd mechanism is not transcendental any more in relation to man, or at any rate to mankind. It is a trap set by man himself into which he has fallen.'[74] Stripped of the absolute, Kott suggests that man's agency can only ever be self-negating. He says that absurdity is like:

> ■ a game in which the probability of [man's] total defeat constantly increases. The Christian view of the end of the world, with the Last Judgement, and its segregation of the just and the unjust, is pathetic. The end of the world caused by the atom bomb is spectacular, but grotesque just the same. Such an end to the world is intellectually unacceptable, either to Christians or to Marxists. It would be a silly ending.[75] □

In the face of inexplicable suffering, Kott suggests that tragedy and the grotesque ask the same questions, but pose different answers. 'Tragedy is the theatre of priests, grotesque is the theatre of clowns.'[76] By this he means that tragedy entertains the possibility of a higher causality which offers at least some kind of consolation. The grotesque, on the other hand, merely *performs* suffering. He continues, 'When established values have been overthrown, and there is no appeal to God, Nature, or History from the tortures inflicted by the cruel world, the clown becomes the central figure in the theatre.'[77]

In a more traditional reading of *King Lear*, William Elton ultimately rejects the Christian optimist view of the play. He says that the play's pagan setting problematises a reading of Christian values which are potentially inscribed in it. If we take it that Shakespeare shapes a pagan world into an implicitly Christian world, Elton argues, 'we are left with the spectacle of a Christian tragic hero who ends as a skeptic blaspheming his Deity, a unique occurrence in the dramatist's work and one fraught with danger, both politically and artistically'.[78] He concludes by suggesting that while Shakespeare offers us a pagan setting, a Jacobean audience would have found it hard to resist mapping onto it aspects of their own Christian faith (and doubt).

Iconoclasm and cultural memory

Several prominent new historicist critics, including Stephen Greenblatt and Robert N. Watson, have argued that the emergence of English Renaissance tragedy in the mid-sixteenth century is intimately connected with the English Reformation. At the Reformation, Catholic rituals of death were abolished and suppressed. These included the practice of saying Masses for the dead to expedite the progress of their souls through Purgatory.[79] Together with this, the rich funerary visual culture of Catholic England was attacked in a wave of Protestant iconoclastic zeal. This meant that the many images of death which adorned churches and graveyards were defaced or shattered as reformers sought to purge the visual landscape not just of graven images of God but of religious iconography more generally. It is argued by new historicist critics that this dramatic change generated cultural nostalgia for old Catholic rites of death, even among those who on a doctrinal level may have subscribed to religious reform. In the emerging Protestant theology, Purgatory no longer had a place. Under the Calvinist doctrine of predestination, it was held that God had decided before all time who would be saved (a group known as 'the Elect') and who would be damned. Prayers for the dead were not only ineffectual but heretical, since no one knew whether the dead person was among the Elect or not and to pray for a soul in hell would be a sin. In contrast, the Catholic faith had preserved a sense of a continuing relationship between living and dead: the living would pray for the dead, and the dead (i.e., the saints) could intercede with God to help the cause of the living. As Greenblatt eloquently puts it:

> ■ Not only doctrine, then, but also chants, gestures, images, and the very air that the faithful breathed said the same thing: the border between this world and the afterlife was not firmly and irrevocably closed. For a large group of mortals – perhaps the majority of them – time did not come to an end at the moment of death. The book was not quite shut ... The living could have an ongoing relationship with one important segment of the dead, and not simply a relationship constituted by memory.[80] □

In Calvinist theology, the point of death was more final and what happened after death, the possible destination of the soul, was polarised and unknown.

New historicists have argued that early modern drama provided a means of expression for the cultural crisis which these religious changes precipitated. In this reading, early modern tragedy emerges as a form which caters to a deep psychological need to contemplate and, even more importantly, to visualise death. According to Michael Neill, this need to visualise death was served by the enactment of spectacles of dying and of death in tragedy. Ghost scenes became in early modern tragedy a way of articulating anxieties about the afterlife. This need is heightened, Neill argues, in a culture that was dealing with the experience of mass mortality through the various outbreaks of plague during the period. The theatre effectively started to perform some of the psychological and philosophical work which had previously been done by the Church. The theatre offered a kind of secular substitute for Church ritual; at the same time, it provided a mechanism for taking up and harnessing the artistic energies which had been displaced from parish churches. Whereas these churches had provided a focus for all kinds of artistry (such as the work of sculptors, painters and stonemasons), these artistic impulses found a new focus in the theatre. As Neill suggests, it is particularly in the form of revenge tragedy that the early modern 'crisis of death' finds its expression:

■ More consistently than any other form, it is now possible to see, it was revenge tragedy that spoke to the anxieties produced by this painful transformation in relations with the dead: its protagonists are haunted by ghosts because they are possessed by memory; the dead will not leave them alone, because the dead cannot bear to be left alone. Alternately disabled by their inability to forget, and driven by their violent compulsion to remember, revenge heroes must wrestle to redeem their dead from the shame of being forgotten, even as they struggle to lay these perturbed spirits to rest, and thereby free themselves from the insistent presence of the past.[81] □

In one of the most influential refractions of this account, Robert N. Watson examines the relationship between mortality and immortality.[82] Watson argues that the Reformation brought with it an intensified fear of death because of the new eschatological uncertainties that Calvinists espoused: with the obsolescence of the doctrine of Purgatory, it was no longer certain what happened to the soul after death. Watson sees Renaissance tragedy as a response to this heightened fear of death because it attempts to deny that death is a kind of end. For Watson, Renaissance tragedy presents a kind of fantasy in which human agency can continue after death, for example, in the form of an injunction to exact revenge.

Stephen Greenblatt's book *Hamlet in Purgatory* explores the subject of cultural nostalgia for the old faith, and ways in which that finds expression in the concept of what he terms 'speaking with the dead'. Greenblatt examines the implications of recalling through the figure of the ghost in *Hamlet* the doctrine of Purgatory which was outlawed in the Protestant regime. Whereas in the old Catholic faith, it was widely believed that ghosts came from Purgatory, the abolition of this doctrine meant that belief in ghosts was no longer sanctioned (or even logically possible). Greenblatt stresses that he is not aiming to resolve the question of whether the Ghost has a Catholic or Protestant identity. Rather, he is interested in the figure of the Ghost as a kind of cultural and ideological anachronism in a Protestant era, and how the play negotiates the tensions which the Ghost presents. As part of his enquiry, Greenblatt proposes that ghosts on the Renaissance stage typically derive from classical sources and that the appearance of the Ghost in *Hamlet* is inflected with particular anxieties relating to the English Reformation.[83] Greenblatt argues that the appearance of the ghost in *Hamlet* is not simply a convenient and popular stage device but is deeply embedded in a larger and highly topical debate.

Against this complex cultural and theological background, Greenblatt focuses closely on the tensions in the Ghost's injunction to Hamlet to 'remember' and to 'revenge' in Act I, Scene v of the play. Greenblatt says that 'what is at stake in the shift of emphasis from vengeance to remembrance is nothing less than the whole play'.[84] He contends that the call to remembrance signifies a general nostalgia for rituals of death which had been suppressed at the Reformation; these have overtaken the Senecan call for revenge as the primary concern of tragedy. Greenblatt concludes by suggesting that funeral rites in Elizabethan and Jacobean England were designed to confer a sense of closure. Ghosts, according to Greenblatt, disrupt this sense of closure. In the figure of the Ghost, he writes, 'the boundary between the living and the dead was not so decisively closed'.[85]

This chapter has been concerned with the relationship between tragedy and its religious frameworks. We have looked at the ritual origins of Greek tragedy in the festival of Dionysus at Athens, and traced a continuing interest in ritual patterns in tragedy, most influentially in Girard's work on sacrifice and the figure of the scapegoat. Thus Girard, as we have seen, is not interested in the religious aspects of ritual but rather its social function. When violence is directed towards a chosen victim in the form of a scapegoat, the potential for further violence is contained and the threat to society at large is minimised.

We have considered whether the religious dimensions of ancient Greek tragedy survive in tragedy's later manifestations, particularly in the Christian contexts of early modern tragedy. Many critics, as we have seen, regard the concept of Christian tragedy as a contradiction in terms, and in Chapter 8 we will return to see how this question fits into a larger debate about the status of tragedy in the modern era. In the final part of the chapter, we looked at the religious crisis of the Reformation and the way that critics such as Stephen Greenblatt have argued that this created conditions which were conducive to the production of tragedy.

As we have seen, this chapter has explored the significance of collective ideologies, as well as those in transition or in crisis. Tragedy, we have seen, reflects and speaks to the beliefs and values of its audiences. In the next chapter, we will look further at the public and political dimensions of tragedy in relation to its audiences and we will see how critics have sought to understand and explain these dynamics in reference to the chorus.

CHAPTER TWO

The Chorus

The role of the chorus

In the *Poetics*, Aristotle discusses the chorus in only the most cursory terms, in his reference to the origins of tragedy in the singing of the dithyramb (discussed previously in Chapter 1). Aristotle thus appears to recognise that tragedy begins with a collective voice, against which an individual performer was differentiated. He goes on to note that Aeschylus added a second actor, and made the role of the chorus less important. It might seem surprising to us that Aristotle does not have more to say about the role of the chorus, given its importance as a feature of Greek tragedy. The most likely explanation for this is that Aristotle is not predominantly concerned with character in the *Poetics*: his main focus is the structural elements of the plot. For further discussion of Aristotle's prioritisation of plot over character, see Chapter 3, 'The Tragic Hero'.

Although Aristotle's discussion of the chorus is heavily abbreviated, modern critics have produced a wealth of material on the subject. George Steiner argues that the importance of the chorus is universally recognised as something which is essential to our understanding of Greek tragedy: 'Readers of Greek tragedy, students, performers, know that the chorus lies at the formal roots and centre of the art.'[1]

As the final part of this chapter will explore, some modern readers and audiences have felt estranged from the idea of the chorus as a non-naturalistic dramatic device. In this final section, we will look at critical arguments in favour of reinstating and reinventing the chorus in new ways that have a fresh relevance to modern audiences. But first, let us focus on the chorus of ancient Greek tragedy, and sketch out some of its principal functions.

The chorus was a body of some 12 to 15 actors, who entered after the Prologue, and took up their place in the *orchestra*, the central performance space in front of the main stage building. They would conventionally remain on stage for the duration of the play, though there are important exceptions to this in Aeschylus' *Eumenides* and Sophocles' *Ajax*. In the

Eumenides, the action of the play relocates from Delphi to Athens, itself a breach of Greek tragic convention. With this relocation, Aeschylus introduces a second chorus of Athenian women who celebrate the acquittal of Orestes and the institution of the judicial system in Athens. In the *Ajax*, Tecmessa, fearing for her husband's safety, asks the Chorus to go in search of him. Their departure leaves the stage empty in preparation for Ajax's suicide, an event which is unparalleled in Greek tragedy because of the convention that death should not be portrayed onstage. The absence of the chorus would therefore have heightened the audience's sense of the extraordinary nature of the scene.

Once the chorus had taken its place in the *orchestra*, each scene was followed by a choral ode, in which the chorus would sing and dance. This pattern of alternation set up an important tension in the role of the chorus: by being (in most cases) continuously present, the chorus promoted a sense of structural coherence in the play. At the same time, the choral odes helped to create some tonal and thematic variations within the larger whole. During the episodes, the chorus leader would engage in dialogue with the main actors.

Although the members of the chorus were not characterised individually, each chorus was assigned a collective identity – for example, old men or young women – and this identity was expressed by means of costume and mask. It would also have influenced the way that particular choruses moved. It is generally agreed that the chorus contributed in considerable measure to the visual and aural appeal of tragedy.

The choral odes did not generally comment in precise analytical terms on the action of the play. Instead, the chorus would often bring a wider mythological perspective to bear on the meaning of the play and on the interpretation of action. Helene Foley describes the role of the chorus as follows:

> ■ The chorus was a repository of cultural memory, largely in the form of traditional myth. It tried to make sense of past, present, and future events through these myths, and through the citation of traditional wisdom, although it rarely succeeded in doing so. Hence the audience could not rely on the chorus's judgement to interpret the action, although it could relate to the choral struggle to do so.[2] □

John Gould argues that the chorus embodies collective memory and experience. He compares this with the chorus of Euripides' *Phoenissae* in which the women are connected not through lived experience but via inherited memories.[3] Given this collective identity, Gould notes that it is a significant moment when the collective, univocal speech of the chorus in the *Agamemnon* breaks down into individual voices and becomes expressive of dissonance.[4]

Critical debate on the subject has largely focused on the relationship between the chorus and the audience. Opinion is divided on the question of how far the chorus is present in order to articulate an orthodox moral or political view on behalf of the assembled Athenian citizenship. Before exploring this further, let us look in some detail at tragedy's institutional role and examine ways in which critics have sought to situate the chorus in this larger political framework. Steiner stresses the versatility of the Greek tragic chorus:

■ Far beyond any turning stage or proscenium arch, the chorus is a device whereby the antique playwright can exactly calibrate and modulate the distances, the sight-lines, between audience and myth, between spectator and scene ... Thus it acts as a kind of drawbridge which the dramatist can raise or lower, shorten or lengthen at will by metrical and choreographic means. Via the chorus, the spectator can be drawn on to the stage or distanced from it; he can be virtually enmeshed in the scenic situation or barred from (naïve) access to it.[5] □

In her influential study of Greeks and barbarians, Edith Hall pays close attention to the role of the chorus, which, she notes, was often characterised as female or barbarian, or both. Of the chorus's marginal status, Hall observes:

■ On one level, of course, the chorus is the voice of the collective, whose well-being is dependent on and jeopardized by the individual characters, but it is paradoxically also estranged from the central *pathos*. It rarely participates or influences decisions and events, for its members remain marginal, standing and dancing on the edges of the actors' space; their medium is song rather than speech, and their role – usually that of social inferior – to sympathize and lament. The chorus' relation to the central figures, simultaneously dependent and marginalized, is thus almost a cultural paradigm of the relation borne in the Greek city-state by women, slaves and metics [resident foreigners] to the body of male citizens.[6] □

Also interested in the chorus's mediation of the main action of the play is Georg Lukács, who uses an architectural analogy to describe the way that the chorus frames the drama:

■ Thus the chorus was able to provide a background which closes the work in the same way as the marble atmospheric space between figures in a relief closes the frieze, yet the background of the chorus is also full of movement and can adapt itself to all the apparent fluctuations of a dramatic action not born of any abstract scheme ... Speaker and chorus in Greek tragedy are of the same fundamental essence, they are completely homogeneous with one another and can therefore fulfil completely separate functions without destroying the structure of the work; all the lyricism of the situation, of destiny, can be accumulated in the chorus, leaving to the players the all-expressive words and all-embracing gesture of the tragic dialectic laid bare – and yet they will never be separated from one another by anything other than gentle transitions.[7] □

Thus Lukács offers a more muted account of the tensions between actor and chorus than many of the other accounts which we have seen in this chapter.

The voice of the *polis*

Many leading political theorists, literary critics and cultural historians have attended to the importance of the Athenian *polis* as an institution. As we started to see in Chapter 1, critics such as Simon Goldhill and Jean-Pierre Vernant stress not only the religious contexts of Greek tragedy but its social and political functions too. Arguably, the religious, social and political contexts of Greek tragedy are almost impossible to separate. As Christian Meier has argued, 'it was essentially *as* citizens that the citizens saw and heard tragedy ...'.[8] In stressing the political dimensions of Greek tragedy, Meier notes Athens' rapid rise to power in the fifth century BC, notably through victories against the Persians at the battle of Marathon in 490 BC and the battle of Salamis in 480 BC. Meier suggests that this rise to power brought with it a radical restructuring of civic and political systems in Athens and through these, in turn, evolved a new sense of the Athenian citizen identity. Tragedy, suggests Meier, offered a vital way of processing urgent questions about the gods, the city and the citizen in this emerging political order.

According to Peter Euben, Athenian citizens expected tragedy to play a role in their social and political education. Euben stresses the political and civic dimensions of tragedy as 'a form of public discourse that inculcated civic virtue and enhanced the citizen audience's capacity to act with foresight and judge with insight'.[9] Describing Greek tragedy as 'a critical consideration of public life', Euben takes issue with the idea that Greek tragedy straightforwardly articulates the views of the masses rather than mounting a critique of them.[10]

Euben suggests that at the time of Plato (whose views on tragedy we discuss in Chapter 6), tragedy was felt to be failing in this role; in response to this, political philosophy came into being in order to take on the task of evaluating the city. While Euben sees political theory as a departure from Greek tragedy, he also argues that it sets out the territory for questions of key social and political relevance to us today: issues of gender, citizenship, nationhood, and the experience of those displaced from their homeland. For further discussion of political approaches to tragedy – especially in relation to Sophocles' *Antigone* – see Chapter 4.

As Jean-Pierre Vernant observes, 'Tragedy is not only an art form; it is also a social institution which the city, by establishing competitions in tragedies, sets up alongside its political and legal institutions.'[11] Vernant sees the chorus as an instantiation and projection of Athenian civic identity. Citing Walter Nestle's observation that 'tragedy is born when myth starts to be considered from the point of view of a citizen', Vernant describes the chorus as 'the collective and anonymous presence embodied by an official college of citizens. Its role is to express through its fears, hopes, questions and judgements, the feelings of the spectators who make up the civic community'.[12] Here Vernant may be overstating the anonymity of the chorus: as we have seen, the chorus was at least partially characterised according to age, gender and other features such as geographical or religious identity. Indeed, Simon Goldhill has commented that 'All too often in the criticism of tragedy a chorus is treated as a disembodied voice.'[13] Yet in spite of his insistence on the status of the chorus as representative of the citizen body, Vernant acknowledges that the chorus does not simply reflect a sociopolitical dimension. Rather, he says, the chorus exists in order to interrogate and to problematise such questions.

Vernant's work on the chorus has provided a touchstone for many subsequent critical accounts. Developing Vernant's model of the chorus, Oddone Longo has stressed the 'collective character of ancient drama'.[14] Longo looks to the origins of tragedy in order to suggest that the perspective articulated by the chorus was very closely aligned with that of the spectators:

■ Inside the structure of the spectacle, the communitarian aspect of dramatic performance had its most distinctive and obvious realization in the chorus. The original matrix for tragedy (and for comedy) is to be sought in choral action. But this carries us back to a stage in which there was as yet no clear separation into two groups – the community of actors (the chorus) and the community of spectators (the public). In the earliest performances there was no split or distinction between the stage area and the auditorium (this was before the construction of stage or auditorium), nor between the actors and the public. The public – that is, the community – was also the collective which acted the 'drama.'... Given this scheme of the genesis of drama – hypothetical, of course, as are all discussions of origins – it remains secure that the essence of the chorus, the essential and distinctive feature of Attic drama, must be recognized in its role as 'representatives of the collective citizen body.'[15] □

John Gould, however, has found fault with Longo's account.[16] Longo proposes that the chorus is present in order to articulate an ideologically and politically standard view against which the transgressions of the protagonist can be debated and measured, but Gould suggests that there is a chronological problem with the argument. Gould points out that tragedy as a dramatic form predates the emergence of the democratic city. In other words, the chorus existed before there could be the kind of coherent ideological standpoint which Longo describes.

In a reply to Gould, Simon Goldhill agrees that Vernant's position is in need of nuance and adjustment.[17] Goldhill challenges Vernant's thesis that the chorus embodies a specialised knowledge or privileged perspective on the action. For Goldhill, the full meaning of the tragedy is only intelligible to the spectator because Greek tragedy regularly exploits the resources of dramatic irony. As Goldhill points out, the chorus does not always share in the audience's access to meaning. As an illustration, Goldhill refers to the so-called Deception Speech in Sophocles' *Ajax*, in which the protagonist tricks the chorus into believing that he does not intend to commit suicide.

Many critics, from the late twentieth century to the present, have been interested in the way that the chorus is constituted by the cultural 'Other'. Helene Foley has influentially argued that the chorus of Greek tragedy is typically composed of marginal groups such as women, slaves, foreigners and old men.[18] Gould stresses that 'otherness' should not be seen as a homogeneous idea, and that we need to pay close attention to the variations from one chorus to another. But he does suggest that the chorus's marginal status tends to mean that it lacks tragic authority. By this he means that we cannot necessarily accept the chorus's perspective as the standard view, or as the one we should adopt.

Like Gould, Helene Foley has questioned the extent to which the chorus can straightforwardly represent the citizen body of Athens. This observation leads Foley to suggest, like Gould, that the often marginal identity of the chorus might compromise its tragic authority. Simon Goldhill proposes that, rather than embodying tragic authority, the chorus has a special function in questioning its locus.

Foley notes that tragedies were performed in the context of a dramatic competition and she suggests that this may have provided an incentive for 'playing the Other'. Such parts placed greater demands on the performance skills of the chorus members, and so displayed their talent to the maximum.[19] In addition, the costumes worn by women or foreigners would have been more decorative than those that would have been worn by ordinary Athenian citizens, and so these choruses helped to enhance the visual appeal of the tragedy. Although some critics have suggested that there was little differentiation in the way that Greek tragic choruses moved, Foley argues that each chorus would dance in a way that was appropriate to its identity within the play. The possibilities for choreographic variation provided an additional reason for dramatists to experiment with different kinds of choruses.

Foley questions the assertion that Greek tragic choruses must be marginal because of the convention that they do not intervene in the action. She argues that the chorus is far less passive than this (particularly in the plays of Aeschylus), and she suggests that a much more nuanced account is needed. Foley notes that 'gender does not correlate clearly with inactivity or lack of assertiveness ... Female choruses in tragedy who act or attempt to act or suffer risk are not less common, and are very possibly more common, than male choruses'.[20] Foley also interrogates an assumption that female choruses are more able to establish an intimate, confidential role with a female protagonist. She argues that female choruses are able to establish a similarly sympathetic relationship with a male protagonist (e.g., in Aeschylus' *Prometheus Bound*), but that male choruses rarely, if ever, form a sympathetic relationship with a female protagonist. Foley suggests that female choruses tend to establish a more private and domestic set of concerns, while male choruses tend to establish a political frame of reference. But she notes that the perspectives afforded by different choruses typically draw on traditional wisdom rather than offering a distinctively gendered point of view. In this respect, she points out that distinctions between male and female choruses are liable to overstatement and emphasises that female choruses are often 'deeply concerned with the status of their city'.[21] These observations lead Foley to a general conclusion that choral identity does not define choral action as markedly as some have suggested.

Jacques Lacan defines the chorus simply as 'people who are moved'. Rather than seeing them as a body which directs or represents audience opinion, he says the chorus vicariously experiences feelings on the audience's behalf:

■ When you go to the theatre in the evening, you are preoccupied by the affairs of the day, by the pen that you lost, by the cheque that you will have to sign the next day. You shouldn't give yourselves too much credit. Your emotions are taken charge of by the healthy order displayed on the stage. The Chorus takes care of them. The emotional commentary is done for you. The greatest chance for the survival of classical tragedy depends on that. The emotional commentary is done for you. It is just sufficiently silly; it is also not without firmness; it is more or less human.

   Therefore, you don't have to worry; even if you don't feel anything, the Chorus will feel in your stead.[22] □

In this reading, Lacan goes much further than critics who have been interested in the mediating role played by the chorus. Lacan suggests that the chorus allows us to remain passive as spectators of the play.

German aestheticism

The chorus has been the subject of a fertile area of criticism in nineteenth-century Germany. In his essay 'On the Use of the Chorus in Tragedy', which first appeared as the preface to his play *The Bride of Messina* (1803), Schiller mounts a polemical attack on naturalism in art. He remarks that 'there has been and still is a long struggle with the vulgar concept of the *natural*, which reduces all poetry and art to naught and destroys them'.[23] He recognises that the chorus, once organic to the performance of ancient drama, has become in the drama of his own age a poetic contrivance. Schiller does not see the chorus as an undesirable anachronism, but rather he argues that the chorus should be reintroduced as part of a necessary struggle against the movement towards naturalism. A particular focus of Schiller's attack is the French neoclassical tragedy of Racine and others, who dispense with the chorus.

In his study of Racine, as we saw in Chapter 1, Lucien Goldmann emphasises that God is always present, but always hidden. One of the main effects of this is to heighten the isolation of the tragic hero, who is estranged both from the world and from God. It is for this reason, Goldmann argues, that Racine dispenses with the chorus whom Goldmann characterises as *'the voice of the human community* and therefore the voice of the gods'.[24] The absence of the chorus in Racine is therefore a sign of the silence of God.

Schiller is unsparingly critical of this move. He writes: 'Abolition of the chorus and the contraction of that materially powerful organ into the characterless and tediously recurrent figure of a sorry confidant was, then, not so great an improvement of tragedy as the French and their blind adherents imagined.'[25] Arguing that it is imperative for tragedians to counter this development, Schiller proposes that:

> ■ The introduction of the chorus would be the final and decisive step – and if it served no other purpose than to declare war openly and honestly on naturalism in art, it would be a living wall which tragedy draws about itself in order to shut itself definitely away from the actual world and preserve for itself its ideal ground and its poetic freedom.[26] □

In the phrase 'living wall', Schiller characterises the chorus as a barrier rather than (as Steiner does) a 'drawbridge' which can allow the audience into the world of the play as well as stand at a distance from it. For Schiller, the chorus adds grandeur and dignity to tragedy. Without the chorus, he suggests, the tone of the play as a whole is less elevated. He remarks that when ancient tragedy took as its setting the world of gods, heroes and kings, the chorus was 'a necessary concomitant'.[27] But the modern tragedian, observes Schiller, 'no longer finds the chorus in nature. He has to create it poetically and introduce it, that is, he has to manipulate an alteration in the story he is treating in order to transpose it back into that childlike time and into that childlike form.'[28]

Schiller suggests that the chorus breaks up the action and allows reflective pauses that give the spectator a chance to recover from the powerful emotions which tragedy incites. Schiller challenges objectors who claim that the chorus breaks the dramatic illusion. He says that this is precisely what is needed: not for the spectator to be lost in the action, but to be able to stand at a remove from it:

> ■ If the blows with which tragedy afflicts our hearts were to follow one upon another uninterruptedly, affliction would prevail over activity. We would be confused amid the subject matter and no longer hover above it. The chorus, by holding the parts separate and by intervening between the passions with its calming observations, gives us back our freedom, which would otherwise be lost in the storm of emotional agitation.[29] □

Schiller also emphasises the singularity of choral identity:

> ■ The chorus is not itself an individual but rather a general concept. This concept is represented by a sensorily powerful mass which impresses the senses by its expansive presence. The chorus abandons the narrow circle of the action to discourse on past and future, distance ages and peoples, the entire range of things human, in order to draw the great conclusions of life and to pronounce the teachings of wisdom ... the chorus, therefore, *purifies* the tragic poem by dissociating reflection from the action and by endowing reflecting itself with poetic power through this very dissociation.[30] □

Writing in the same decade as Schiller, Schlegel in his *Lectures on Dramatic Art and Literature* (1809–11) influentially describes the chorus of Greek tragedy as 'the ideal spectator'.[31] He says of the chorus: 'We must consider it as a personified reflection on the action which is going on; the incorporation into the representation itself of the sentiments of the poet, as the spokesman of the whole human race.'[32] Schlegel sees the chorus as both abstracted and anonymous, and at the same time representative of a broad base of humanity; this stands in marked contrast to the more recent accounts by Helene Foley and Edith Hall which have sought to stress the specificities of choral representation in individual plays. In keeping with this emphasis on abstraction and generality, Schlegel argues that the chorus 'represented in general, first the common mind of the nation, and then the general sympathy of all mankind'.[33] In characterising the chorus as the ideal spectator, Schlegel suggests that 'it conveys to the actual spectator a lyrical and musical expression of his own emotions, and elevates him to the region of contemplation'.[34] In other words, he sees the chorus not as a constitutive body of Athenian political life, articulating views which are culturally and temporally distant from Schlegel and his contemporaries, but as embodying wisdom that transcends its own historical moment.

Like Aristotle, Nietzsche takes the view that tragedy grows out of the chorus and he argues that the chorus represents the lifeblood of Greek tragedy. In *The Birth of Tragedy* (1872), Nietzsche asserts that tragedy confronts suffering in the world in a way that is not consoling but rather life-affirming. In other words, tragedy is not escapist but brave and defiant in the face of the presence of overwhelming suffering in the world. For Nietzsche, music – which he associates with the concept of the 'Dionysian' – is a key constituent in tragedy's capacity to affirm life. The idea of the Dionysian in Nietzsche's account receives a more detailed discussion in Chapter 5, 'Tragic Dualities', but, briefly summarised, Nietzsche uses the concept of the Dionysian to refer to states of intoxication, ecstasy as well as the primordial cry of pain.

It is through the concept of the Dionysian that Nietzsche explicates an account of the powerful communal experience of watching tragedy; according to Nietzsche, we have a sense of individuation in the world (*principium individuationis*) which is painful. Tragedy allows us to transcend our individuated existence and to experience something profoundly communal. Nietzsche argues that the chorus is crucial in facilitating this dissolution of boundaries between ourselves and others. The chorus allows the audience to experience 'an overwhelming feeling of unity leading back to the very heart of nature ... For the rapture of the Dionysian state with its annihilation of the ordinary bounds and limits of existence contains, while it lasts, a *lethargic* element in which all personal experiences of the past become immersed.'[35]

Nietzsche attacks Schlegel's characterisation of the chorus as the 'ideal spectator', and argues that there is a profound disjunction between the perspective of the chorus and that of the spectator: 'For we had always believed that the right spectator, whoever he might be, must always remain conscious that he was viewing a work of art and not an empirical reality. But the tragic chorus of the Greeks is forced to recognize real beings in the figures on stage.'[36] Nietzsche also objects to Schlegel's account as ahistorical. He says that the primitive chorus existed without the stage, and in view of this, Schlegel's account makes no sense. Nietzsche argues, 'What kind of artistic genre could possibly be extracted from the concept of the spectator, and find its true form in the "spectator as such"? The spectator without the spectacle is an absurd notion.'[37] Nietzsche approves of Schiller's declared intention to wage war on naturalism in art and concurs that 'it is not sufficient that one merely tolerates as poetic license what is actually the essence of all poetry'.[38]

The chorus and its modern (in)equivalents

Schlegel pessimistically remarks that 'Modern critics have never known what to make of the Chorus.'[39] He suggests that critics who have failed to grasp the true function and purpose of the chorus 'have censured it as a superfluous and cumbersome appendage, expressing their astonishment at the alleged absurdity of carrying on secret transactions in the presence of assembled multitudes'.[40] From this basis, Schlegel is sceptical about the viability of any modern attempt to reinstate the chorus. He argues that modern dramatists 'seem to have forgotten that we have neither suitable singing or dancing, nor, as our theatres are constructed, any convenient place for it. On these accounts it is hardly likely to become naturalized with us.'[41]

The chorus of Greek tragedy was in decline from the middle of the fifth century BC. Schlegel himself notes that Euripides diminishes the role of chorus to 'a mere episodical ornament'.[42] The Roman tragedian Seneca includes choruses in his plays; but Senecan drama is generally believed to have been recited by a single performer rather than fully staged. This effectively signalled the end of the chorus, at least in terms of a group of performers who sang and danced, as an organic feature of tragedy. Where the chorus appears after this point, it is frequently as a self-conscious archaism or a dramatic device.

It is through the Senecan influence (rather than Greek) that early modern English dramatists continue to include choruses in their plays. It is a device used by Shakespeare in *Henry V* and *Romeo and Juliet*, for example. Significantly, during this period, the term 'chorus' no longer refers to a group of people, but more typically to a single actor. By this point the plural identity of the chorus – something which we might think is essential to the very concept of 'choral' performance – has been lost.

With this history in mind, Steiner acknowledges that the question of the virtual obsolescence of the chorus is a complex one. Steiner shies away from offering a precise explanation for the way that the chorus has receded from post-classical tragedy. But he suggests that an important factor in this is the evolving emphasis on individuality which Western tragedy has witnessed since the sixteenth century. We have, he suggests, become resistant to thinking in terms of collective identity and community and this has had the effect of displacing the chorus from the crucial role it once occupied in ancient tragedy. We will look more closely at these evolving notions of individuality, selfhood and subjectivity in Chapter 3.

It is clear that Steiner takes a pessimistic view of the potential for the chorus to be meaningfully reinvented. In an essay on the chorus in modern interpretations of Greek tragedy, Helene Foley observes that 'Many performances of Greek tragedy include a chorus of one to three actors that neither sings nor dances and, for an audience accustomed to realistic theatre, often appears to impede the action and awkwardly clutter the set.'[43] Foley acknowledges that there are major difficulties for modern audiences in relating to the idea of a chorus. She says that 'creating any undifferentiated collectivity on stage runs counter to modern ideas about the individual's complex and ambivalent relation to social groups and the representation of this relation in performance'.[44]

Foley notes that the expense of staging a full chorus can be prohibitive for modern commercial productions, and this has contributed to a trend towards scaled-down choruses, or indeed productions in which the part of the chorus is spoken by just a single actor. Foley acknowledges that the dense mythological content of Greek choral odes can be difficult for audiences to grasp, even when the plays are performed in translation, but she suggests that programme notes and supertitles for choral songs can help to overcome cultural distance.[45]

Foley also recognises that the predominance of the modern indoor proscenium arch theatre has militated against the flourishing of the chorus on the modern stage. She does, however, vigorously contest the common claim that modern audiences are so thoroughly attuned to naturalistic theatre that they struggle to accept the non-naturalistic device of the chorus: here Foley points out that by no means all modern theatre is naturalistic.

In a claim that echoes Steiner's stances on modern tragedy (discussed in Chapter 8, 'Modern Tragedy'), Foley points out that 'The chorus's religious and ritual dimension and its complex political relation to its original community cannot be recreated for an eclectic modern audience that does not have the shared historical and cultural experience of the Attic polis.'[46] But here she suggests that:

■ Choral reactions of the kind represented in tragedy are also not unknown in modern contexts and performances can explore these possibilities. Interviews with survivors of the 9/11 disaster by the Columbia University oral history program, for example, show a consistent effort to understand each miraculous survival in terms of divine causes, luck, or sheer human ingenuity. At their best, the media or journalists also create from similar interviews a kind of choral reaction to current events that preserves the integrity of individual voices.[47] □

Foley notes that:

■ The chorus's unified group personality and the supposed limitations on its engagement in the action have raised complex class and other ideological and theatrical issues for Western audiences. Nineteenth-century European critics of the chorus, for example, began to find the chorus's group identity problematic in a world where the individual had apparently become paramount and communal consciousness on all issues, whether religious, social, or political, was thought to be divided or non-existent.[48] ☐

Foley comments here that such was Wagner's antagonism to the chorus that he 'came to reject the chorus even in opera, where it was a fixture, and proposed to replace it with the relation between singer and orchestra'.[49] Foley suggests that nineteenth-century thinkers created a legacy of ambivalence about the chorus as a viable institution, but asserts that twentieth-century productions have sought out new ways of negotiating 'the problem of staging a collective voice/identity in an era firmly attached to preserving individual ones'.[50] Foley contends that twentieth-century performances and adaptations of Greek tragedy have been able to explore the way that the chorus 'can play off individual voices against a collective one created by war and suffering',[51] and argues that Euripides' *Trojan Women* has become an important vehicle for projects of this kind.

Modern performance criticism is already starting to register the impact of experiments with the chorus. In a discussion of a stage adaptation of Dimitris Dimitriadis's novella *Pethaino san chora* ('I am Dying as a Country') (1978), directed by Michael Marmarinos at the Athens Festival 2008, Vassilis Lambropoulos describes how the production utilised a chorus of 200 volunteers of different ages and from varying ethnic groups and social backgrounds.[52] Lambropoulos characterises the director's approach as 'anti-theatrical': he argues that it served to collapse distinctions between audience and chorus. The audience was invited not to relate to the performance on stage but instead – more radically – to become part of it. According to Lambropoulos, this was not an attempt to recover or reanimate Greek tragic tradition, but to call into question the viability of establishing a collective identity in a postmodern age. For Lambropoulos, this performance resonated with many of the doubts about the legitimacy of the chorus in contemporary drama which we have been examining in this chapter. In his concluding remarks, Lambropoulos asks whether the performance confirmed that the traditional notion of the chorus has fundamentally disintegrated, and whether it heralded the search for a new device which might replace it. He suggests that the performance invited the people of Athens to think about new forms of collective action and public participation. Although Lambropoulos does not press a causal connection, he notes that, shortly afterwards, thousands of Greek citizens took to the streets in a collective act of political protest: it is implied that instead of a chorus being something political within a play, it spurred the audience to be more politically active outside the play.

Marmarinos's production took a sceptical view of the capacity of a chorus to embody and express collective identity. As we saw earlier in the chapter, not all choruses are figured as groups, yet the single-figure chorus embodies something of a contradiction in terms. For some writers, choral figures represent a detached voice of commentary on the actions of the main protagonists. In an early study of its kind, H. C. Montgomery surveys the history of choral development since the Greeks. He suggests that O'Neill's *Mourning Becomes Electra* (1931), a play that is closely imitative of Greek tragic models, draws on the device of the chorus, although none of the characters is formally defined as such. Montgomery argues that the role played by the chorus is dispersed among minor characters, and the sea shanty 'Shenandoah' is used as a refrain.[53]

Several critics have been interested in the way that Thomas Hardy utilises choric figures in his novels. It has now become almost a critical commonplace to refer to the 'chorus of rustics' in his novels. In a recent study of *The Return of the Native* (1878), Trish Ferguson has remarked, 'As is typical of Hardy's novels, the laborers of Egdon act primarily as a rustic chorus commenting on the actions of the principal characters.'[54]

Carol Reed Anderson looks at ways in which Hardy provides a larger context for his main plot. Anderson suggests that two of the ways in which Hardy achieves tonal variation is through references to the landscape, and through his use of a chorus of local Wessex characters who act as a foil for the pessimism of the protagonists: 'Emotional balance is achieved also by the chorus of rustics and their necessary ironic counterweight to the main characters' extremities of introspection.'[55] Another critic, C. M. Jackson-Houlston, has suggested that this technique becomes more problematic in the development of Hardy's career, and that in his later novels he was less ready to embody local or traditional wisdom in this choric device: 'As Hardy became more and more interested in the social and economic exploitation of the ordinary man he was less and less able either to create what sometimes looks like a separable chorus of quaint, lovable rustics or to allow his main characters to escape into a world that is less and less that of the present.'[56] We will look in more detail at relationships between the novel and tragic conventions in Chapter 7.

This chapter began by reviewing the ancient Greek chorus as an historical phenomenon, rooted in the cultural and performance conditions of the fifth century BC. We have traced a debate about how far the chorus can be seen as manifestation of the audience's own perspective on the drama. Vernant holds that the chorus represents the citizen view; others have wanted to offer a more nuanced account which recognises that the chorus is typically composed of outsider figures, such as slaves or women, who do not represent the 'official' male citizen perspective in any obvious way. Thus there are tensions and ambiguities in the way that the chorus articulates its position.

Some of the most important work on the chorus originates in nineteenth-century Germany. Schiller celebrates the chorus as a non-naturalistic device, a 'living wall' designed to separate drama from reality. In seeing the chorus as an abstract, anonymous 'ideal spectator', Schlegel suggests that the perspective of chorus and audience is unified and harmonious, a view which accords with Vernant's later account. Hegel sees the chorus not as a distanced, reflective figure, but at the heart of tragedy itself. Nietzsche concurs with Hegel in seeing the chorus as a vital element in Greek tragedy. While these German philosophers have wanted to emphasise the crucial role played by the chorus in Greek tragedy, several critics have wondered whether the chorus is now obsolete and defunct in modern drama. Other critics, such as Helene Foley, have identified ways in which the device of the chorus is being reconstituted and reinterpreted in modern drama and the novel.

This look at the collective voice of the chorus brings us to a consideration of individual tragic experience over the next two chapters. Vital to our understanding of the chorus is the protagonist, with whom the chorus is in dialogue. In the next chapter, we turn to the tragic hero.

CHAPTER THREE

The Tragic Hero

Character and subjectivity

We noted in the previous chapter on the chorus that Aristotle has relatively little to say on the subject of dramatic character and that he understands character primarily as a vehicle for the plot. In the *Poetics*, Aristotle claims that, 'A tragedy is ... a *mimesis* not of people but of their actions and life ... [By definition] a work could not be a tragedy if there were no action. But there could be a tragedy without *mimesis* of character ...'[1]

Since Aristotle, the consensus has changed radically and critics, particularly during the last century, have sought to situate the protagonist more prominently in their readings of tragedy. As Sidney Zink has argued, 'tragedy, whatever else it requires, requires a protagonist of great dimensions. The tragic hero must be an extraordinary human specimen.'[2] Anticipating Zink by some half a century, A. C. Bradley suggests that Shakespearean tragedy is:

> ■ pre-eminently the story of one person, the 'hero', or at most of two, the 'hero' and 'heroine'. Moreover, it is only in the love-tragedies, *Romeo and Juliet* and *Antony and Cleopatra*, that the heroine is as much the centre of the action as the hero. The rest, including *Macbeth*, are single stars.[3] □

For Bradley, it is not just that the protagonist occupies a place that is structurally central to the tragedy; Bradley proposes a reading of tragedy as essentially character-driven:

> ■ The centre of the tragedy, therefore, may be said with equal truth to lie in action issuing from character, or in character issuing in action ... What we do feel strongly, as a tragedy advances to its close, is that the calamities and catastrophe follow inevitably from the deeds of men, and that the main source of these deeds is character.[4] □

As an extension of this claim about the relationship between action and character, Bradley argues:

> ■ The suffering and calamity are, moreover, exceptional. They befall a conspicuous person. They are themselves of some striking kind. They are also, as a rule, unexpected, and contrasted with previous happiness or glory. A tale, for example, of a man slowly worn to death by disease, poverty, little cares, sordid vices, petty persecutions, however piteous or dreadful it might be, would not be tragic in the Shakespearean sense.[5] □

What is significant about Bradley's analysis here is that he is not just referring to the status of the hero, but insisting that the hero's sufferings need to be elevated or amplified in their scope. This idea came under considerable pressure later in the twentieth century, through the work of dramatists such as Arthur Miller, as we shall see later in the chapter.

Like Bradley and Zink, Felski also emphasises the centrality of the protagonist as the locus of tragic conflict:

> ■ Such a conflict, moreover, is often enacted in the divided desires and psyche of a single protagonist rather than being parceled out among a dramatic cast of allegorical types. Robert Heilman writes: 'It is in tragedy that man is divided; in melodrama, his troubles, though they may reflect some weakness or inadequacy, do not arise from the urgency of unreconciled impulses. In tragedy the conflict is within man; in melodrama, it is between men, or between men and things.'[6] □

In one of the most influential discussions of tragic characterisation, Bernard Knox argues that Sophocles' plays follow a distinctive pattern: 'the presentation of the tragic dilemma in the figure of a single dominating character'.[7] Insofar as Sophocles can be credited with this invention, Knox suggests, he can also be credited with laying the foundations for the Western tragic tradition. Knox attributes this in part to Sophocles' movement away from the tragic trilogy, the form that had been practised by Aeschylus, towards the composition of individual plays. Knox argues that Sophocles is characteristically interested in the 'tragic dilemma in terms of a single personality facing the supreme crisis of his life', unlike Euripides who, Knox claims, diffuses his attention through an ensemble of characters.[8] Thus Knox suggests:

> ■ The Sophoclean hero acts in a terrifying vacuum, a present which has no future to comfort and no past to guide, an isolation in time and space which imposes on the hero the full responsibility for his own action and its consequences. It is precisely this fact which makes possible the greatness of the Sophoclean heroes; the source of their action lies in them alone, nowhere else; the greatness of the action is theirs alone. Sophocles

presents us for the first time with what we recognize as a 'tragic hero': one who, unsupported by the gods and in the face of human opposition, makes a decision which springs from the deepest layer of his individual nature, his *physis*, and then blindly, ferociously, heroically maintains that decision even to the point of self-destruction.[9] ☐

While acknowledging that there are variations between the plays, Knox posits a clear pattern in Sophocles' characterisation of the tragic hero. With extensive supporting evidence from the plays, he suggests that each of the heroes exhibits an amplified determination or resolve which manifests itself in a refusal to yield to persuasion by others. This resolve, when under pressure, turns to anger. One of the main consequences of this intransigence is the hero's isolation, a central idea in Knox's account which Michelle Gellrich suggests is indebted to the Romantic concept of the sublime.[10] As Gellrich notes, 'Schiller's Kantian ideas stress the individual hero and his isolation in the face of potentially annihilating powers such as fate.'[11] In developing this concept of heroic isolation in relation to his reading of Sophocles, Knox argues that in his most extreme moments, the hero 'speaks neither to man nor to gods, but to the landscape, that unchanging presence which alone will not betray him'.[12]

The natural extension of this isolation is found in death:

■ The hero chooses death. This is after all the logical end of his refusal to compromise. Life in human society is one long compromise; we live, all of us, only by constantly subduing our own will, our own desires, to the demands of others, expressed as the law of the community or the opinion of our fellowmen ... But in Sophoclean tragedy the hero faces an issue on which he cannot compromise and still respect himself. Surrender would be spiritual self-destruction, a betrayal of his *physis*; the hero is forced to choose between defiance and loss of identity. And in the Sophoclean hero the sense of identity, of independent, individual existence, is terribly strong. They are, all of them, exquisitely conscious of their difference from others, of their uniqueness. They have a profound sense of their own worth as individuals, and this exasperates the anger they feel at the world's denial of respect. In the crisis of their lives, abandoned by friends, ringed by enemies, unsupported by the gods, they have nothing to fall back on for support but this belief in themselves, their conception of their own unique character and destiny.[13] ☐

Thus Knox proposes the presence of recurrent patterns in Sophoclean tragedy and its presentation of character. In his study of Senecan tragedy, Braden also identifies a highly consistent approach to characterisation which, he suggests, can be traced in each of the plays. Seneca's characters are, he says, 'titanic figures of insatiable appetite for conquest and destruction; the vehemence of their desire all but wrecks the classical forms into which they are put, and expresses itself in set pieces of hyperbolic rant that seem bent on violating all sensible standards of literary decorum'.[14] Although Braden might seem in this passage to be mounting an attack on the aesthetics of Senecan drama, he sees this powerful rhetoric as crucial to our understanding of the texts. There is in Senecan drama, he argues, a shift away from conventional narrative structures towards an intense and sustained focus on the interior world of the emotions: 'The basic plot of a Senecan play is that of inner passion which bursts upon and desolates an unexpecting and largely uncomprehending world, an enactment of the mind's disruptive power over external reality ...'[15]

For Linda Bamber, the tragic hero exerts a much more precarious position within the narrative. Tragic conflict exists not as a process which revolves around the hero, but as one which ultimately displaces him from his place in the narrative:

■ The tragic world thwarts and opposes the hero, refusing to rearrange itself around him. What the hero desires is centrality; what we see is his displacement from the center of his own story. Antony is displaced by Caesar, Lear by old age and bad children, Hamlet by his uncle's ambition and his mother's remarriage. The world grinds on, having its own purposes, indifferent to the suffering its progress is causing our hero.[16] □

In this account, tragedy is not about the centrality of the hero, but his marginalisation. Raymond Williams, like Bamber, queries the centrality of the hero but from a different perspective. He argues that we focus too much on the tragic hero and on his death as the culminating event in the play. Williams argues: 'We think of tragedy as what happens to the hero, but the ordinary tragic action is what happens through the hero. When we confine our attention to the hero, we are unconsciously confining ourselves to one kind of experience which in our own culture we tend to take as the whole.'[17] For further discussion of tragedy's anthropocentrism, see Joseph Meeker in the Conclusion to this Guide.

Over the last century or so, the field of character study has negotiated two opposing ways of thinking about character and individual identity. The structuralist account of the French anthropologist Claude Lévi-Strauss has provided an influential theoretical basis for arguments about the universality of human experience. Lévi-Strauss is interested the way that myth expresses aspects of human experience and structures it in terms of binary oppositions. As Charles Segal has suggested, Lévi-Strauss sees the function of myth as 'to mediate fundamental contradictions in human existence, man's relation to man in society, and man's relation to nature in the external world'.[18] The work of Lévi-Strauss has been particularly influential on Jean-Pierre Vernant and other scholars of Greek tragedy following him. (For further discussion of binary oppositions, see Chapter 5.)

Competing with this emphasis on archetypal modes of human experience, there has arisen a more recent interest in historical specificity. Critics from Marxist and associated schools of thought have all sought to interrogate the way in which subjectivity is constructed by social, political and cultural forces. Marxist literary theorists take the view that character is formed in relation to particular historical conditions and not human nature. This is a view which has been particularly prevalent in the scholarship of early modern English tragedy. In his influential book on the subject, *Radical Tragedy*, Jonathan Dollimore argues that, 'Because informed by contradictory social and ideological processes, the subject is never an indivisible unity, never an autonomous, self-determining centre of consciousness.'[19] For this reason, he writes, materialist critics (among whom he is numbered) tend to prefer the term 'subject' to 'individual'.

The title of Catherine Belsey's book, *The Subject of Tragedy: Identity and Difference in Renaissance Drama*, plays on two, interrelated meanings of the subject: both as the human subject, the self, and subject as the subject matter or topical concern of tragedy as an art form. Like Dollimore, Belsey counters the view that human nature can be understood in terms of eternal patterns or archetypes:

■ The history of the subject in the sixteenth and seventeenth centuries indicates, however, that there are radical discontinuities. On this reading the past affirms the possibility (the inevitability?) of change. It demonstrates that subjectivity as liberal humanism defines it is not natural, inevitable or eternal; on the contrary, it is produced and reproduced in and by a specific social order and in the interests of specific power-relations.[20] □

Belsey is interested in the way early modern tragedy creates a sense of 'intimations of the construction of a place which notions of personal identity were later to come to fill'.[21] She quotes as the classic case in point Hamlet's assertion: 'I have that within which passes show – / These but the trappings and the suits of woe' (*Hamlet*, I.ii.85–6). She notes that the play initially seems to present itself as a narrative which is concerned with questions of identity, self-realisation and agency; but by Act V these are abandoned as the play 'surrenders to providence'.[22] Belsey suggests that the play poses questions of selfhood which are far ahead of its time; the play fundamentally lacks the philosophical and cultural tools to pursue these questions to a conclusion. As she says: 'The play, which has begun to define an interiority as the origin of meaning and action, a human subject as agent, cannot produce closure in terms of an analysis which in 1601 does not yet fully exist'.[23] As such, the play's investigation of subjectivity is, in a very real sense, before its own time.

In her discussion of Vittoria in Webster's *The White Devil* (1612), Belsey refers to what she calls a 'discursive mobility' of character, noting that Vittoria speaks from different perspectives and subject-positions in the play.[24] Belsey argues that tragedy is moving towards an understanding of character as complex, flexible, and sometimes even demonstrating inconsistencies as individuals do in real life.

Belsey notes the way that the shift from a medieval worldview to the early modern worldview has a profound effect on the evolving concepts of identity and subjectivity:

> ■ In the Middle Ages knowledge was ultimately knowledge not of the world and the self but of God, by means of theology, the queen of the sciences, culminating discipline of the trivium and the quadrivium. To know God was not to master an object of knowledge, but to apprehend a meaning which was also truth. God, the *Logos*, at once divinity, concept and word, was pure meaning and pure being, the transcendental signified and referent, and fully to know God was not to differentiate oneself from the objects of knowledge but, on the contrary, to become absorbed in total presence, to be transformed and ultimately dissolved.[25] □

Belsey suggests that this rising sense of subjectivity is one of several conditions which promote the rise of tragedy in the early modern period and that, in turn, tragedy contributes to the evolving sense of the subject. It is worth noting that other commentators do not see this kind of subjectivity as a crucial element in earlier forms of tragedy. Hegel, for example, argues that Greek tragedy precisely lacks this kind of subjectivity; rather he sees characters as embodying positions within an ethical system. As Segal suggests: 'The Greek tragic hero, then, is not a "character" quite in the sense of the hero of a modern fiction or drama, an individual with a three-dimensional personality. He is, rather, both an individual caught in a moral conflict and a symbolic element in a complex socio-religious structure.'[26]

Sharing some affinity with this emphasis on the moral content of drama, medieval and early Tudor drama had taken a more diagrammatic view of character: prior to the early modern period, character was understood primarily in terms of its symbolic function of a figure in a moral didactic narrative. Typographical names (e.g., Crafty Conveyance in Skelton's *Magnificence*, written *c.*1515) emphasised the priority of a single characteristic which would remain fixed for the duration of the play. Belsey argues that the emergence of the soliloquy as a dramatic device marks a fundamental shift from the moral allegories of Tudor drama to signify a new emphasis on interiority:

> ■ As the literal drama discards allegory, and morality personifications give way to social types, concrete individuals, the moral conflicts externalized in

> the moralities are internalized in the soliloquy and thus understood to be confined *within* the *mind* of the protagonist. The struggle between good and evil shifts its centre from the macrocosm to the microcosm.[27] □

Soliloquy is an important vehicle for character development, since self-expression requires us to suppose the presence of a prior self with its own interior life of desire, fear, anger and so on. Analysis of the tragic hero's self-expression has led several critics to comment on the heightened significance of the first-person pronoun in the utterances of the tragic hero, both in soliloquy and in dialogue. In reference to the Senecan Medea's assertion, 'Medea superest' ('Medea is left'), Gordon Braden notes, 'That triumphant utterance of her own famous name is pure Seneca, the most stunning instance of a habit that runs through all the plays …'[28] The Senecan legacy is important in shaping similar moments of self-assertion in early modern tragedy.

Belsey comments on what she calls 'the self-assertion of Elizabethan and Jacobean protagonists when they proclaim the continuity of inviolable identity: "I am / Antony yet" (*Antony and Cleopatra*, III.xiii, 92-3); "I am Duchess of Malfi still" (*The Duchess of Malfi*, IV.ii, 142).'[29] The prominent assertion of the first-person pronouns is not simply confined to the speeches and soliloquies of early modern drama, but, as John Gould has demonstrated, it can be traced back to Greek tragedy where it is also a noticeable feature of heroic self-expression.[30] Gould also argues that there is heightened importance attached to utterances of the protagonist's name in plays such as *Philoctetes* and *Oedipus Tyrannus*. For Gould, this investment in the 'I' of tragedy, and in the hero's name, reflects the way that tragedy is often concerned with a struggle to maintain individual identity in a changing world.

Conversely, in her comparative study of ancient Greek and modern Irish tragedy, Fiona Macintosh notes that in final speeches, the tragic protagonist has a marked tendency to refer to himself in the third person. During his dying moments, the protagonist experiences a crisis in his sense of self which is articulated through his use of the third person. It is as if the hero is already constructing self-references in terms of the reported narrative that will survive him. As an illustration of this, Macintosh suggests that Heracles in Sophocles' *Trachiniae* manifests what she calls this 'hyperconsciousness of self' that is characteristic of the dying protagonist.[31] This phrase recalls T. S. Eliot's reference to the 'attitude of self-dramatization assumed by some of Shakespeare's heroes at moments of tragic intensity', which he says is derived from Seneca.[32] In his discussion of Senecan self-dramatisation, Eliot suggests that it reflects a Stoical attitude which is fundamentally opposed to Christian ideals of humility. Eliot says that this attitude is exemplified in Othello's last great speech (V.iii), in which he adopts an *'aesthetic* rather than a moral attitude, dramatizing himself against his environment'.[33]

While the work of Belsey and others investigates the notion of subjectivity and interiority, it is worth remembering that tragic heroes exist as bodies on the stage as well in the realm of an interior self which is accessible to us via the self-disclosures of soliloquy. While the idea of an exterior body and an interior self, capable of agency and self-expression, might seem to exist in tension with one another, several critics have demonstrated that the hero's physical self and mental self are intimately connected. Writing about the mind and manifestations of consciousness in Greek tragedy, Ruth Padel has shown that these abstract concepts are frequently figured in reference to parts of the body and internal organs such as the heart, liver, lungs and gallbladder as sites of emotional activity. As she remarks, 'Greek tragedy describes what happens inside human beings … biologically, in ways that read to us like metaphor.'[34] Padel points out that this construction of emotional experience in corporal terms is not, as it first appears, a metaphor, but is indicative of a different way of expressing interiority and emotion that is historically determined. Padel argues:

> ■ If you sit on the hillside above the theater of Dionysus, you see why inward rather than external experience matters to tragedy. In the physical performance, crowded by the bodies of thousands of other people, peering a long way down to the stage, a spectator was distant from the actors' bodies, which were hidden in their tokens of representation, the mask, the long costume. These bodies were very small. What the spectators received were the external and rhetorical trappings by which tragic language made apparent what they could not see: the stage figures' inwardness.[35] □

Padel suggests that in Homeric war, the body is the primary site of damage, whereas in Greek tragedy, the focus shifts to interior suffering, particularly in the form of madness.[36]

Nobility

The idea that tragedy charts a fall from greatness derives from Aristotle's *Poetics*. As George Steiner has observed, 'The very rubric "tragedy" in its Senecan and medieval demarcation is that of "the fall of illustrious men." Tragedy argues an aristocracy of suffering, an excellence of pain.'[37]

Aristotle suggests that tragedy and comedy deal with different types of character: he observes that comedy represents those who are 'baser than us' while tragedy represents those who are 'greater than us'.[38]

There is considerable ambiguity about what Aristotle means here and whether he is referring to an ethical hierarchy or a social one.[39]

The idea that tragedy and comedy deal with different social classes entered the critical mainstream through the commentary tradition of Donatus-Evanthius: 'But many things distinguish comedy from tragedy, especially the fact that comedy is concerned with the average fortunes of people, the onset of moderate risks, and actions with happy endings. But in tragedy, everything is the opposite: great people, immense terrors, and deathly endings.'[40] In this construction, comedy is seen as the genre of the man next door, while tragedy is seen as the genre of the ruling classes, a convention that was influential in shaping Renaissance ideas about tragedy. When, in the sixteenth century, Philip Sidney complains that contemporary English dramatists are guilty of 'mingling kings and clowns' in their plays, this reflects a critical orthodoxy (albeit one which was rarely observed in practice) that kings were the proper subject for tragedy and clowns belonged to the world of comedy.[41] For Sidney, the segregation of the two genres went hand in hand with the segregation of characters of different social rank. Shakespeare does not subscribe to neoclassical ideals but, as Bradley remarks, Shakespeare's tragedies are broadly concerned with 'persons of "high degree"; often with kings or princes; if not, with leaders in the state like Coriolanus, Brutus, Antony; at the least, as in *Romeo and Juliet*, with members of great houses, whose quarrels are of public moment.'[42]

On the face of it, Bradley is suggesting that *Romeo and Juliet* is concerned with broadly the same class of characters as the other tragedies. At the same time, the concessive phrase 'at the least' shows some hesitation on his part. Ruth Nevo more boldly asserts that *Romeo and Juliet* is less tragic than a play like *King Lear* because 'Here all is at a lower pitch; nearer to the commonplace and ordinary.'[43] As we have seen, Bradley suggests that the Montagues and the Capulets, as aristocratic families, are figures of public importance in the world of the play. However, it is clear that the play's location in Verona constitutes a more provincial setting than many other tragedies of the period in which the action is located in a royal court. Indeed, although the play includes a prince among its characters, he plays a relatively marginal role in the action. Still further, the action does not focus on Lord Montague or Lord Capulet as the heads of their respective families, but rather on Romeo and Juliet, who as adolescents are among the least powerful members of the two families. Thus the play represents a shift away from the idea of a fall from greatness as defined in terms of rank or political power, and instead demonstrates a view of nobility which accords with Bradley's account of the 'exceptional' nature of the tragic protagonist.

Although, as we have seen, Bradley adopts a fairly orthodox position on the subject of tragedy and high rank, he does offer some important qualifications. He observes that Shakespeare's tragic heroes 'are exceptional beings'. By 'exceptional', Bradley is not abandoning the notion of royal blood or high political status. Rather, he is suggesting that attendant upon high rank is another kind of greatness:

> ■ We have already seen that the hero, with Shakespeare, is a person of high degree or of public importance, and that his actions or sufferings are of an unusual kind. But this is not all. His nature is also exceptional, and generally raises him in some respect much above the average level of humanity ... [Shakespeare's] tragic characters are made of the stuff we find within ourselves and within the persons who surround them. But, by an intensification of the life which they share with others, they are raised above them; and the greatest are raised so far that, if we fully realize all that is implied in their words and actions, we become conscious that in real life we have known scarcely any one resembling them.[44] □

In this emphasis on intensity is a distinct echo of Hegel's pronouncement on tragic character:

> ■ Throughout they are what they can and must be in accordance with their essential nature, not an ensemble of qualities separately developed epically in various ways; on the contrary, even if they are living and individual themselves they are simply one power dominating their own specific character; for, in accordance with their own individuality, they have inseparably identified themselves with some single particular aspect of those solid interests we have enumerated above, and are prepared to answer for that identification. Standing on this height, where the mere accidents of the individual's purely personal life disappear, the tragic heroes of dramatic art have risen to become, as it were, works of sculpture ...[45] □

For Hegel the greatness of the tragic character does not exist in terms of amplification of emotion as much as in the intense commitment to an ethical standpoint.

Like Knox in his study of the Sophoclean hero, Lukács suggests that the man of high rank is inextricably figured in terms of isolation, and that this amplifies the tragic potential of the conflicts which he experiences. It is only in the king's suffering that the suffering of the whole community is symbolised and distilled:

> ■ In tragedy the hero must be a king simply because of the need to sweep all the petty causalities of life from the ontological path of destiny – because the socially dominant figure is the only one whose conflicts, while retaining the sensuous illusion of a symbolic existence, grow solely out of the tragic problem; because only such a figure can be surrounded, even as to the forms of its external appearance, with the required atmosphere of significant isolation.[46] □

From Hegel to Bradley, we can see an emerging idea that tragic nobility might not consist exclusively or even primarily in terms of rank. This possibility allowed writers to experiment with new forms of tragedy. In her study of tragedy in the Victorian novel, discussed in more detail in Chapter 7, Jeanette King notes the importance of the publication of Wordsworth and Coleridge's *Lyrical Ballads* (1798), which was radical in its attention to the experience of ordinary characters.[47] Although Wordsworth and Coleridge are not writers of tragedy, King suggests that the publication of this text had the effect of refocusing literary attention onto the lives of homely or humble characters, a concern which is particularly marked in the novels of George Eliot, for example.

Steiner argues that Buchner's *Woyzeck* (published posthumously in 1879) is 'the first real tragedy of low life' and contends that the play:

■ repudiates an assumption implicit in Greek, Elizabethan, and neo-classic drama: the assumption that tragic suffering is the sombre privilege of those who are in high places. Ancient tragedy had touched the lower orders, but only in passing, as if a spark has been thrown off from the great conflagration inside the royal palace. Into the dependent griefs of the menial classes, moreover, the tragic poets introduced a grotesque or comic note. The watchman in *Agamemnon* and the messenger in *Antigone* are lit by the fire of the tragic action, but they are meant to be laughed at. Indeed, the touch of comedy derives from the fact that they are inadequate, by virtue of social rank or understanding, to the great occasions on which they briefly perform.[48] □

In *The Origin of German Tragic Drama* (1928), a study of the German Trauerspiel (mourning play), Walter Benjamin sets out to differentiate the aesthetics of the baroque Trauerspiel from those of classical tragedy. Benjamin proposes that while tragedy is rooted in myth, the Trauerspiel is rooted in history. It is important to Benjamin's argument that the Trauerspiel – which he sees as displacing tragedy in the eighteenth century – is not concerned with the transcendental but instead with the more worldly realm of political intrigue. As part of this discussion, Benjamin suggests that noble rank is not an integral feature of tragedy: 'It would be otiose to point out that the sublimity of the content is not explained by the rank and lineage of the characters ... [I]t could not be more obvious that it is an incidental factor, arising from the material of the tradition on which tragic poetry is based.'[49] On this point, Benjamin quotes the anonymous author of *Die Glorreiche Marter Joannes von Nepomuck*:

■ 'For the heroes of their tragedies the Greeks generally took royal persons and the moderns for the most part have done the same. This is certainly not because rank gives more dignity to the person who acts or suffers; and as it is merely a question of setting human passions in play, the relative worth of the objects by which this is done is a matter of indifference, and farms achieve as much as is achieved by kingdoms ... Persons of great power and prestige are nevertheless best adapted for tragedy, because the misfortune in which we should recognize the fate of human life must have sufficient magnitude, in order to appear terrible to the spectator, be he who he may ...'[50] ☐

The anonymous writer concludes that 'the misfortunes of the great and powerful are unconditionally terrible ... [T]he fall is greatest from a height. Bourgeois characters lack the height from which to fall.'[51]

Raymond Williams suggests that while tragedy has historically differentiated between the death of a king and the death of a servant (the former seeming a worthy subject for tragedy while the latter has not seemed to rise above the level of mere accident), the middle class of twentieth-century culture is beginning to reject this social stratification and thus 'the tragedy of a citizen could be as real as the tragedy of a prince'.[52] Of the 'man of rank', Williams observes:

■ His fate was the fate of the house or kingdom which he at once ruled and embodied. In the person of Agamemnon or of Lear the fate of a house or a kingdom was literally acted out. It was of course inevitable that this definition should fail to outlast its real social circumstances, in its original form. It was in particular inevitable that bourgeois society should reject it: the individual was neither the state nor an element of the state, but an entity in himself ...

Rank in tragedy became the name-dropping, the play with titles and sonorities, of costume drama. What had formerly been a significant relationship, of the king embodying his people and embodying also the common meanings of life and the world, became an empty ceremonial ...[53] ☐

One of the most important interventions in the debate about tragic nobility comes in Arthur Miller's 'Tragedy and the Common Man' (1949), in which Miller interrogates the traditional formulation of tragedy as a genre concerned with kings and ruling houses. Miller acknowledges that it presents an apparent problem for the modern dramatist since audiences are no longer as deeply concerned with affairs of state and the fortunes of monarchs:

■ Insistence upon the rank of the tragic hero, or the so-called nobility of his character, is really but a clinging to the outward forms of tragedy. If rank or nobility of character was indispensable, then it would follow that the problems of those with rank were the particular problems of tragedy. But surely the right of one monarch to capture the domain from another no longer raises our passions, nor are our concepts of justice what they were to the mind of an Elizabethan king.[54] □

Miller argues that modern psychoanalysis has demonstrated the universality of certain human conditions, for example the Oedipus complex. For Miller, Sophocles' Oedipus is not an exemplar of unique suffering; rather, in the wake of Freudian psychoanalytic theory, Oedipus has come to represent and embody psychological impulses which are commonly implicated in childhood sexual development:

> ■ I believe that the common man is as apt a subject for tragedy in its highest sense as kings were. On the face of it this ought to be obvious in the light of modern psychiatry, which bases its analysis upon classical formulations, such as the Oedipus and Orestes complexes, for instances, which were enacted by royal beings, but which apply to everyone in similar emotional situations.[55] □

Miller acknowledges that Freudian theory has effected a fundamental shift in the way we think about suffering: according to Freud, processes of psychological conflict – between the conscious realm of reason and social constraint and the unconscious realm of desire – are universal. Writing in a recent collection of essays, Felski echoes Miller's claim by remarking on the universality of suffering in a post-Freudian world: 'In this democratized vision of suffering, the soul of a bank clerk or a shop girl becomes a battleground on which momentous and incalculable forces play themselves out.'[56]

Miller elaborates on his claim about the universality of human suffering as 'the underlying struggle ... of the individual attempting to gain his "rightful" position in his society' – a struggle which unites those of all ranks.[57] He argues:

> ■ there are among us today, as there always have been, those who act against the scheme of things that degrades them, and in the process of action everything we have accepted out of fear or insensitivity or ignorance is shaken before us and examined, and from this total onslaught by an individual against the seemingly stable cosmos surrounding us – from this total examination of the 'unchangeable' environment – comes the terror and the fear that is classically associated with tragedy ... And such a process is not beyond the common man. In revolutions around the world, these past thirty years he has demonstrated again and again this inner dynamic of all tragedy.[58] □

Although Miller begins his essay by suggesting that psychoanalysis has opened up the potential relevance of legendary figures such as Oedipus, conversely he also suggests that modern psychiatry and sociology have had a detrimental effect on the production of tragedy: 'If all our miseries, our indignities, are born and bred within our minds, then all action, let alone the heroic action, is obviously impossible.'[59] In this construction, tragedy becomes a battle within the self, rather than a battle against external conditions such as Fate. The tragic conflict has become internalised, and through this very struggle, the possibility of action is negated, a theme which Shakespeare radically anticipates in *Hamlet* (1601). For Miller, tragedy explores the hero's single-minded determination to realise his humanity. In this process, Miller claims, must lie the possibility of victory. For Miller, such a possibility destabilises conventional definitions of tragedy as a story with a sad ending and says, on the contrary, 'in truth tragedy implies more optimism in its author than does comedy'.[60]

The fatal flaw and tragic guilt

Bradley defines tragedy as 'a story of exceptional calamity leading to the death of a man in high estate', a conception of tragedy which has long endured.[61] This formulation originally derives from the following passage in Aristotle's *Poetics*:

> ■ So it is clear that one should not show virtuous men passing from good to bad fortune, since this does not arouse fear or pity, but only a sense of outrage. Nor should one show bad men passing from bad to good fortune, as this is less tragic than anything, since it has none of the necessary requirements; it neither satisfies our human feeling nor arouses pity and fear. Nor should one show a quite wicked man passing from good to bad fortune; it is true that such an arrangement would satisfy our human feeling, but it would not arouse pity or fear, since the one is felt for someone who comes to grief without deserving it, and the other for someone like us (pity, that is, for the man who does not deserve his fate, and fear for someone like us); so this event will not arouse pity or fear. So we have left the man between these. He is one who is not pre-eminent in moral virtue, who passes to bad fortune not through vice or wickedness, but because of some piece of ignorance, and who is of high repute and great good fortune, like Oedipus and Thyestes and the splendid men of such families.[62] □

The word which is translated in this passage as 'some piece of ignorance' is the Greek term *hamartia*, perhaps more usually translated as 'error'. In its original context, *hamartia* does not refer to a character flaw but to an action committed in error. It is essential to Aristotle's conception of tragedy that the hero in some measure contributes to his downfall, but at the same time, the hero is not fully accountable for his misdeeds because they are committed in ignorance. As this passage illustrates, Aristotle would not see the punishment of a bad man as a suitable subject for tragedy.

Aristotle's observations on *hamartia* have provided the basis for many subsequent accounts of human agency and tragic guilt. Fitz says: 'The most significant difference between Shakespeare's mature tragic practice and Aristotle's tragic theory is that while Aristotle at one point says that "pity is aroused by unmerited misfortune," Shakespeare insists on eliciting audience sympathy for characters who, to a greater or lesser degree, have brought their misfortune on themselves.'[63] Like Fitz, Bradley also insists on the role of human agency and responsibility in tragic falls: the hero 'always contributes in some measure to the disaster in which he perishes'.[64] Interestingly, Bradley says the characters of Shakespeare's late plays (such as *Cymbeline* and *The Winter's Tale*) could never be tragic because they show a capacity to change and learn from their mistakes. In his account of tragedy that we have just been discussing, Arthur Miller argues that the 'tragic flaw' is akin to a feeling of indignation in the face of injustice. Defined as such, he argues that the tragic flaw is 'not necessarily a weakness', nor is it the preserve of elevated characters. Other critics have asked whether the fatal flaw might be understood as a particular characteristic. Bradley acknowledges that the faults of the tragic heroes may be various, but that underlying all these is 'a marked one-sidedness, a predisposition in some particular direction; a total incapacity, in certain circumstances, of resisting the force which draws in this direction; a fatal tendency to identify the whole being with one interest, object, passion, or habit of mind. This, it would seem, is, for Shakespeare, the fundamental tragic trait.'[65] Bradley's emphasis on the single-mindedness of the tragic hero reverberates in other accounts, particularly Bernard Knox's analysis of the Sophoclean hero and in Hegel's suggestion that the tragic hero is utterly committed to – may even be seen as an embodiment of – an ethical standpoint.

The question of tragic guilt has been a fertile area for philosophical readings of tragedy. Kierkegaard figures Aristotle's account of *hamartia* in terms of a tragic collision:

> ■ Aristotle, as we know, requires the tragic hero to have *hamartia* ... But just as the action in Greek tragedy is something intermediate between activity and passivity, so too is the guilt, and in this lies the tragic collision. On the other hand, the more the subjectivity becomes reflected, or the more one sees the individual, in the Pelagian manner, left to himself, the more the guilt becomes ethical. Between these two extremes lies the tragic. If the individual is entirely without guilt, the tragic interest is removed, for the tragic collision loses its power. If, on the other hand, he is guilty absolutely, he can no longer interest us tragically.[66] □

For Kierkegaard, tragedy must negotiate a fine line between guilt and innocence in order to retain our sympathy and interest. It is a view also affirmed by Hegel whose account of tragedy – discussed further in Chapter 5, 'Tragic Dualities' – argues that Greek tragedy consists in this collision of equally justified ethical powers. It is essential to Hegel's vision of tragedy that it dramatises a collision of right with right, rather than right with wrong. In a claim which resonates with Hegel, Kierkegaard suggests that modern tragedy places a heightened emphasis on individual guilt, and that this distorts the balance between tragedy's aesthetic and ethical concerns:

> ■ So it is surely a misunderstanding of the tragic that our age strives to have the whole tragic destiny become transubstantiated in individuality and subjectivity. One turns a deaf ear on the hero's past life, one throws his whole life upon his shoulders as his own doing, makes him accountable for everything; but in so doing one also transforms his aesthetic guilt into an ethical guilt. The tragic hero thus becomes bad. Evil becomes the real object of tragedy. But evil has no aesthetic interest, and sin is not an aesthetic element.[67] □

While Kierkegaard constructs the ethical collision in tragedy in terms of guilt and innocence, Hegel rejects these categories:

> ■ In all these tragic conflicts, however, we must above all place on one side the false notion of the *guilt* or *innocence*. The heroes of tragedy are quite as much under one category as the other ... The strength of great characters consists precisely in this that they do not choose, but are entirely and absolutely just that which they will and achieve. They are simply themselves, and never anything else, and their greatness consists in that fact.[68] □

In an adjacent passage, however, Hegel appears to qualify his initial suggestion that the notions of guilt and innocence should be set aside. He argues that tragic heroes exhibit a profound resolution about what they do. Guilt is willingly assumed:

> ■ They have no desire to avoid the blame that results therefrom. On the contrary, it is their fame to have done what they have done. One can in fact urge nothing more intolerable against a hero of this type than by saying that he has acted innocently. It is a point of honour with such great characters that they are guilty.[69] □

Other critics have approached the subject of tragic guilt not in terms of action but in terms of knowledge and existence. Karl Jaspers argues, 'Tragedy becomes self-conscious by understanding the fate of its characters as the consequence of guilt, and as the inner working out of guilt itself. Destruction is the atonement of guilt.'[70] Jaspers argues that it is possible for man to experience destruction when he is guiltless. But, he says, 'this whole heart-rending, gruesome reality is not tragic, in so far as disaster is not the atonement of a guilt and is unconnected with the meaning of this life'.[71] Jaspers stresses the collective nature of guilt and suggests that because of inexplicable, undeserved suffering in the world, we have come to a sense of complicity in guilt: 'I am responsible for all the evil that is perpetrated in the world, unless I have done what I could to prevent it, even to the extent of sacrificing my life. I am guilty because I am alive and can continue to live while this is happening.'[72] Jaspers suggests that tragic knowledge posits two kinds of guilt. The first is existence: 'man's greatest guilt is to have been born'.[73] According to Jaspers, merely by living, we impose on others. Here Jaspers refers to the idea of inherited guilt which is common to Greek and Judaeo-Christian traditions. Jaspers cites a notable instance of this in the figure of Antigone, who he says is 'born contrary to the law as the daughter of Oedipus and his own mother. The curse of her descent is active within her.'[74] Second, Jaspers identifies guilt in the form of action. This he describes as performing an action freely, but he argues that tragic knowledge entails recognition of guilt: 'Man cannot escape his guilt through right and truthful conduct: guilt itself seems incurred guiltlessly. Man takes this guilt upon himself. He does not try to evade it. He stands by his guilt, not out of personal stubbornness, but for the sake of the very truth, which is destined for failure in his necessary sacrifice.'[75] Jaspers concludes that 'Tragedy depicts a man in his greatness beyond good and evil.'[76] Here he echoes the Nietzschean position that Greek tragedy transcends the realm of moral questioning.

Jaspers' construction of tragic guilt as consisting in the fact of mere existence has recently been echoed by George Steiner. In an essay in which he reflects on his major work, *The Death of Tragedy*, Steiner suggests that at the heart of tragedy is 'A legacy of guilt, the paradoxical, unpardonable guilt of being alive'.[77] He elaborates on this idea as follows:

■ This nucleus [*Ur-grund*] is that of 'original sin'. Because of that fall or 'dis-grace,' in the emphatic and etymological sense, the human condition is tragic. It is ontologically tragic, which is to say in essence. Fallen man is made an unwelcome guest of life or, at best, a threatened stranger in this hostile and indifferent earth (Sophocles' damning word, dwelt on by Heidegger, is *apolis*). Thus the necessary and sufficient premise, the axiomatic constant in tragedy is that of an ontological homelessness – witness this motif in Beckett, in Pinter – of alienation or ostracism from the safeguard of licensed being. There is no welcome to the self. That is what tragedy is about.[78] □

Paul Hammond has recently expanded on this idea of man's alienation from the world around him.[79] Hammond takes as his starting point Freud's essay 'The "Uncanny"' (1919) to suggest that the Freudian concepts of the *heimlich* (what is familiar, comfortable) and the *unheimlich* (usually translated as 'the uncanny') provide a theoretical basis through which we can better understand tragedy's characteristic interest in themes of alienation.[80] Hammond argues that the tragic protagonist is displaced into the realm of the *unheimlich*; and he takes a line from Seneca's *Hercules* ('Quis hic locus?' 'What place is this?' l. 1138) as a choric-like refrain in his text and uses this as a way of reflecting on tragedy's exploration of space.

Hammond, like Steiner, is inclined to see the tragic struggle in terms of how – and where – existence is possible. However, in the twentieth century, tragic guilt has not always been approached in terms as all-encompassing as these, and there has been continuing interest in possible constructions of *hamartia* in terms of a specific error. Like Kierkegaard, the Brazilian theatre practitioner Augusto Boal argues that the audience must engage sympathetically with the protagonist's *hamartia*:

> ■ It is necessary to understand also that the presentation of the error of weakness was not designed to make the spectator, in his immediate perception of it, feel repugnance or hatred. On the contrary, Aristotle suggested that the mistake or weakness be treated with some understanding. ... indeed, the efficacy of a dramatic process would be greatly diminished if the fault were presented from the beginning as despicable, the error as abominable. It is necessary, on the contrary, to show them as acceptable in order to destroy them later through the theatrical, poetic processes.[81] □

In the case of Oedipus, Boal emphasises the significance of acting knowingly:

> ■ ... what is his true flaw (hamartia)? His tragedy does not consist in having killed his father or married his mother. Those are not habitual acts either, and habit is one of the basic characteristics of virtuous or vicious behaviour. But if we read the play with care, we will see that Oedipus, in all the important moments of his life, reveals his extraordinary pride, his arrogance, the vanity which leads him to believe that he is superior to the gods themselves. It is not the Moirai (the Fates) that lead him to his tragic end; he himself, by his own decision, moves towards his misfortune.[82] □

In Chapter 6, we revisit Boal's account of tragedy and see how he connects the notion of *hamartia* with another Aristotelian concept, that of *catharsis*.

Also with the figure of Oedipus in mind, Martha Nussbaum makes an important distinction between the way Greek tragedy presents *hamartia* and the way it presents character flaws:

> ■ Thus Oedipus' shortness of temper is not the cause of his decline; but it is one thing about Oedipus that makes him a character with whom we can identify. It is not a 'tragic flaw'; but it is instrumental to the tragic response. So, indeed, are Philoctetes' self-pity, Creon's self-ignorance and his mistaken ambition, Antigone's relentless denial of the civic, Agamemnon's excessive boldness.[83] □

With this analysis, Nussbaum challenges twentieth-century accounts of the fatal flaw in terms of individual characteristics, and returns the discussion to the realm of tragedy's larger ethical schemes.

As we saw in the Introduction to this Guide, critical attempts to define tragedy are many and various. Amid these diverging views, some critics have identified the tragic hero as a means of anchoring their analysis of tragedy. As we saw in Chapter 2, the chorus was once integral to the performance of Greek tragedy but is not organic to the tragedy of later periods. Many of the most important critical debates on this subject from the nineteenth century onwards turn on the value of reintroducing or reconstituting the chorus in new ways. The tragic hero, on the other hand, is a relatively constant presence in forms of tragedy from the Greeks to the present day. Yet, as we have seen in this chapter, there are different tragic heroes for different historical moments.

In the figure of the tragic hero, many critics have sought to explore questions of human agency and the complex interplay of innocence and guilt. In Shakespeare's tragedies, Bradley sees the tragic hero's flaws as the essential motor that drives the play, an idea which is picked up by Bernard Knox in reference to Sophoclean tragedy. Knox's interest in the figure of the protagonist facing a great crisis leads him to characterise the tragic hero as a figure in isolation.

Other critics have assimilated Marxist thinking about the way that social identity is constructed by the social, cultural and political processes that shape us. Both Dollimore and Belsey see the early modern period as a crucible in which ideas about agency and selfhood are being forged with particular urgency. While much of this chapter is concerned with ideas of selfhood as something that is intangible and hard to locate – sometimes hard to articulate – we have also looked at relationships between mind and body in tragedy. As we saw, Greek tragedy tends to concretise emotional experience in reference to physical experience: as Ruth Padel has shown, this is a different way of expressing interiority.

In this chapter, we have also interrogated the concept of nobility. Aristotle characterises tragedy in terms of a fall from greatness, an idea which was traditionally understood in terms of rank. Writing about Shakespearean tragedy, Bradley suggests that this nobility may instead refer to an intensity of feeling; in this reading, Shakespeare strikingly anticipates nineteenth- and twentieth-century conceptions of tragedy which are concerned with characters of bourgeois or humble status. In his own defence of this practice, Arthur Miller argues that Freud has profoundly democratised the experience of suffering so that tragic theatre can no longer be the exclusive domain of kings and princes.

We have also been looking at the idea of *hamartia*, an idea which also derives from Aristotle's *Poetics*. Most critics agree that the tragic hero must carry some responsibility for his own downfall. For Kierkegaard, the tragic hero treads a fine line between guilt and innocence. Both Boal and Nussbaum reject the idea that the tragic downfall is attributable to a particular character flaw such as jealousy or greed. Others such as Jaspers and Steiner see tragic guilt in the mere fact of existence. In the next chapter, we consider the tragic fall in relation to female experience and examine Western tragedy's recurrent interest in tragic women.

CHAPTER FOUR

Tragic Women

Gender and genre

In her book *The Subject of Tragedy*, Catherine Belsey devotes separate sections to her discussion of 'Man' and her discussion of 'Woman'. Her aim in this, she says, is to demonstrate that:

■ at the moment when the modern subject was in the process of construction, the 'common-gender noun' largely failed to include women in the range of its meanings. Man is the subject of liberal humanism. Woman has meaning in relation to man. And yet the instability which is the result of this asymmetry is the ground of protest, resistance, feminism.[1] □

In our last chapter, 'The Tragic Hero', we largely took the term 'hero' to function as a common-gender noun. In the passage above, Belsey suggests that the assumptions that underlie this practice are problematic. Our discussion of the tragic hero was not framed specifically in reference to issues of masculine experience. However, to talk of the tragic heroine typically foregrounds issues of gender and sexual identity.

Tragedy's interest in female experience and female agency confronts us with a paradox. On the one hand, tragedy has flourished in cultures (such as those of fifth-century Athens or sixteenth-century England) which have largely consigned women to domestic roles. At the same time, these cultures have sought to bring female characters into the public gaze by putting them on stage. In Greek tragedy, female parts were played by adult men; and in the theatre of Shakespeare and his contemporaries, female parts were played by boys. In that sense, the stage was not a public space to which women had privileged access. However, it is striking that cultures which, broadly speaking, sought to silence or to prescribe female roles also repeatedly generate in their tragedies images of women which are complex and interesting. It is a paradox that has been noted by Helene Foley:

■ Greek tragedy was written and performed by men and aimed – perhaps not exclusively if women were present in the theater – at a large, public,

61

male audience. Masculine identity and conflicts remain central to the enterprise, but the texts often explore or query these issues through female characters and the culturally more marginal positions that they occupy.[2] □

In his study of Greek tragedy, Michael Shaw argues that the staging of female characters is not at odds with the presence of misogyny in the culture at large; it can be a direct manifestation of it: 'women in drama are all doing what women should not do. (Indeed, by the very act of being in a drama, which always occurs outside the house, they are doing what women should not do) ... They are *all*, to borrow T. B. L. Webster's phrase, "bad women"'.[3]

The presence of female characters like Antigone or Clytaemnestra standing symbolically outside the house, in the public space of the theatre, would have struck the original audience as a subversive image. Shaw's reading radically displaces some of the ethical questions surrounding Greek tragedy (which we discussed in the section on *hamartia* in the last chapter): by merely *being* in a tragedy – let alone acting – the female character is 'bad'. Shaw's reading of Greek tragedy relies on a heavily polarised account of male and female values, an antithesis which will be discussed further in Chapter 5, 'Tragic Dualities'.

In his own analysis of Greek tragedy, and the space which it affords women, Rush Rehm notes that Greek culture associated women with rites of passage such as death rituals, marriage and childbirth. Through these roles, he suggests, female characters in Greek tragedy are able to explore emotional extremes which the culture would regard as unbecoming in men. Rehm argues that the phenomenon of male actors playing female roles reinforces a 'closed system of male cultural production'.[4] Thus, Rehm argues, Greek tragedy only seemingly affords women a voice in its performance; in reality, it projects an account of female experience which has been authorised by men. Rehm's study of the cultural and sexual politics of Greek tragedy draws on the work of gender theorists such as Judith Butler, who propose that gender itself is a performance.[5]

As we saw at the beginning of this chapter, Foley suggests that Greek tragedy often carries out its exploration of male identity obliquely; its concentration on female characters allows us to draw inferences about the status of men. Later in the same study, Foley suggests that female experience naturally lends itself to scrutiny in the context of tragedy:

> ■ by being even more confined to their social roles and more dependent on others, [women] can serve to embody in a particularly self-conscious form the tragic image of the human, whose actions and decisions are often nullified by a series of uncontrollable contingencies, including ignorance and misfortune. Awareness of the corrosive effects of cultural prejudice can

weigh particularly heavily with female characters (i.e., Phaedra or Medea), as can a sense of tragic self-division. No male character faces an extended internal debate between two compromised alternatives in the fashion of the heroic and androgynous Medea ...[6] ▫

Foley suggests that the representation of such self-debates 'both affirms the danger of allowing women to make choices independent of men and, because men have put them in the impossible positions in which they find themselves, reveals the dangers of not educating them to do so'.[7]

In an important essay on gender roles in Greek tragedy, Froma Zeitlin asserts that the Self in tragedy is identified as male, and the Other as female. (For further analysis of this idea, see the work of Linda Bamber, discussed later in the chapter.) Zeitlin concedes: 'There are other "others" to be sure on the Athenian stage (e.g. barbarians, servants, enemy antagonists, and even gods), but the dialectic of self and other is consistently and insistently predicated on the distinctions between masculine and feminine, far more even than in Shakespeare.'[8] Zeitlin argues that the basic gender categories are 'too limited to encompass the woman's double dimensions – she is a model of both weakness and strength, endowed with traits and capacities that have negative and positive implications for self and society'.[9] Looking at the cross-dressing scene in Euripides' *Bacchae*, Zeitlin contends that Dionysus and Pentheus, although male characters, embody different facets of femininity: 'one on the side of femininity as power and the other on the side of femininity as weakness'.[10] Zeitlin suggests that this scene distils an important preoccupation of Greek tragedy: feminised males and masculinised women (e.g., Clytaemnestra, Medea and Agave). These role reversals, Zeitlin claims, have typically been seen as the staging of 'a temporary reversal before its decisive correction'.[11]

As we saw earlier, some critics have explored the apparent discrepancy between the way that tragedy often highlights female experience on the one hand, while on the other, tragedy has thrived in cultures in which women are marginalised or oppressed. Zeitlin reiterates the view that women in tragedy never, in fact, take centre stage:

> ■ *functionally* women are never an end in themselves, and nothing changes for them once they have lived out their drama onstage. Rather, they play the roles of catalysts, agents, instruments, blockers, spoilers, destroyers, and sometimes helpers or saviors for the male characters. ... their experience of suffering or their acts that lead them to disaster regularly occur before and precipitate those of men.[12] ▫

In this reading, Zeitlin suggests that female characters act as satellites to their male counterparts. Significantly, she contends that audiences may closely engage with female characters on an emotional level, but that the central narrative (at least in Greek tragedy) is always a male one. Developing this idea, Zeitlin argues that a woman's protection of domestic concerns often places her, paradoxically, in a highly political struggle with a male antagonist. In the passage that follows, Zeitlin pays attention to conventions of staging in the Attic theatre that mean that all the dramatic action takes place outside the house:

> ■ As a result, however, of the stand she takes, the woman also represents a subversive threat to male authority as an adversary in a power struggle for control which resonates throughout the entire social and political system, raising the terrifying specter of rule by women. Here we might note how strongly alien is the presence of this feminine other who, in asserting the legitimate values most associated with her social role, is also perceived as illegitimately asserting the rights reserved for the masculine project of self. She never achieves these in any permanent way. But in the contest over rights to control domestic space that the stage conventions exploit, it is the woman and not the man who, by reason of her close identification with the house as her intimate scene, consistently rules the relations between inside and outside and shows herself as standing on the threshold betwixt and between.[13] □

Like Greek tragedy, English Renaissance drama offers powerful representations of female characters, for example in Webster's *The Duchess of Malfi* (written *c.*1612), or Beatrice-Joanna in Middleton's *The Changeling* (1622). For Lisa Hopkins, these images constitute a radical critique of misogyny: 'Ironic though it may seem, the staging of a constant stream of bad or fallible women worked not to reinforce misogyny, but to prise it open, revealing the grounds on which it was constructed.'[14] Jonathan Dollimore is more qualified in his appraisal: 'Certainly in Jacobean drama we find not a triumphant emancipation of women but at best an indication of the extent of their oppression.'[15]

If we recall Bradley's account of Shakespeare's female characters as adjuncts to men, he does not recognise any of them as protagonists in their own right. Bradley's account of Desdemona now makes for uncomfortable reading. He describes Othello in Act V Scene i: 'The deed he is bound to do is no murder, but a sacrifice. He is to save Desdemona from herself, not in hate, but in honour; in honour, and also in love.'[16] Here Bradley's critical voice seems to merge with the chaotic inner voice of Othello himself: it is not a clear-minded analysis of motivation but an over-sympathetic allegiance with the protagonist. There is an interesting ambiguity in the term 'bound'. On one level, it suggests simply 'heading towards'. On another level, for all Bradley's emphasis on responsibility, the word 'bound' suggests a moral necessity: implicit in it is the language of the homosocial 'bond' of friendship between fellow-warriors to which Othello himself refers in the scene.

It is difficult for modern readers to tolerate, let alone agree with, Bradley's attempt to exonerate Othello from the act of killing his wife. Equally, Bradley's account of Desdemona seems to turn on a highly idealised notion of feminine passivity which would persuade few critics of the present generation:

> ■ ... when we watch her in her suffering and death we are so penetrated by the sense of her heavenly sweetness and self-surrender that we almost forget that she had shown herself quite as exceptional in the active assertion of her own soul and will. ... She appears passive and defenceless, and can oppose to wrong nothing but the infinite endurance and forgiveness of a love that knows not how to resist or resent. She thus becomes at once the most beautiful example of this love, and the most pathetic heroine in Shakespeare's world.[17] □

Thus Bradley reads Desdemona's death in terms of her virtue rather than in terms of the violence that is done to her; and indeed, Bradley posits a disturbing connection between the two. Bradley's account is not far from Linda Fitz's mind in her evaluation of critical responses to Shakespeare's Cleopatra. Interestingly, she chooses not to proceed through her critical analysis chronologically, for the reason that 'there has been no real critical development on this issue, and modern critics are just as sexist in their views as nineteenth-century critics'.[18] Pointing out that Antony dies in Act IV and that the dramatic climax is with the death of Cleopatra in Act V, Fitz challenges what she describes as 'the almost universal assumption that Antony alone is [the play's] protagonist'.[19] She goes on to argue:

> ■ A favorite game among Shakespeare critics has always been to compare characters from one play with characters from another ... With whom is Cleopatra compared? Lear? Macbeth? Othello? No, Cleopatra is compared only with female characters – Viola, Beatrice, Rosalind, Juliet. Juliet is most frequent, and it must be confessed there are certain similarities. Both appear in tragedies (the rest of the women used for comparison are comic heroines); both are allegedly in love; and they share the distinction of being two of the three women to have made it into the titles of Shakespeare plays. Otherwise, the two are as apt for comparison as Mae West and St. Cecilia.[20] □

Fitz argues that critics pay insufficient attention to the fact that Shakespeare treats his women as individuals rather than as a species. In her account of *Antony and Cleopatra*, she acknowledges that Cleopatra's behaviour is undesirable but suggests that we are invited to evaluate her actions in human terms, rather than in specifically gendered ones. In her characterisation of Cleopatra as a tragic hero, Fitz sees her as a particular refraction of traditional male heroic values. Fitz's reading is in direct conflict with Bamber's construction of Cleopatra as the tragic 'Other', the antithesis of the male tragic Self.

Fitz is part of a generation of feminist critics who have had a major impact on the field of Shakespeare studies in recent years. Like John Gould, whose work on Greek tragedy we looked at earlier in the book, the feminist Shakespeare critic Dympna Callaghan remarks on what she calls the 'hypervisibility of women in the dramatic literature' as opposed to their limited visibility in life.[21] At the same time, she recognises that the figures we see on stage are female characters and not women. Callaghan is interested not in the presence of women in Shakespeare's plays but in their absence: she argues that the playing of female parts by boy actors means that, in a literal sense, there are no women in Shakespeare. She argues that *representing* women on stage is not the same as giving them a voice; echoing the point made by Rush Rehm in relation to Greek tragedy, that male authorship of female characters tends in the very opposite direction. Callaghan is interested in the implications of this tension between representation and inclusion for the production of difference in early modern tragedy. Callaghan is also among those who have insisted that discourses about gender are implicated in discourses about other categories, such as race and class: for further discussion, see Chapter 9.

Linda Bamber argues that the male heroes of Shakespearean tragedy are aligned with the idea of the Self and female characters are defined in relation to the male Self. She says: 'The hero is to begin with *concerned* with himself; the first privilege of the Self is to have an *extra* Self who comments on or is simply aware of the original one.'[22]

Whereas masculinity is a flexible category in the plays, Bamber argues, the female role is fixed insofar as it is always defined in relation to the male. She asserts that 'Women do not change in Shakespearean tragedy; they do not respond to the events of the play, to the suffering, with new capabilities.'[23] Bamber identifies what she sees as a discrepancy between Shakespeare's presentation of women in the tragedies and in the comedies. She formulates this distinction as follows:

■ In the comedies Shakespeare seems if not a feminist then at least a man who takes the woman's part. Often the women in the comedies are more brilliant than the men, more aware of themselves and their world, saner, livelier, more gay. In the tragedies, however, Shakespeare creates such nightmare figures as Goneril, Regan, Lady Macbeth, and Volumnia. How are we to account for these terrible portraits, charged as they are with sexual antagonism? For these characters are not just women who happen to be evil; their evil is inseparable from their failures as women. Again and again Shakespeare darkens their cruelty by locating it on the very site of our expectations of a woman's kindness.[24] □

Bamber argues that misogyny in the plays emerges as a consequence and as an expression of fissures in the male sense of self. In *Lear, Hamlet, Othello* and *Antony and Cleopatra*, Bamber suggests, misogyny is a projection of a crisis within the male psyche. For the male heroes of these plays, misogyny is 'a signal of the chaos inside them at their worst moments'.[25] In *Macbeth* and *Coriolanus*, however, misogyny does not emerge as a symptom of male crisis: rather it is pervasive throughout the whole world of the play: 'Only in these two plays is the feminine *actually* as bad as the heroes of the other four plays imagine it to be.'[26]

In an important case study of Ophelia, Elaine Showalter takes as a point of departure Lacan's 1959 psychoanalytical study of *Hamlet* in which he casts Ophelia narrowly as the object of Hamlet's desire.[27] Lacan claims that the etymology of Ophelia is 'O-phallus': Ophelia is forever seen, Lacan suggests, as an extension of Hamlet and a projection of his desire. In her essay, Showalter contends that Ophelia is a relatively neglected figure in literary criticism and that her visibility in art and popular culture 'is in inverse relation to her invisibility in Shakespearean critical texts'.[28] Ophelia represents a problem for feminist critics since she appears in only five scenes out of *Hamlet's* total of 20 and her tragedy is subordinated to that of the male protagonist. Very little is known about Ophelia's story from the play's beforetime. Showalter goes on: 'I would like to propose instead that Ophelia *does* have a story of her own that feminist criticism can tell; it is neither her life story, nor her love story, nor Lacan's story, but rather the *history* of her representation.'[29]

Showalter unfolds the iconography of Ophelia in relation to the history of psychoanalysis, gender and cultural representation. She revisits Gaston Bachelard's theoretical formulation of the 'Ophelia complex' in which he posits symbolic connections between women, water, death and drowning.[30] In the stage history of the play in the eighteenth century, Showalter notes, Ophelia's madness was often represented in terms of 'polite feminine distraction'.[31] This changes in the nineteenth century as Ophelia's madness was staged with greater passion and intensity. At this time, there was a new interest in possible links between madness and female sexuality. Crucially, Showalter suggests, early photographers working in asylums in the 1850s began to impose the paradigm of Ophelia on their photographic subjects. In the wake of Freudian theory, Ophelia's madness was understood as a symptom of traumatic experience of female sexuality, ensuing either from guilt at an illicit sexual relationship with Hamlet that does not result in marriage or a repressed Oedipal attachment to her father Polonius. In either of these

Freudian readings, Showalter suggests, Ophelia has failed to fulfil her authorised sexual and cultural role as a married woman. The 1970s saw Ophelia as an image of rebellion against patriarchal culture. Far from trying to resolve these different representations of Ophelia into a single, stable and authorised view of character, Showalter concludes that each refraction sheds important light on the social conditions and ideological perspectives of its time.

In another important feminist study of Shakespeare, Philippa Berry takes issue with Michael Neill's claim that one of the teleological goals of tragedy is to confirm male identity at its conclusion.[32] Berry argues that puns, wordplay and feminised figures of speech (i.e., relating to the female body) disturb tragedy's conventions of closure. Berry affirms that both literal and metaphorical images of female death in Shakespeare:

> ■ figure death repeatedly, not as an ending, but as a process: an *interitus* or passing between ... So the body of the living Juliet (who by her marriage is no longer a Capulet) proves to be an uncannily disruptive force in her own family vault, while the 'maimed rites' of Ophelia's corpse generate social and political disturbances on a comparable scale in the Elsinore graveyard. As they hover disturbingly upon the borders of death and life, Cordelia and Desdemona likewise have peculiarly equivocal 'ends'.[33] □

Berry argues that Shakespeare's exploration of feminine tropes in his tragedies poses a challenge to conventional boundaries of both gender and tragic form:

> ■ The Freudian definition of the *Unheimlichkeit*, or uncanny, encompasses any moment when meaning has proceeded so far in the direction of ambivalence that it effectively coincides with its opposite, in a disturbing collapse of semantic differences. In their exploration of death through a series of feminine, or what might best be described as *feminized* figures (since they invariably problematize the boundaries of both gender and desire), the tragedies privilege similarly uncanny moments of semantic ambiguity, in what seems a deliberate exploitation of the contemporary uncertainty as to death's meaning that was felt by many at this liminal moment of religious and intellectual crisis.[34] □

To take an illustrative example from Berry's discussion, she argues that the death of Ophelia, as narrated by Gertrude, draws extensively on references to Mayday festivities. Ophelia's death thus 'affords a striking instance of the tragedies' figurative entwining of the complex duality of woman's erotic dying', a duality which is expressed as 'a process of natural decay which is nonetheless "indued" with the sexual vitality of the May games'.[35] Berry contrasts this with Hamlet's death, which, she argues:

> ■ is troped, not in terms of nature and the body, and certainly not as pleasure, but rather as a compulsory submission to a strict masculine force of law and judgement – 'this fell sergeant, Death, / Is strict in his arrest' (5.2.341–2) – that is associated with a more absolute or final 'rest': 'And flights of angels sing thee to thy rest' (5.2.365).[36] □

In positing an antithesis between masculine (closed) representations of death and feminine (open and indeterminate) images of death, Berry argues that the polar opposites of male/female in Shakespearean tragedy are constitutive of a wider interrogation of tragic teleology and eschatology. Thus her study is not just concerned with the subject of gender in tragedy (complex though that topic might be): it is concerned with the way that tragedy as a form might itself be gendered through its presentation of different modes and images of death.

Heroines and female heroes

A number of important critics have considered the extent to which heroism, as a code of values and a code of behaviour, is the privilege of men. Insofar as the concept originates in the world of military prowess – as in Homer's *Iliad* – this seems to be self-evidently the case. If, however, the term 'hero' is simply synonymous with the term 'protagonist', where does this leave tragedy's female characters?

We will return to the semantics of female heroism in a moment. First, it should be noted that some important critics have suggested that Greek tragedy reflects a dialogue between (male) heroism and female responses to heroism and its consequences. According to John Gould, Euripides regularly aligns a female tragic protagonist with a female chorus, with the result that the principal dialectic in these plays is not between protagonist and chorus but between a female world and the male. In this reading, the whole play becomes a critique of the male heroic code.[37]

In her study of Greek tragedy, Foley argues that the experience of the Peloponnesian War heightened the need for expressions of grief. She shows how, during this period, Athens appropriated the private funerals of wealthy aristocrats in the service of glorifying the city's military losses. According to Foley, this marginalised and suppressed the cultural role of female lamentation which had traditionally 'stressed the cost of death and heroic values to family and loved ones'.[38] Greek tragedy, argues Foley, provided a mechanism for restoring the female lament to a central role. Foley identifies key moments of intervention by female characters in Greek tragedy, which she organises around the themes of lamentation, marriage and 'ethical interventions by women at different stages of their reproductive lives (as virgin, wife, and mature mother)'.[39] Foley argues that Greek tragedy stages moments of disruption in the performance of these traditionally prescribed roles, moments at which there is a female incursion into traditional male roles governed by the pursuit of *kleos* (honour): 'Tragedy often (if not exclusively) allowed women and barbarians like Medea or Hecuba to explore the full negative or ambivalent consequences of pursuing such traditional honor-related goals. Women's pursuit of *kleos* consistently endangers male interests and threatens to masculinize the women themselves ...'[40]

In a seminal essay on women and death in Greek tragedy, Nicole Loraux argues that in death, the Greek male achieved *kleos* or fame: he was publically commemorated for his sacrifice.[41] Conversely, in death, a woman is celebrated by being remembered only by her husband and in a brief epitaph. Public recognition could only ever be synonymous with disgrace. 'Women in tragedy died violently. More precisely, it was in this violence that a woman mastered her death, a death that was not simply the end of an exemplary life as a spouse. It was a death that belonged to her totally ...'[42] Loraux claims that tragedy disrupts the social conventions of the time by providing a public narrative of women's deaths in a public arena. Central to Loraux's argument is that in Greek tragedy men usually die by murder, but women die by sacrifice or suicide. Loraux suggests that in Greek tragedy women are associated with particular modes of death, namely hanging and throat-cutting. She points out that men in Greek tragedy never hang themselves. In Loraux's reading, these methods of dying and of being killed have cultural significance. In the *Agamemnon*, for example, Clytaemnestra claims that on many occasions she has tried to hang herself in response to reports coming back from the Trojan War. Loraux suggests that by uttering this false claim, Clytaemnestra is travestying traditional expectations of female grief: 'The murdering queen denied the law of femininity, that in the extreme of misery a knotted rope should provide the way out.'[43]

In the case of hanging, Loraux suggests that in Greek tragedy female clothing and paraphernalia are typically used to carry out the deed. She argues that, in contrast, dying by the sword is an approved, male mode of suicide, in which the instrument of death is appropriated from the male world of battle. She suggests that sacrificial throat-cutting is 'insistently opposed to the language of hanging'.[44] Whereas men never hang themselves, a woman can choose between the noose and the sword. In the case of the sword, Loraux proposes that the woman is effectively 'stealing' a man's death. Death is an aspect of male experience which is available to women; conversely, female experiences of death are never available to men.

Loraux argues that female silence prefigures a woman's disappearance through death. Like Zeitlin, Loraux suggests that female suffering and death are predicated on that of men. Women in tragedy die at the hands of men and kill themselves for men: 'So the death of women confirms or reestablishes their connection with marriage and maternity.'[45] Virgins are almost universally killed: they do not kill themselves. This is one of the things that makes Antigone an important exception to Greek tragic norms. For Loraux, Greek tragedy reflects and constructs a world in which 'Glory indeed is essentially virile.'[46] When women die in tragedy, 'there are no words available to denote the glory of a woman that do not belong to the language of male renown'.[47]

Loraux's work investigates the relationship between female modes of dying and an heroic code which is understood as male. As the focus of tragedy shifts away from the myths surrounding the Trojan War, the concept of heroism becomes less securely rooted in a martial context. This opens up new spaces for questioning how heroism might be constituted, and what stake women might have in heroism as an ideology, an identity or a code of behaviour. In a book that focuses on English drama of the seventeenth century, Lisa Hopkins suggests that in the period from 1610:

> we find a rush of female tragic protagonists on the English stage, including Webster's Duchess of Malfi and Vittoria Corombona, Middleton's Bianca and Beatrice-Joanna, and Ford's Annabella and Calantha, all of whom are the eponymous heroes of their plays. The rise of the female protagonist is not incidental, but can be linked to a specific historical moment and to particular and highly contested debates within early modern culture and drama in England, including changing ideas about the relationship between bodies and souls and between men's bodies and women's, marriage and mothering, the law, religion and the nature of theatrical representation itself.[48]

Hopkins discusses her reasons for choosing to refer to these characters as 'female heroes' rather than 'heroines'. She points out that the word 'heroine' was not used in its modern sense until 1662, and indeed the dramatist Margaret Cavendish coined the term 'Heroickesses' to refer to the female characters in her play *Bell in Campo*. In addition, Hopkins points out that many of the female tragic characters she discusses would more properly be described as 'villainesses' than 'heroines'. As she argues, 'it was an essential part of the contemporary conception of what was possible for women that this should be so, since action, even heroic action, was seen as unsuitable for women and indeed as unsexing them.'[49]

Also addressing the question of what to call the female protagonist, Naomi Conn Liebler takes up the debate:

> ■ The female tragic hero engages in a struggle exactly as rigorous, exactly as dangerous, and exactly as futile as that of any of her masculine counterparts. That the space where her agon is staged is sometimes (but not always) domestic rather than public does not in any way diminish either its rigor or its social and political significance. To assume, as many critics – including many feminists – have done, that the representation of the tragic agon in a domestic or interior setting is somehow degraded or trivialized is to impose a particular set of (de)valuations on that representation.
>
> ... [I]t is not surprising that critics feminist and otherwise, have refused to recognize the female tragic protagonist as heroic, and have assumed that the very term 'hero' is a masculine form belonging properly only to masculine representations, and, further, that a feminine 'version' of that representation must be only and exactly that: a version, a poor imitation, an 'inauthentic copy.' To ensure that we see her as such, she has traditionally been given the diminutive suffix *-ine*, so that there could be no mistaking the derivative, diminished, and 'different' ontology of the hero*ine*. From this perspective, males would own the title of 'hero,' and any attempt to locate a 'female tragic hero' would be futile because such a figure could only be a naturalized or misappropriated version of a masculine category or status.[50] □

According to Liebler, male authorship should not be seen as an insuperable bar to representation of female experience. She suggests that some feminist critics have done a disservice to the very discourse they have tried to advance, for example in the way that Bamber's theory of Otherness constructs female characters in deeply negative terms. Dympna Callaghan sees misogyny (either implied or explicit) in every representation of women, and in their absence too: according to Callaghan, images of powerful women on stage are transparently fictitious when set against the actual role of women in the patriarchal culture of the early modern period. However, Liebler argues that women's relationship with power is not just reducible to the position of victimhood. She is troubled by what she sees as an exaggerated critical polarisation of male and female identities, which she suggests has led to a tendency to see female identity as predicated on what men are not. In contrast, she sees masculinity and femininity as 'reciprocal images'.[51] She says, 'I can think of no tragedy, ancient, early modern, or modern, that rests on such a static, artificially binary, structure.'[52] Liebler links her work on the female tragic hero with her earlier work on ritual and sacrifice (discussed in Chapter 1). As she points out, the tragic protagonist needs to be a surrogate for the community, and this substitution only works if the community can identify with her/him. Within the terms of this argument, a community could not identify with a female scapegoat whom it regarded as markedly inferior.

Antigones

Sophocles' Antigone is arguably the most celebrated tragic heroine of all. *Antigone* is the subject of numerous adaptations, and has generated a significant body of critical and theoretical work in its own right. In the final section of the chapter, we will be looking at the critical approaches which the play has prompted. We will not be attempting a comprehensive analysis of the play, but rather looking at ways in which different critics have engaged with the text in the context of broader tragic theory.

The title of George Steiner's seminal work *Antigones* uses the plural form in recognition of the many and varied accounts of the play. As he says, 'Antigones past and present have proved beyond inventory.'[53] Bonnie Honig's recent book concurs that the play is 'the most commented-upon drama in the history of philosophy, feminism, and political theory'.[54] Steiner suggests that attention to the *Antigone* is particularly concentrated in the nineteenth century, and that the play is widely cited by major philosophers and authors of this period.

Reception studies by Steiner and others testify to the rich importance of the play for major English and Continental writers. In the Preface to his *Poems* (1853), Matthew Arnold vigorously argues for the relevance of classical literature to contemporary literature and culture. Yet Arnold, strikingly, acknowledges the difficulty for a modern audience to sympathise with what is at stake in Sophocles' play. He writes: 'An action like the action of the *Antigone* of Sophocles, which turns upon the conflict between the heroine's duty to her brother's corpse and that to the laws of her country, is no longer one in which it is possible that we should feel a deep interest.'[55]

In his analysis of Arnold's text, Gerhard Joseph challenges this assessment of the play as intellectually and historically irrelevant to modern audiences, noting that 'Even in our enlightened times, few tribes of the race can accept with equanimity the prospect of unburied kin.'[56] Joseph posits that the source of Arnold's objection to the play is in his own vision of political stability:

> ■ As the defender of stable community in its collective and corporate character, as the embattled polemicist of *Culture and Anarchy* with its trumpeting of the state as the means by which 'the best that is said and thought in the world' can be widely dispersed, Arnold might be expected to have difficulties with a play that treats as heroic an individual's defiance of the state's claim to primacy ... [Antigone's resolve] significantly anticipates Doing As One Likes, the anarchic self-assertion that Arnold attacks so vehemently in his analysis of the Victorian culture crisis.[57] □

As Joseph also demonstrates, the *Antigone* figures recurrently in the work of George Eliot. In *Middlemarch* (1874), Dorothea is described as 'a sort of Christian Antigone' and George Eliot quotes the most famous line from the play ('I cannot share in hatred, but in love') in *Daniel Deronda* (1876), chapter 32. The same line was inscribed on the flyleaf of her commonplace notebook. In her essay 'The *Antigone* and Its Moral' (1856), George Eliot singles out the play as one of the finest tragedies and contemplates its relevance to her own age:

> ■ We said that the dramatic motive of the Antigone was foreign to modern sympathies, but it is only superficially so. It is true we no longer believe that a brother, if left unburied, is condemned to wander a hundred years without repose on the banks of the Styx; we no longer believe that to neglect funeral rites is to violate the claims of the infernal deities. But these beliefs are the accidents and not the substance of the poet's conception.[58] □

George Eliot suggests that the play is not concerned with the importance of burial rites per se, but in dramatising the conflict between 'the impulse of sisterly piety' and 'the duties of citizenship'.[59] In a Hegelian reading, she contends that both these claims have their validity. She continues:

> ■ It is a very superficial criticism which interprets the character of Creon as that of a hypocritical tyrant, and regards Antigone as a blameless victim. Coarse contrasts like this are not the materials handled by great dramatists. The exquisite art of Sophocles is shown in the touches by which he makes us feel that Creon, as well as Antigone, is contending for what he believes to be the right, while both are also conscious that, in following out one principle, they are laying themselves open to just blame for transgressing another; and it is this consciousness which secretly heightens the exasperation of Creon and the defiant hardness of Antigone.[60] □

While George Eliot interprets the play in the Hegelian terms of right versus right, Virginia Woolf appropriates the figure of Antigone in the service of a more radical cause. In Virginia Woolf's anti-war essay *Three Guineas* (1938), she alludes to Antigone as an image of 'female rebellion against patriarchal tyranny' and as 'the classical forerunner of Mrs. Pankhurst and of the anti-Fascist martyr':[61]

> ■ Consider Antigone's distinction between the laws and the Law. That is a far more profound statement of the duties of the individual to society than any our sociologists can offer us. Lame as the English rendering is, Antigone's five words ['I cannot share in hatred, but in love'] are worth all the sermons of all the archbishops.[62] □

Steiner emphasises the role of the French Revolution in creating the cultural conditions for this interest in the play and the ethical problems which it poses. According to Steiner, the play 'dramatizes the meshing of intimate and public, of private and historical existence. It is the historicization of the personal which is the commanding truth and legacy of the French Revolution.'[63]

One of the most important studies on which Steiner draws is Hegel, whose account of the play is discussed further in Chapter 5 ('Tragic Dualities'). Hegel establishes the play as a test case for ethical questions in tragedy, which many other critics have subsequently explored. While Hegel tends to emphasise Antigone and Creon as equal and opposite presences in the play, Bernard Knox suggests that there is a profound imbalance. Antigone, he says, 'goes to her death unrepentant. It is Creon whose will is smashed and broken. It is Creon who gives in.'[64] Indeed, Knox poses a further challenge to Hegel's position by suggesting ways in which the aims and values of the *polis* are not fundamentally opposed to those of the *oikos*: Antigone's actions are political and Creon's motives are partly religious. In a close reading of the language of the play, Knox observes that Antigone speaks of her loyalty to Polyneices in political terms such as 'treason'. Knox notes that Athenian democracy grew out of a tribal system, so the play does not explore value systems which are essentially opposed, but ones which prioritise different conceptions of political life.

While Knox suggests that a sense of antithesis in the *Antigone* is often overstated, he nonetheless argues that an Athenian audience would have vehemently sided with the views articulated by Creon. Knox contextualises his arguments as follows:

■ In 1939 E. M. Forster, who knows his Sophocles well and surely had an eye on Creon's speech, wrote the famous and scandalous sentence: 'I hate the idea of causes, and if I had to choose between betraying my country and betraying my friends, I hope I should have the guts to betray my country.' This is of course a polemical statement, inspired by bitter memories of the crass propaganda used in the First World War, and deliberately couched in shocking terms, but it none the less expresses, in extreme form, a feeling which has its place in the consciousness of civilized modern man.

It could not have been written, much less said in public, in fifth-century Greece; its author would have been treated as criminally insane. Loyalty to the *polis* was not an abstract 'cause'; it was a practical necessity.[65] □

Following Hegel and Knox, critical attention to the play has largely turned on the figure of Antigone herself and to what extent her defiance of Creon is to be commended or condemned. In her study of Antigone as moral agent, Foley suggests that when Greek tragedies show women making ethical decisions, this constitutes 'at least a partial break from a cultural ideal ... [tragic poets] use female characters to explore ambiguous and often dangerous moral frontiers.'[66] Foley notes that this poses a challenge to Aristotle's view that tragic characters should be fundamentally good. As Foley observes, it is widely recognised that Antigone and Creon have a common ethical vocabulary: each talks in the highly polarised terms of 'friend' and 'enemy'. But Foley draws fresh attention to the way in which Antigone and Creon have different modes of making ethical decisions.

Foley suggests that Antigone's controversial speech (lines 904–20) in which she says she would only defy the city to bury a brother, and not a husband or her child, is crucial for our reading of the play: 'In insisting that there was only *one* case in which her action is in her own view fully justifiable, Antigone's speech probably capitalizes on cultural presuppositions about exceptional circumstances – whether these circumstances are real or a tragic topos – in which women could be expected to act autonomously.'[67] Foley suggests that without this emphasis on the highly specialised circumstances in which Antigone acts, she would have 'become a cultural monstrosity rather than a subversive yet admirable anomaly'.[68] Foley argues that the play demands a sense of historical and ethical specificity, which some of Antigone's advocates have been dangerously inclined to ignore:

> ■ To accept Antigone's argument that there are only specific circumstances in which a virgin daughter should contemplate taking autonomous action in life-threatening circumstances requires her audience to accept that her heroic action cannot serve in any simple sense as a timeless, gender-free model for civil disobedience. At the same time, it does not diminish her heroism and her moral audacity. Within the context of a Mediterranean morality that offers to a woman specific exceptional opportunities to win honour by acting on behalf of the natal family, Antigone's choice to accept a challenge that requires her death still defines her as heroic.[69] □

In her essay on the *Antigone*, Christiane Sourvinou-Inwood attempts to strip away our modern preconceptions, and to approach the play as its contemporary audience might have done. She argues that our knowledge of the play's outcome can distort our reading of the play by producing a tendency to 'read backwards'.[70] If we start from the premise that Antigone is right, then we organise all our responses around this assumption and become less attuned to nuances and ambiguities in the play. Sourvinou-Inwood sees character as a series of shifting constructs rather than a fixed essence, and says that we should not misinterpret the concept of the *polis* simply as 'the state', which she suggests can carry for modern readers an anachronistic impression of a secular institution. Sourvinou-Inwood reminds us that the *polis* is an organ of religious belief and practice. She says that critics have set up a number of false oppositions between Antigone and Creon, and falsely suggest that the two characters have different religious loyalties. As she demonstrates, the *polis* was in fact the institution through which all religious activity was sanctioned and performed: the *polis* observed both Olympian and chthonic deities, and sanctioned the performance of funeral rites.

Sourvinou-Inwood is one of very few critics to attend to the dramaturgy of the play in relation to the ethical questions which it poses. She suggests that particular details of staging would have alerted a contemporary Athenian audience to the transgressive nature of Antigone's position from the first moments of the play: the conversation between Antigone and Ismene with which the play opens takes place in the dark and beyond the gates of the courtyard – that is, in a place in which women could not legitimately be. In other words, the staging of the play figures Antigone in conspiratorial terms; and Sourvinou-Inwood argues that discussions of abstract morality fail to take adequate account of these issues of dramaturgy through which the ethical questions of the play are explored. Antigone's actions are 'self-willed, disordered and disordering' and she is punished accordingly.[71] She not only dies, she is buried alive and commits suicide: it is a double death which reflects the gravity of her crime. By dying before marriage, Sourvinou-Inwood argues, Antigone has not fulfilled her role as a woman; by writing her out of the play well before its close, the play pronounces a stern judgement on her actions.

Philip Holt says that, as modern readers, we are predisposed to see Antigone as 'a martyr for a cause, and our age is rather drawn to causes and martyrs'.[72] He suggests that a view of Antigone as right and Creon as wrong and tyrannical has now become orthodox. This is in part, Holt claims, a reaction to the twentieth-century experience of totalitarian regimes: in the post-Romantic age we favour resistance to oppressive forms of political rule. Holt takes the view that this is anachronistic. Like Sourvinou-Inwood, Holt wants to situate his reading of the play specifically in terms which would be relevant to a contemporary audience. His argument offers an exposition of the positive view that Athenians held of the *polis* as an institution which upheld rule by consensus rather than oppression. He also notes that the refusal to bury traitors in Athenian territory was a well-established and approved Athenian practice. The play, he argues, simply does not consider possible alternatives and compromises, such as burying Polyneices outside Theban territory. As Holt demonstrates, the Greeks do not have a neatly equivalent concept for what we term 'conscience' and their experience of religion was mainly built on actions (such as prayer and ritual) rather than inner, personal beliefs. With this in mind, it is difficult to support a reading of the play as a drama of conscience, which is how many critics have seen it.

Having established that the Athenians would not approve of Antigone's actions in real life, Holt goes on to offer some significant qualifications: tragedy mediates and complicates our response to actions and their moral implications. He argues that the audience would in fact have sympathy for Antigone, even if this reaction would sit uneasily with their sense of civic identity and duty. One of the things that is most powerful about this play, he suggests, is the way it sets up and explores contradictions between an audience's response to Antigone's actions in a dramatic context, and its likely response to the same ethical questions if they were to arise outside the theatre.

Judith Butler's book *Antigone's Claim* has been one of the most widely discussed accounts of the play and its central character in recent years.[73] In this book, Butler asks what kind of figure Antigone represents for feminist critics. She has been celebrated as a figure of opposition to male sovereignty; but she has become, Butler proposes, a far less radical figure, invoked by feminists seeking the endorsement of the state. Butler dismantles the Hegelian tradition which posits an antithesis in the play between kinship and state. She questions the extent to which Antigone, as the offspring of an incestuous union, can neatly represent the values of 'family' in the way that Hegel and others following him would suggest. Butler points out that Antigone speaks the language of the state, just as Creon does; conversely, Creon is ruler by virtue of family lineage. Butler suggests that kinship and state 'are metaphorically implicated in one another in ways that suggest that there is, in fact, no simple opposition between the two'.[74] In Butler's reading, Antigone is a figure who does not embody but transgresses both gender and kinship norms. For Butler, Antigone's declaration that it is only on behalf of her brother that she would act in defiance of the state (not a husband or children) is highly revealing. In stressing the singular, exceptional circumstances of her action, Antigone is not acting in conformity with the law since laws enshrine general principles and obligations rather than exceptional ones.

Butler argues that her rereading of *Antigone* is pertinent at a time when constructions of the family are changing: in the contemporary world, she suggests, children may move from one family to another because of divorce and remarriage; children may be raised by same-sex parents. It is important for Butler's reading of the play that Antigone's non-normative kinship status is not resolved in a heteronormative union with Haemon, something which, she points out, Antigone refuses. Yet at the same time Antigone does not achieve sovereignty and, for Butler, Antigone's living death in the tomb is an image of the liminality of non-normative kinship. Thus Antigone's story offers:

> ■ an allegory for the crisis of kinship: which social arrangements can be recognized as legitimate love, and which human losses can be explicitly grieved as real and consequential loss? Antigone refuses to obey any

law that refuses public recognition of her loss, and in this way prefigures the situation that those with publicly ungrievable losses – from AIDS, for instance – know too well.[75] □

Bonnie Honig's book *Antigone, Interrupted* looks at receptions of the play in political theory, and pays particular attention to the responses of feminist and queer theorists to the text. She looks at the way that Antigone is invoked as an archetypal figure of mourning, and argues that Antigone is particularly identified with the image of the mourning mother, even though Antigone is emphatically not a mother and never will be.[76] Honig argues that this practice of constructing Antigone archetypally – and, by extension, figuring grief and mourning as universal experiences – is unhelpful. Antigone, she says, is habitually contrasted in political theory (either explicitly or implicitly) with Oedipus: while Oedipus stands for rationality, sovereignty, hierarchy and patriarchy, Antigone is regularly opposed to these values so that she represents what is instinctive, anti-sovereign and feminine. This paradigm polarises relations between mourning and politics, an opposition which Honig traces back to Freud. His suggestion that the process of mourning involves turning away from the world, Honig suggests, has created assumptions that political activism is at odds with the act of mourning.[77] She is at pains to reinstate a sense of connection between mourning and politics and to this end repeatedly and urgently contrasts what she calls 'the politics of *lamentation*' with 'the *politics* of lamentation'. With this sense of mourning as a political act, Honig rejects constructions of Antigone as an archetypal figure of grief as sentimental. These images, she suggests, neutralise the political charge which mourning – for example, those killed in war or those who have died from AIDS-related illnesses – should carry.

In a very different reflection on the same question about the politics of mourning, Mark Sanders traces parallels between the action of the *Antigone* and human rights abuses during the period of apartheid in South Africa.[78] Sanders notes the frequency with which those testifying to the Truth and Reconciliation Commission report violations of burial rites. For Sanders, these experiences resonate with the *Antigone* in the way that 'law' is figured as a multivalent concept. In these human rights violations, the law of the state is profoundly in conflict with the law of custom. For Sanders, Antigone is not evoked as the kind of sentimental archetype which Honig rejects. Rather, the play's discourse is seen to shed light on political processes in post-apartheid South Africa.

Antigone is often seen as capitulating in death: retreating from her political challenge to Creon to a different mode of being, a lamentation of the loss of marriage which suggests a turn towards more conventional feminine priorities. Honig is interested in recuperating Antigone from this reading. She questions the way that critics have tended to polarise Antigone's actions (conspiracy or open defiance) and suggests that Antigone negotiates another course of action, which Honig characterises as a 'conspiracy with language'.[79] Creon, she suggests, hears Antigone's words as lamentation; he hears her words as a retreat from the world of political engagement. But Honig insists that Antigone's words continue to be a radical critique of the state, intelligible as such to other audiences, if unintelligible to Creon himself.

In Chapter 3, we looked at the term 'hero' as a common gender noun. This chapter has sought to unravel many of the assumptions that are bound up in such a practice. Many critics have commented on the prevalence of female characters in the tragic canon; at the same time, it is widely recognised that many of the societies which generate these images of tragic women (such as classical Athens or early modern England) are fundamentally patriarchal. For some critics, this presents something of an anomaly insofar as cultures that largely deny women a public voice consistently give women a high profile on stage. As others have noted, female characters in Greek tragedy are not 'women' but rather male bodies in female costume. In Shakespeare, female parts are played by boys. This significantly complicates the way that tragedy stages female experience: tragic heroines do not have a voice that is independent of male systems of cultural production. The words that they speak have been written by – authorised by – men, though there are some notable exceptions to this, for example in early modern closet drama written by Mary Sidney, Elizabeth Cary and others.

In this chapter, we have also seen how critics have evaluated the relative merits of the term 'heroine' and 'female hero'. Loraux suggests in her reading of Greek tragedy that heroism is an essentially masculine sphere of operation. For some critics, the term 'female hero' is a way of resisting this point of view, and reclaiming for the female protagonist a sense of agency that withstands the connotations of passivity or martyrdom which female tragic experience is sometimes taken to imply.

In the final part of this chapter, we looked at critical responses to Sophocles' *Antigone*. Its protagonist, it is claimed, has been written about more extensively than any other tragic heroine. The play sets up a pattern of binary oppositions between male and female, city and state, living and dead. For some, these dualities exemplify a patterning which is at the heart of tragedy itself. In the next chapter, we turn to the subject of tragic dualities and tragic conflict.

CHAPTER FIVE

Tragic Dualities

Conflict and synthesis

According to Goethe, 'All tragedy depends on an insoluble conflict. As soon as harmony is obtained, or becomes a possibility, tragedy vanishes.'[1] In his analysis of modern tragedy, Raymond Williams argues that conflict in the modern age is serving to renew and revitalise tragedy as a form: 'Man can achieve his full life only after violent conflict; man is essentially frustrated and divided against himself; while he lives in society; man is torn by intolerable contradictions, in a condition of essential absurdity.'[2] Charles Segal is among critics who have drawn attention to the dualities of Greek tragedy, an important theme in our previous discussion of Sophocles' *Antigone*:

■ Throughout Greek tragedy systems of linked polarity – mortal and divine, male and female, man and beast, city and wild – operate within the dense fabric of the language and the plot to include not just the emotional, interior world of the character or spectator but the whole of society in its multiple relationships to the natural and supernatural order.[3] □

Many critics, such as Vernant, have noted that tragedy embodies an essentially dialectical form in the relationship between chorus and protagonist.[4] Goldhill argues that the alternating pattern between choral song on the one hand and the speech of individual actors on the other produces a vital tension in tragedy, and he further suggests that this tension is a model for the relationship between the individual and society in the Athenian democracy.[5] With these and other dialectics in mind, this chapter looks at the way that conflict and dualities have figured in the critical tradition.

Michelle Gellrich has pointed out that the idea of conflict – which we now see as integral to theories of tragedy – is absent in Aristotle.[6] For Gellrich, Aristotle establishes a powerful precedent for theorists of tragedy by suggesting that tragedy manifests patterns which conform to our expectations of order. On the other hand, Gellrich is sensitive to the presence of *disorder* in tragedy and she suggests that we cannot restructure tragedy's inherent disorderliness into neat philosophical formulations. Thus, although Hegel is explicitly concerned with conflict, Gellrich argues, his 'traditional assumptions about unity and coherence are nonetheless so binding on his views that he ends up taming conflict and reducing it to his own philosophical terms of order'.[7] In other words, much that is written about tragedy prioritises a sense of its coherence over a sense of its dissonances and, in doing so, essentially misrepresents tragedy as a form. Gellrich argues that the now-familiar emphasis on opposition and conflict in tragedy, so notably absent in Aristotle, emerges in the eighteenth century under the influence of the Romantic concept of the sublime. She identifies Edmund Burke's *A Philosophical Enquiry into the Origin of our Ideas of the Sublime and Beautiful* (1756) as a key text in this process. This shifted attention away from neoclassical values of restraint and the importance of proportion and form towards a new emphasis on intensity of feeling 'that cannot be adequately presented in conventional artistic structures'.[8] The Romantic conception of the sublime, she suggests, posed a challenge to neoclassical conceptions of form. (For further discussion of neoclassical form, see Chapter 7; and for further discussion of Gellrich's account of the sublime, see Chapter 3).

It should be noted that tragedy itself is often understood as operating as part of a binary system through which it is opposed to comedy. One of the best illustrations of this kind of thinking can be found in the commentary of Donatus-Evanthius, which we briefly encountered in Chapter 3:

> ■ But many things distinguish comedy from tragedy, especially the fact that comedy is concerned with the average fortunes of people, the onset of moderate risks, and actions with happy endings. But in tragedy, everything is the opposite: great people, immense terrors, and deathly endings. Furthermore, in comedy what is stormy at first becomes smooth at the end; in tragedy the action has the opposite pattern. Then, too, tragedy presents the kind of life that is to be avoided, whereas the life of comedy is one which we are drawn towards. Finally, in comedy, everything comes from fictional plots, whereas in tragedy, we often look to the facts of history.[9] □

Theorists such as Aristotle have posed a challenge to this stark polarisation of tragedy and comedy by admitting the presence of variant forms such as 'happy-ending tragedy', as we saw in the previous chapter. But the traditional antithesis of tragedy and comedy has, to some extent, prevailed. Reflecting on this dichotomous relationship between tragedy and comedy, Joseph Meeker argues that tragedy and comedy deal with conflict in different ways:

> ■ As patterns of behavior, both tragedy and comedy are strategies for the resolution of conflicts. From the tragic perspective, the world is a battleground where good and evil, man and nature, truth and falsehood make war, each with the goal of destroying its polar opposite. Warfare is the basic metaphor of tragedy, and its strategy is a battle plan designed to eliminate the enemy. That is why tragedy ends with a funeral or its equivalent. Comic strategy, on the other hand, sees life as a game ... When faced with polar opposites, the problem of comedy is always how to resolve conflict without destroying the participants. Comedy is the art of accommodation and reconciliation.[10] □

The 'polar opposites' which Meeker suggests are essential constituents of tragedy have been identified and characterised in many different ways. George Steiner suggests that Sophocles' *Antigone* uniquely encapsulates 'all the principal constants of conflict in the condition of man':

> ■ the confrontation of men and of women; of age and of youth; of society and of the individual; of the living and the dead; of men and of god(s). The conflicts which come of these five orders of confrontation are not negotiable. Men and women, old and young, the individual and the community or state, the quick and the dead, mortals and immortals, define themselves in the conflictual process of defining each other.[11] □

At the same time, Steiner recognises that within this pattern of conflict is also reciprocity:

> ■ In essence, the constants of conflict and of positive intimacy are the same. When man and woman meet, they stand against each other as they stand close. Old and young seek in each other the pain of remembrance and the matching solace of futurity. Anarchic individuation seeks interaction with the compulsions of law, of collective cohesion in the body politic. The dead inhabit the living and, in turn, await their visit. The duel between men and god(s) is the most aggressively amorous known to experience. In the physics of man's being, fission is also fusion.[12] □

Thus Steiner draws attention to the way that antithesis can often be preliminary to synthesis or resolution, an idea that is important in Hegelian dialectics (considered in the final section of this chapter). To begin, however, with the first of the various binary relationships which Steiner identifies as crucial to the *Antigone*, let us consider the dualities of male and female in tragedy. We saw in Chapter 4 how several critics, such as Linda Bamber, suggest that the categories of masculine and feminine, although existing in antithesis, are always in contact with one another and are mutually defining and reinforcing.[13] In his study of gender in Greek tragedy, Michael Shaw also explores this basic antithesis of male and female values. He suggests that femininity is governed and determined by a woman's place in the *oikos* (house), while conversely masculinity is determined by a man's place in the *polis* (city):

> ■ The wife's virtues are those demanded by the *oikos*, mother love, industry, and the ability to create harmony. There are certain negative virtues as well. She will not normally be known in public, because this implies that something is wrong inside the house which is driving her outside ....
>
> Similarly, the image of man is determined by the fact that his sphere lies outside the house. His basic duty is to defend the *oikos* in the outside world. He does this by means of associations with other men, the heads of other households, the largest association being the *polis* itself.[14] □

Thus from a basic set of observations about the male–female antithesis, Shaw adumbrates a second set of binary oppositions between private and public: the inner world of the house and the public world of the city. In a highly schematic Hegelian account, Shaw suggests that Greek tragedy dramatises a threat to the categories of masculine and feminine which is then resolved in a new synthesis:

> ■ (1) a man, acting as pure male, does something which threatens the pure female; (2) the pure female comes out of the *oikos* and opposes the male; (3) there is an impasse; (4) the female, taking some male attributes, acts; (5) a previously invisible feminine aspect of the male (e.g., his love for his children) is destroyed; (6) there is a new formation, with male and female no longer pure.[15] □

In a reply to Shaw, Helene Foley questions the security of his initial antithesis of male–female and *polis–oikos*. Taking the celebrated example of *Antigone* – a play which is often seen perfectly to exemplify the kinds of antithesis to which Shaw refers – Foley suggests that Antigone's values are not narrowly defined in terms of her attachment to the *oikos*, but that she reflects the interests of the *polis*, for example in questioning the city's policy towards traitors. Foley argues that it is often 'a woman's movement from the household [that is] consistently destructive not only to herself but to the very oikos-related interests that she is ideally meant to protect ... How can women be understood to represent an institution from which they frequently describe themselves in tragedy as alienated?'[16] Here Foley cites the examples of Medea and Clytaemnestra and notes many examples in Greek tragedy in which women demonstrate reluctance to marry (e.g., in Aeschylus' *Suppliants*) or vulnerability to adultery. Foley goes on to argue that the equation of female–male and *oikos–polis* does not hold and that 'Male and female ideally share an interest in the preservation of the oikos and its values ... Order in one sphere is inextricably related to order in the other.'[17]

We can see in both Shaw's and Foley's essays that an attempt to insist upon a rigid dichotomy between male and female is fraught with difficulty. Shaw posits a Hegelian pattern in which thesis–antithesis leads to synthesis, while Foley questions the basis on which women are assigned to the domestic sphere while men are assigned a public or political role. As she suggests, these facets of ideology and experience are crucially intersecting.

Critical attention to the relationship between the *oikos* and the *polis* shows how tragic dualities are often configured in spatial terms. In a seminal article on the representation of place in Greek tragedy, Froma Zeitlin identifies a powerful dialectic between Athens (the place of performance) and Thebes as what she calls a 'conceptual category'.[18] Zeitlin suggests that:

> ■ Thebes functions in the theater as an anti-Athens, an other place ... [W]ithin the theater, Athens is not the tragic space. Rather, it is the scene where the theater can and does 'escape' the tragic, and where reconciliation and transformation are made possible. Thebes and Athens are, in fact, specifically contrasted to one another in several plays, such as Sophokles' *Oidipous at Kolonos* and Euripides' *Suppliant Women*, and implicitly juxtaposed in Euripides' *Herakles* when Theseus comes to lead the broken hero away to sanctuary and protection in Athens. But Thebes is also the obverse side of Athens, the shadow self, we might say, of the idealized city on whose other terrain the tragic action may be pushed to its furthest limits of contradiction and impasse. As such, it also furnishes the territory for exploring the most radical implications of the tragic without any risk to its own self-image.[19] □

Zeitlin suggests that in frequently adopting Thebes as a dramatic location, Attic tragedy projects a:

> ■ negative model to Athens' manifest image of itself with regard to its notions of the proper management of city, society, and self. As the site of displacement, therefore, Thebes consistently supplies the radical tragic terrain where there can be no escape from the tragic in the resolution of conflict or in the institutional provision of a civic future beyond the world of the play. There the most serious questions can be raised concerning the fundamental relations of man to his universe, particularly with respect to the nature of rule over others and of rule over self, as well as those pertaining to the conduct of the body politic.[20] □

In a highly authoritative study of ethnic and racial otherness in Greek tragedy, Edith Hall asks why the drama should return so frequently and insistently to images of the barbarian. The Greek term *barbaros*, Hall notes, 'was simply an adjective representing the sound of incomprehensible speech'; the term 'barbarian', she suggests, became a way in which the Greeks could identify *'all* who did not share their ethnicity'.[21] Hall argues that 'Greek writing about barbarians is usually an exercise in self-definition, for the barbarian is often portrayed as the opposite of the ideal Greek'.[22]

Hall suggests that Aeschylus' *Persians* is 'the earliest testimony to the absolute polarization in Greek thought of Hellene and barbarian which had emerged at some point in response to the increasing threat posed to the Greek-speaking world by the immense Persian empire'.[23] She contends that the play proposes:

> ■ the theme of hubris and its punishment as inseparable from the evocation of barbarism. In this play at least, the argument runs, Aeschylus implies not that all men are subject to the same human laws, but that the barbarian character, *in contrast* with the free and disciplined Hellene, is luxuriant and materialistic, emotional, impulsive, and despotic, and therefore especially liable to excess and its consequences.[24] □

In one of the most radical accounts of duality in Shakespearean tragedy, Norman Rabkin draws on the concept of complementarity, an idea originally formulated in the field of quantum mechanics.[25] J. Robert Oppenheimer coined the term 'complementarity' to refer to the idea that 'an electron must sometimes be considered as a wave, and sometimes as a particle', an idea that was subsequently popularised by Oppenheimer's fellow physicist Niels Bohr.[26] Complementarity therefore expresses the idea that something can simultaneously exist as two opposite and irreconcilable versions of reality. Oppenheimer himself recognised that this concept had a wide range of possible applications outside the field of physics.

For Rabkin, the model of complementarity is highly suggestive as a way of understanding Shakespeare's plays, which he says 'are built on visions of complementarity'.[27] Rabkin stresses that complementarity is 'a way of seeing, not an idea or an ideology'.[28] He suggests ways in which the plays exhibit this complementarity, for example in terms of the double plot in *Troilus and Cressida*, *King Lear* and *Hamlet*.

Rabkin's identification of complementarity as a critical tool for reading Shakespeare has paved the way for other studies of its kind. Explicitly building on Rabkin, Bernard McElroy also argues that Shakespeare's plays are structured around a principle of complementarity.[29] Whereas Rabkin proposes that there is a different dialectic in each of the plays, McElroy contends that there is an overarching pattern in Shakespeare's mature tragedies (*Hamlet, King Lear, Macbeth* and *Othello*). He asserts that the basic tension in these four tragedies can be traced to the intellectual and theological upheavals of the period and the transition from the medieval worldview to the early modern. 'The issues involved do not take the form of questions, still less of theories, but rather of diametrically opposed possibilities about the nature of reality, about man's relation to the world and the cosmos, about the value of his actions and the limitations of his capabilities.'[30]

From this larger claim, McElroy identifies several specific 'opposed possibilities' which he says inform the themes and structure of the four tragedies. In one view, he suggests, the plays offer us a view of man's identity as fixed within the natural order; in the opposite view, man is seen as free while social bonds are merely arbitrary. To take another example, man has a special dignity in the natural hierarchy; set against this is the view that man is simply another animal, governed by his appetites.

After mapping out these conflicting ideologies, McElroy proposes that these dialectics manifest themselves in different ways in the four plays that are the subject of his book. He argues:

■ In *Hamlet*, for instance, the dialectic takes place almost exclusively in the mind of the hero, whose most fundamental character trait is a propensity for seeing reality from several different vantage points at once ... Hamlet's mind is complementary, that is, he is quite capable of believing simultaneously two things which logically should cancel each other out. This unique quality of mind largely accounts for the many contradictions and internal inconsistencies which render him such a fascinating and endlessly debatable character.[31] □

McElroy argues that in *Othello*, the protagonist is caught between the twin poles of Iago and Desdemona: Othello believes first one account of reality, then another. In *King Lear*, 'the world of the play is itself complementary', that is, it entertains multiple accounts of the truth. In *Macbeth*, McElroy suggests:

■ dialectical tension is generated between the ideas of reality held by the two principal characters at the beginning of the play. Early in the action, however, the hero commits himself irrevocably to the view of nature and man set forth by his wife. Yet he does so without ever being able to abandon his inner adherence to the opposite view, and, hence, for the remainder of the play is forced to judge himself and his deeds by a set of values from which his own actions have estranged him.[32] □

Tom McAlindon argues that the concepts of duality and polarity play a pivotal role in Shakespeare's tragedies: instability in the tragedies, he says, comes from 'the violent conflict and confusion of opposites'.[33] Among the examples of duality that McAlindon considers is the antithesis of Roman and Goth in *Titus Andronicus*, which he suggests is a figure for a debate about the categories of civilisation and barbarianism. He also looks at the example of Turco-Christian conflict in *Othello*, a play which he says invokes the myth of Mars (Roman god of war) and Venus (Roman god of love). He reads Othello's relationship with Desdemona as one of 'complementary opposition'.[34]

Post-Shakespearean readings of the tragedies have explored the importance of conflict and duality in tragedy; McAlindon suggests that Hegel and Nietzsche's interest in dialectics constitutes a self-conscious return to the precepts of ancient cosmology. He shows how this tension is derived from models of the cosmos inherited from classical antiquity which supported the idea of a 'dynamic system of interacting opposites'.[35] Ancient philosophers and natural scientists had formulated a system of binary opposites (hot/cold, moist/dry) which characterised man and nature at large. The classical legacy was vital in the emergence of Renaissance cosmology, which posited the idea of man as microcosm of the universe: 'Thus Renaissance culture abounded in brilliant emblems of the universe where man is always given a central place, and brilliant emblems of man which emphasise his physical and psychological subjection to cosmic influences.'[36] McAlindon stresses that the Globe theatre itself evokes a sense of these cosmic emblems. He takes issue with E. M. W. Tillyard's hierarchical construction of the Elizabethan worldview and argues that early modern cosmologists saw these tiers within the natural order as interacting.[37] While Rabkin and McElroy argue that Shakespeare reconciles the various binary oppositions in his plays, McAlindon suggests that the sense of antithesis is preserved.

Nicholas Grene takes a different approach to the idea of dialectic in Shakespeare in suggesting that there is 'a doubleness in Shakespeare's tragic imagination'.[38] Like Kenneth Muir (see the Introduction to this book), Grene is explicitly concerned with dismantling the notion of 'Shakespearean Tragedy'. While Muir constructs the Shakespeare canon in terms of a sequence, Grene suggests that within this sequence, Shakespearean tragedies can be paired chronologically. He argues: 'In the tragedies from 1599 on there appears to be a dialectic between these two modes of tragic imagination. Cognate themes, related situations and dramatic images are pursued alternately in sequent plays, now in one mode, now in another. When Shakespeare wrote *Hamlet*, he evidently still had *Julius Caesar* in mind.'[39] Elaborating his claim that there is a strong relationship between these two plays, Grene refers to the Ghost that appears near the end of *Julius Caesar* and at the beginning of *Hamlet*. He notes that critics have often seen *Hamlet* as a play that 'represents a historical moment of transition' towards modernity.[40] He suggests ways in which *Hamlet* bypasses the historical modes of thinking that are so important in *Julius Caesar*. Instead of the play's modernity, Grene emphasises the way the play engages with 'more atavistic, and primitive patterns of meaning', particularly through images of pollution and guilt.[41] In his final assessment of *Hamlet*, Grene suggests that 'Against the imaginative historicity of *Julius Caesar* it reaches back through metaphor towards myth.'[42]

Social and ethical conflict

Grene's contrasting of history and myth is a good moment at which to reflect on theoretical constructions of human history in terms of conflict, struggle and revolution, particularly in the intellectual history of the nineteenth century. One of the most significant contributors to this narrative is Charles Darwin (1809–82). His formative work on evolutionary biology brought new urgency to questions of heredity and class struggle, questions with which nineteenth- and twentieth-century dramatists were much concerned. In formulating the concept of the 'struggle for existence' (a phrase which refers to competition in the animal world for vital resources such as food), Darwin radically proposed that strife was part of the natural order of things and not (as the established Church had held) a failure of Christian charity and therefore a consequence of sin. Critics such as Gillian Beer have shown that Darwin's work had a powerful impact on the literary imagination of the period, particularly in the novel.[43] In recent years, Joseph Meeker has taken issue with the idea that Darwin presents a tragic vision of the world, insisting that the narrative of evolutionary biology is comic because it is a story of survival: 'Tragedy demands that choices be made among alternatives; comedy assumes that all choice is likely to be in error and that survival depends upon finding accommodations that will permit all parties to endure. Evolution itself is a gigantic comic drama, not the bloody tragic spectacle imagined by the sentimental humanists of early Darwinism.'[44]

While Darwin was proposing an account of inevitable conflict in the natural world, Marx and Engels were advancing radical new claims that society is structured by cycles of conflict. According to Marxism, there is a basic division in society between the capitalist ruling bourgeoisie, who control the basis of economic power, and the labouring proletariat. Marx and Engels constructed the relationship between these two classes in terms of a dialectic; their exposition of this dialectical relationship is itself indebted to the work of Hegel, whose work is discussed in the final section of this chapter. Marxist theory has been highly influential in shaping successive generations of literary theorists, who have been attentive to the way that power relations are constructed and expressed in texts. Among those indebted to Marxist theory are Brecht and members of the Frankfurt School (discussed in Chapter 8), as well as more recent Marxist critics, whose work is discussed throughout this Guide, such as Georg Lukács, Terry Eagleton and Jonathan Dollimore.

Through the circulation of Marxist ideas, the theme of class struggle was highly topical for writers of the nineteenth century. In 1888, the Swedish playwright August Strindberg wrote his play *Miss Julie*, which explores the relationship between Miss Julie and her servant, Jean. In the preface to the printed edition of the play, Strindberg radically argued that class struggle is 'suitable matter for tragedy'. He writes, 'the problem of social ascent and decline, of higher or lower, better or worse, man or woman, is, has been and will be of permanent interest'.[45] Like subsequent critics such as Ania Loomba and Dympna Callaghan (whose work is discussed in Chapter 4), Strindberg recognises that different discourses of power and hierarchy are implicated in one another: his play explores the complex shifting of both class and gender relations in the period. So although Jean is of a lower social rank than Miss Julie, Strindberg says that Jean 'has the whipping hand of Miss Julie simply because he is a man. Sexually he is an aristocrat by virtue of his masculine strength, his more finely developed senses and his ability to seize the initiative.'[46] At the same time, Strindberg expresses his disgust at Jean's social ambition. Jean, he says, 'is polished but coarse underneath; he knows how to wear a tail-coat, but can offer us no guarantee that his body is clean beneath it'.[47] On the question of tragic nobility, Strindberg suggests that the noble class is being reconstituted under the influence of social and cultural pressures of the time:

■ But Miss Julie is also a relic of the old warrior nobility, which is now disappearing in favour of the new neurotic or intellectual nobility; a victim of the errors of her age, of circumstances, and of her own flawed constitution, all of which add up to the equivalent of the old concept of Destiny or the Universal Law.[48] □

We recall that in Chapter 1, Eugene O'Neill observed the difficulty of finding concepts in modern drama which could satisfactorily correspond to the Greek tragic idea of fate. Strindberg, on the other hand, suggests that social laws are even more powerful than the old concept of nemesis (divine retribution) in which the Greek tragedians once dealt. He writes that Miss Julie has:

■ that innate or acquired sense of honour which the upper classes inherit ... It is the nobleman's *hara-kiri*, the Japanese law of inner conscience which commands a man to slit his stomach when another has insulted him, and which survives in a modified form in that ancient privilege of the nobility, the duel. Thus, the servant, Jean, lives; but Miss Julie cannot live without honour.[49] ☐

In the intellectual history of the nineteenth century, therefore, writers such as Strindberg were becoming highly alert to the presence of a host of dialectical relationships in nature and in society. One of the most important philosophical formulations of such a dialectic is by Hegel, in whose account, as we saw in Chapter 3, tragedy dramatises a conflict between two opposing ethical powers:

> ■ The original essence of tragedy consists then in the fact that within such a conflict each of the opposed sides, if taken by itself, has *justification;* while each can establish the true and positive content of its own aim and character only by denying and infringing the equally justified power of the other. The consequence is that in its moral life, and because of it, each is nevertheless involved in *guilt*.[50] ☐

Central to Hegel's conception of tragedy is the resolution of these two opposite points of view. He argues:

> ■ However justified the tragic character and his aim, however necessary the tragic collision, the third thing required is the tragic resolution of this conflict. By this means eternal justice is exercised on individuals and their aims in the sense that it restores the substance and unity of the ethical life with the downfall of the individual who has disturbed its peace.[51] ☐

Hegel suggests that in this resolution, 'the *one-sided* particular which had not been able to adapt itself to this harmony, and now ... unable to renounce itself and its intention, finds itself condemned to total destruction, or, at the very least, forced to abandon, if it can, the accomplishment of its aim.'[52] Where moral absolutes are fundamentally opposed to one another, there can be no possibility of compromise or mutual accommodation, only annihilation. In a variation on this idea, Hegel writes:

> ■ The final result, then, of the development of tragedy conducts us to this issue and only this, namely, that the twofold vindication of the mutually conflicting aspects is no doubt retained, but the one-sided mode is cancelled, and the undisturbed ideal harmony brings back again that condition of the chorus, which attributes without reserve equal honour to all the gods. The true course of dramatic development consists in the annulment of contradictions viewed as such, in the reconciliation of the forces of human action, which alternately strive to negate each other in their conflict.[53] ☐

Hegel's account of tragedy prioritises ethical conflict over the individual subject.

This view of character as an embodiment of an ethical absolute is crucial to Hegel's reading of the *Antigone*: 'This sort of development is most complete when individuals who are at variance appear each of them in their concrete existence as a totality, so that in themselves they are in the power of what they are fighting, and therefore they violate what, if they were true to their own nature, they should be honouring.'[54] While Hegel's reading of the play is contingent on the notion of antithesis embodied in the ethical conflict of Antigone and Creon, he resists any simple construction of this antithesis. Indeed Hegel anticipates Foley's argument, discussed earlier in this chapter, that both Creon and Antigone find themselves in a matrix of overlapping obligations. Hegel notes that Antigone is bound by her duty to the *polis* and, as a member of the ruling family, to royal command: she has obligations to the very system which she defies. Similarly Creon, as a father and husband, should show reverence for blood ties and the piety which they demand in ancient Greek culture. From these observations about the complexity of both Antigone and Creon's obligations, Hegel argues:

■ So there is immanent in both Antigone and Creon something that in their own way they attack, so that they are gripped and shattered by something intrinsic to their own actual being. Antigone suffers death before enjoying the bridal dance, but Creon too is punished by the voluntary deaths of his son and his wife, incurred, the one on account of Antigone's fate, the other because of Haemon's death. Of all the masterpieces of the classical and the modern world ... the *Antigone* seems to me to be the most magnificent and satisfying work of art of this kind.[55] □

Apollo and Dionysus

Like Hegel, Nietzsche's philosophical work on Greek tragedy concerns its dualities. Whereas Hegel's primary interest is in the ethical dimensions of tragedy, Nietzsche's primary concerns in *The Birth of Tragedy* (1872) are aesthetic. Indeed, Nietzsche reveres and celebrates Greek tragedy as an art form which transcends questions of morality. For Nietzsche, Greek tragedy's transcendent amorality provides a model of life affirmation. It is a way of countering the so-called 'wisdom of Silenus', a legendary story in which Silenus, companion of Dionysus, observes: 'What is best of all is utterly beyond your reach: not to be born, not to *be*, to be *nothing*. But the second best for you is – to die soon.'[56]

In *The Birth of Tragedy*, Nietzsche argues that tragedy is a synthesis of what he calls its Dionysian (or Dionysiac) and Apollonian (or Apolline) elements. In an important critique of the text, Silk and Stern note that 'the Apolline and the Dionysiac are not translatable into constant analytical equivalents: the embodiment of each varies according to the embodiment of the other'.[57] Broadly speaking, the Dionysian is associated with the art of music and intoxication, and the Apollonian with dreams and sculpture. The Dionysian is conceived of as the raw horror of existence; through the Apollonian, Greek tragedy draws a veil over this horror and provides it with a form that enables us to confront life's painful reality. Thus the Apollonian is vital to our ability to tolerate the Dionysian, since, as Silk and Stern argue, 'an unmediated Dionysiac artistic experience would be a totally shattering one'.[58] Central to Nietzsche's account of the Dionysian is the close association he posits between Dionysus and music, as embodied in the performance of the chorus. Nietzsche argues that music is more capable of expressing pain than language is: 'Language can never adequately render the cosmic symbolism of music, because music stands in symbolic relation to the primordial contradiction and primordial pain in the heart of the primal unity ... *language*, as the organ and symbol of phenomena, can never by any means disclose the innermost heart of music.'[59]

Returning to the idea of tragic pleasure, for Nietzsche this is experienced as a form of metaphysical consolation. In reference to the so-called *principium individuationis* which he takes from Schopenhauer, Nietzsche understands the condition of individuation to be painful. He argues that tragedy effects the collapse of the *principium individuationis* and allows man to experience a profound unity with his fellow man and with the world itself: 'at this collapse of the *principium individuationis*, we steal a glimpse into the nature of the *Dionysian*, which is brought home to us most intimately by the analogy of intoxication'.[60] In an extension of this idea, Nietzsche argues:

■ Under the charm of the Dionysian not only is the union between man and man reaffirmed, but nature which has become alienated, hostile, or subjugated, celebrates once more her reconciliation with her lost son, man ... Transform Beethoven's 'Hymn to Joy' into a painting; let your imagination conceive the multitudes bowing to the dust, awestruck – then you will approach the Dionysian. Now the slave is a free man; now all the rigid, hostile barriers that necessity, caprice, or 'impudent convention' have fixed between man and man are broken. Now, with the gospel of universal harmony, each one feels himself not only united, reconciled, and fused with his neighbor, but as one with him ...[61] □

This idea of mystical union is central to Nietzsche's conception of tragic pleasure, the topic that we address in Chapter 6. As Silk and Stern argue:

■ In one sense the Dionysiac–Apolline dialectic represents an answer – and a quite original answer – to a question which had occurred to Plato and which clearly concerns Aristotle: why do we get pleasure from tragedy? ... Nietzsche's answer is coherent and impressive. Tragedy, he argues, presents us with the destruction of individuals in a way which is exalting, because it gives us a glimpse of the underlying deeper power of life ... in which we share, but which is only glimpsed when individuality is transcended.[62]

While Nietzsche's account of the duality of Dionysus and Apollo is central to his account of tragedy, it is important to recognise that Dionysus embodies important dualities in his own right. In one of the most significant studies of this topic, Charles Segal argues that the basic tension in Euripidean drama between the extremes of reason and emotion is embodied in the spirit of Dionysus himself.[63] Segal adumbrates a matrix of contradictions inherent in Dionysus as both local and foreign, Hellene and barbarian, divine and bestial, male and female. He sees in this pattern of contradiction the possibility for boundaries to be dissolved:

■ As Apollo imposes limits and reinforces boundaries, Dionysus, his opposite and complement, dissolves them. From the *Iliad* on, Apollo embodies the distance between god and man. Dionysus closes that distance. His worshipers identify themselves with the god, and in the ecstasy of his cult they experience something like the divine joy and power. Dionysus and the Dionysiac bridge the gap that Apollo so threateningly guards.[64]

Segal expounds an idea which is derived from Nietzsche's account of Dionysiac communion:

■ In the Dionysiac performance, as in the Dionysiac ritual, the individuality of personal identity gives way to fusion. The actor, wearing the mask that has close associations with the Dionysiac cult from early times, fuses to some extent with the personage whom he represents in the theater. The spectator, watching the performance, at some point loses his separateness and identifies with the masked figure before him.[65]

Segal suggests that this 'process of symbolic identification and dissolution of self into other' extends as far as the boundaries of tragedy itself: 'there is a curious fusion of comic and satyric with tragic elements in the *Bacchae*, another aspect of the crossing of boundaries and fusion of opposites characteristic of this god'.[66] In his evaluation of Nietzsche, Segal suggests that his discussion fails to take adequate account of issues of androgyny and sexual ambiguity in relation to both Dionysus and Apollo. Claiming that Dionysus 'dissolves generational as well as sexual boundaries', Segal notes that the god is particularly associated in Athenian culture with the *ephebe* (a youth just approaching maturity, between the ages of about 16 and 20).[67] Segal argues that the figure of Dionysus in the *Bacchae* destabilises and frustrates Pentheus' rite of passage into adulthood. Drawing on Vidal-Naquet's anthropological work on Athenian rites of passage, Segal suggests that Pentheus' excursion to Mount Cithaeron, where he is brutally dismembered by a group of Dionysiac worshippers, including his own mother, is figured as an attempted (and indeed frustrated) rite of passage.[68]

Segal's account of Dionysus thus draws together many different facets of tragic theory relating to the ritual context, the role of the spectator and ideologies of gender. For Segal, this most meta-theatrical of Greek tragedies allows us, through the figure of Dionysus, to gain insight into the heart of Attic drama, the boundaries which it honours and the boundaries which its violence transcends.

In this chapter we have looked at a series of dialetics which recur in tragedy: male and female, public and private. For many, *Antigone* – which received extended discussion in Chapter 4 – is the play which best exemplifies these dialectical processes in action. In considering dialectics of space in this chapter, we have seen how Froma Zeitlin characterises Thebes as a kind of 'anti-Athens' in Greek tragedy: for Zeitlin, Thebes is a projected negative image of the kind of city that Athens aspires to be. Like Zeitlin, Edith Hall is interested in the way that dialectics of place – and in her case, representations of ethnicity – can play a role in processes of self-definition. For her, the binary opposition between Greek and barbarian is a central impetus in Greek tragedy. Turning to Shakespeare, we encountered Norman Rabkin's influential model of complementarity. For Rabkin, the central dichotomy in Shakespeare's tragedies is in the way that each play entertains two different and irreconcilable accounts of reality.

Conflict and dialectic, as we have seen, are major preoccupations in nineteenth-century thinking about the world. Whereas in Christian orthodoxy, strife is seen as a breach of the natural order, Darwin presented a revolutionary current of thinking in which strife is seen as an essential function in nature. Writing in the same period as Darwin, radical political theorists Marx and Engels argue that class struggle is a dialectic that profoundly shapes social change. These ideas helped to fertilise tragedy of the late nineteenth century and figure explicitly as themes in the drama of Strindberg and others.

Finally, in this chapter, we turned to look at Nietzsche's *Birth of Tragedy*. At the heart of Greek tragedy, Nietzsche proposes, is a synthesis of two elements, the Apollonian and the Dionysian. Among critics who have thought closely about the role of Dionysus, Charles Segal has shown that Dionysus is himself a figure that embodies many of the dualities which emerge in his tragic theatre.

In Chapter 8, we will return to Nietzsche's account and his claim that Euripides' rational approach to tragedy causes its demise. In the next chapter, however, we consider the role of the emotions in tragedy as we turn to the subject of tragic pleasure.

CHAPTER SIX

Tragic Pleasure

Pleasure and pain

'"Why does tragedy give pleasure?" is among the hoariest of philosophical questions, akin to "Why is there anything at all?" or "Why is there evil in the world?" There has been no shortage of answers.'[1] So remarks Terry Eagleton on the subject of tragic pleasure. This chapter will offer a survey of some of the most important accounts of tragic pleasure which philosophers and literary critics have proposed.

Theories of tragic pleasure begin with Aristotle. As we shall see in this chapter, his comments on 'the pleasure proper to tragedy' and on *catharsis* – ideas which we will explicate in some detail – sought to establish that watching tragedy was beneficial both to individual spectators and to the state as a whole: in other words, the benefits of watching tragedy were both psychological and political. To understand why Aristotle formulates his argument in this way, we need to go back to his teacher, Plato.

In *The Republic*, one of the earliest surviving philosophical accounts of poetry and drama in the Western tradition, Plato argues that almost all forms of mimetic art (i.e., imitative art, including poetry and drama) are harmful to the development of good citizens, and he recommends that poets should therefore be banished from his ideal state. In advocating such a negative view of the value of mimetic art, Plato prompted generations of critics to write in defence of poetry and drama.

It is widely believed that Aristotle's account of *catharsis* was formulated specifically in response to Plato's attack on art. Briefly summarised, Aristotle argues that tragedy promotes emotional good health in the spectator. If individual citizens are emotionally well regulated, Aristotle implies, the city as a whole stands to benefit. This is how A. D. Nuttall frames Aristotle's reply to Plato: '[Aristotle] is thinking like a civic governor and is saying to his dead teacher, Plato, "You've got the psychology wrong; people leaving a tragic performance don't smash shops and beat up peaceable passers-by; they are strangely quiet."'[2] Or, as Terry Eagleton puts it: 'Tragedy can perform the pleasurable, politically valuable service of draining off an excess of enfeebling emotions such as pity and fear, thus providing a kind public therapy for those of the citizenry in danger of emotional flabbiness ... [T]ragic theatre is a refuse dump for socially undesirable emotions, or at least a retraining programme.'[3]

The idea that theatre can operate, at least potentially, as an instrument for social and political conservatism was particularly attractive to Renaissance critics. In sixteenth-century Italy, the critics Ellebodius, Speroni and Giacomini all argued that tragedy can promote civic order by purging the spectators of their passions; this reflects views assimilated from Stoic thinking about the dangers of emotional excess.[4] In England, Philip Sidney's *Defence of Poetry* allows the principle that poetry should be pleasurable – something of a concession to the life of the emotions – but at the same time stresses the didactic function of drama. This dual emphasis on pleasure and learning comes from Horace's *Ars Poetica*, a text that heavily influenced Sidney's thinking. Tragedy, according to Sidney, is the form of drama:

■ that openeth the greatest wounds, and showeth forth the ulcers that are covered with tissue; that maketh kings fear to be tyrants, and tyrants manifest their tyrannical humours; that, with stirring the affects of admiration and commiseration, teacheth the uncertainty of this world, and upon how weak foundations gilden roofs are builded ...[5] □

In this passage, Sidney's attention to the emotional response of the audience is relatively muted; it is also striking here that he considers the didactic potential of tragedy not primarily in terms of the masses but those at the centre of power. Like Aristotle's *Poetics* – a text which Sidney knew through sixteenth-century Italian commentaries, if not in the original – the *Defence* mounts its own counter-argument to Plato's concern that poetry is a destabilising influence in a well-ordered society.

Let us look now in some detail at Aristotle's comments on tragic pleasure. In a complex passage, Aristotle suggests that tragedy and comedy each affords the spectator a distinct kind of pleasure:

■ Second is the kind of composition which is said by some to be the best, that is, one that has a double composition like the *Odyssey*, and which ends with opposite fortunes for good and bad characters. It is held to be the best, because of the weakness of the audience, since poets follow the audience, and write according to what pleases them. But this is not the pleasure proper to tragedy, but rather to comedy; for in comedy those who are complete enemies throughout the story, such as Orestes and Aegisthus, become friends at the end and leave the stage, and nobody is killed by anybody.[6] □

This passage is essentially an adverse comment on the composition of tragedies with happy endings such as the *Ion*, the *Helen* and the *Iphigeneia in Tauris*.[7] Aristotle claims that such plays do not deliver 'the pleasure proper to tragedy'. It is a phrase which embodies potential contradictions between the subject matter of tragedy (typically death and suffering) and our response to it in the form of the pleasure that we derive. Commenting on the contradictions that are inherent in the idea of tragic pleasure, Nuttall argues:

> ■ 'The pleasure of tragedy' is an immediately uncomfortable phrase. Quite apart from the original basic collision between terrible matter and a delighted response, there is an awkwardness, somehow, in the very mildness of the term 'pleasure' – it seems a puny word to set beside the thunderous term 'tragedy', adding a species of insult to injury. The Nietzschean oxymoron, 'tragic joy' is, oddly, easier to accept because it fights fire with fire.[8] □

First published in 1757, David Hume's essay 'Of Tragedy' investigates precisely this paradox:

> ■ It seems an unaccountable pleasure, which the spectators of a well-written tragedy receive from sorrow, terror, anxiety, and other passions, that are in themselves disagreeable and uneasy ... They are pleased in proportion as they are afflicted, and never are so happy as when they employ tears, sobs, and cries to give vent to their sorrow, and relieve their heart, swoln with the tenderest sympathy and compassion.[9] □

In exploring this question, Hume gives some weight to L'Abbé Dubos's argument that the worst thing of all is to feel nothing: thus, even to feel negative emotions is better than feeling none at all. Elaborating on this initial thought that we find the mere sensation of emotion to some degree pleasurable, Hume suggests that tragedy gives pleasure because we are emotionally distanced from it: we are protected by our awareness that it is not real. In a later refraction of this idea, Eagleton observes:

> ■ Some of our pleasure in tragedy no doubt springs from simple curiosity. We don't witness brutal murders every day, and are thus intrigued to come across them even in fictional form. Indeed, the fact that they are fictional is the basis of one theory of tragic pleasure: for David Hume, in his essay on tragedy, we enjoy in art what we wouldn't in life.[10] □

It is a characteristically succinct paraphrase from Eagleton, but perhaps one which does not do full justice to Hume's argument. Hume does not entirely think that we can explain tragic pleasure in terms of being artistically distanced from an object that is potentially distressing to us. He argues that the 'eloquence' of the creation transfigures the negative potential inherent in our response to the sadness of tragedy into something pleasurable. He argues:

> ■ tragedy is an imitation; and imitation is always of itself agreeable. This circumstance serves still farther to smooth the motions of passion, and to convert the whole feeling into one uniform and strong enjoyment. Objects of the greatest terror and distress please in painting, and please more than the most beautiful objects, that appear calm and indifferent.[11] □

Hume argues that it is not simply distance which allows sorrowful events to seem pleasurable. Rather, he insists, 'It is thus the fiction of tragedy softens the passion, by an infusion of a new feeling, not merely by weakening or diminishing the sorrow. You may by degrees weaken a real sorrow, till it totally disappears; yet in none of its gradations will it ever give pleasure ...'[12] In other words, in real life, negative emotions such as grief fade over time, but they do not evolve into something more pleasurable. Tragedy does not rely on this diminution of strong feelings into weaker ones: it takes the passions and transforms them, as it were, at source. Hume concludes that 'the pleasure, which poets, orators, and musicians give us, by exciting grief, sorrow, indignation, compassion, is not so extraordinary or paradoxical, as it may at first sight appear'.[13] Central to this, he suggests, is the delight and admiration which we naturally derive in contemplating a work of art.

In his essay 'On the Art of Tragedy' (1792), Friedrich Schiller poses a radical rebuttal of this argument.[14] He suggests that spectacles of suffering do not yield pleasure because they are imitative; here Schiller points out that we may feel a certain attraction to spectacles of real-life suffering, such as watching a ship wrecked in a storm. Thus it is not as imitation but in themselves that spectacles of suffering engender pleasure. Schiller denies that this pleasure comes from a sense of our own safety relative to those who are in mortal danger. Rather, he suggests, the pleasure comes from our empathy with those who are afflicted, that is, from our moral nature. In this account, Schiller recognises that emotions are pleasurable in themselves, but at the same time, he stresses the role of reason in relation to the emotions. Tragic pleasure, he suggests, comes from the moral stimulation we feel when confronted with spectacles of suffering and in our urge to act. For Schiller, tragic pleasure can surpass joyful emotions because we are happiest when our moral faculties are engaged.

The idea of *catharsis* has become influential in the psychoanalytic tradition. In the theory of abreaction formulated by Sigmund Freud and his mentor Josef Breuer, the patient is understood to have an accumulation of emotion after the experience of trauma, particularly in cases where the memory of the original trauma has been repressed. According to Freud and Breuer, this emotion seeks to be discharged and released, thereby bringing the patient relief. This thinking was important in Freud's pioneering work on the treatment of hysteria and continues to inform psychotherapeutic practices today.[15]

Freud's foundational work on the psychology of pleasure and pain has been a significant influence on theorists of tragedy. In another essay, 'Beyond the Pleasure Principle' (1920), Freud looks at patterns of repetition in children's play.[16] He reports a case study in which he observed a child repeatedly throwing away and then retrieving a beloved toy. Freud suggests that by repeating the distressing experience of being parted from a desired object, the child is able to act out the more profound experience of being parted from the mother and anticipating her return. By confronting loss voluntarily, Freud suggests, the child develops mastery over his own distress. Among critics to make use of this Freudian essay is Lionel Trilling, who formulates a version of the so-called Mithridatic account of tragedy. In this account, Trilling refers to the way that 'tragedy is used as the small and controlled administration of pain to inure ourselves to the greater doses which life will force upon us'.[17]

In a very different reading of the same essay by Freud, Fiona Macintosh discusses the pleasure of repetition and its role in tragedy. She suggests that one of the ways in which tragedy excites pleasure is through its iteration of certain structures, motifs and themes across time and across cultures. On this basis, Macintosh suggests that understanding the archetypal nature of what she calls 'the big speech' (i.e., the protagonist's death speech) is key to our understanding of tragic pleasure.[18] We will return to Macintosh's discussion of Greek and Irish tragedy in Chapter 9.

Catharsis: purification or purgation?

In the *Poetics*, Aristotle defines tragedy in the following terms: 'Tragedy is the *mimesis* of an action that is serious and complete in its scope ... bringing about through pity and fear the purging of these and suchlike emotions.'[19] There has been a longstanding dispute as to whether we should understand *catharsis* to signify *purification*, a process of refinement, in which some elements of the emotions are removed while others are left behind, or *purgation*, a more radical process by which certain emotions – typically taken to be pity and fear – are expunged altogether.

Among recent critics, the case for purgation has been robustly argued by A. D. Nuttall.[20] In developing his account of Aristotle, Nuttall states:

> ■ I do not believe that Aristotle is offering a Galenic account of emotions as physical humours, requiring actual excretion from time to time. Rather he is proposing an analogy: as the body seeks to ease its load of waste matter, so the soul – the higher faculty if you like terms of value – seeks to ease its burden of emotion. That is why, apparently against all the odds, the audience leaving the theatre after *Oedipus Rex* feels relief. What they have seen is terrible; what they feel is a kind of ease. This is not simply a feeling of relief that the suffering has stopped. Rather, the relief is integrated with the full process of the drama, with the complete discharging of the tragic sequence from beginning to end.[21] □

There have been prominent dissenters, however. Arguing in favour of the purification theory, Martha Nussbaum suggests that:

> ■ if we look briefly at the whole history of *katharsis* and related words ... it becomes quite evident that the primary, ongoing, central meaning is roughly one of 'clearing up' or 'clarification', i.e., of the removal of some obstacle (dirt, or blot, or obscurity, or admixture) that makes the item in question less *clear* than it is in its proper state.[22] □

Although adhering to an interpretation of *catharsis* as 'purification' (a concept which forms the basis of the main rival to the purgation theory), Nussbaum suggests that in any case 'purgation' means something very close to 'purification':

> ■ The medical use [of the term *catharsis*] to designate purgation is a special application of this general sense: purgation rids the body of internal impediments and obstacles, clearing it up. And the connection with spiritual purification and ritual purity appears to be another specialized development, given the strong link between such purity and physical freedom from blemish or dirt.[23] □

Writing in response to Nussbaum, Nuttall argues:

> ■ It will be observed that Nussbaum and I are converging on a pretty simple idea of washing. When washing occurs something is cleaned and something is washed away. Do we then agree? No. Nussbaum's error is to misplace emotion in this scheme. She seems to think that the emotions are washed. In fact they are what is washed away, or purged. *They* are the obstacle, the dirt, the obscurity (or obscurers).[24] □

Nuttall goes on to insist that, 'For Aristotle it is not the emotions which are purified but the organism. The emotions themselves are, precisely, the impurity which is removed. That emotions are unpleasant for Aristotle seems to me a direct and inescapable implication of the medical term here used.'[25]

As we have seen, Nussbaum suggests that *catharsis* might best be understood as 'clarification'.[26] Like Nussbaum, Leon Golden contends that Aristotle's definition of tragedy may be translated as 'achieving, through the representation of pitiful and fearful situations, the clarification of such incidents'.[27] Here too, Nussbaum follows Golden and paraphrases Aristotle's definition of tragedy as follows: 'the function of a tragedy is to accomplish, through pity and fear, a clarification (or illumination) concerning experiences of the pitiable and fearful kind'.[28]

Jonathan Lear is one of several recent critics who have sought to challenge the hard dichotomy between purification and purgation, and to suggest alternative translations for the term *catharsis*.[29] Lear himself suggests that *catharsis* might be understood as 'release', although this seems remarkably close to the traditional notion of 'purgation' which he ostensibly repudiates. Also rejecting the purgation theory, Eva Schaper poses the valid question, 'Is it very likely that Aristotle really wants to say no more than that the end of tragedy is to arouse emotions in us in order to purge us of them?'[30] Like Lear, Schaper rejects the binary distinction between purification and purgation, and argues that in the *Poetics*, Aristotle employs *catharsis* in a sense which is specific to an aesthetic context.

One of the most authoritative commentators of recent times, Stephen Halliwell, synthesises elements of both purgation and purification theories in his claim that *catharsis* 'entails both an expenditure of emotion and an amelioration of the underlying emotional disposition'.[31] He further argues that it is unhelpful to translate the term *catharsis* at all, and it is now common practice among philosophers and literary critics not to do so. Halliwell argues that *catharsis* should be understood as an educational process, rather than a purely evacuative one. Here we can identify the presence of some common ground with Nussbaum and Golden, whose accounts of *catharsis*, as we have just seen, also place an emphasis on the educative potential of *catharsis* as a form of intellectual clarification. In Halliwell's reading, the purpose of *catharsis* is to bring emotional response into alignment with reality, and so to inculcate a proper perception of the world. The educational view of *catharsis* has found support from critics who favour one or other of the traditional interpretations of *catharsis*, such as Nussbaum, as well as those, like Halliwell, who want to abandon the old dichotomy, or to suggest ways in which its apparently opposing terms might be synthesised.

It is interesting to note that current support for the educational interpretation has brought the commentary tradition full circle: the overwhelming majority of Aristotle's earlier critics took *catharsis* to operate on a didactic model, primarily in terms of a stimulus to repentance. Guarini suggests that a spectator experiences the 'purging terror of tragedy' when he sees the fate that befalls Oedipus, and confronts the magnitude of his mental anguish:

> ■ This is a spectacle that makes us consider and repent of our sins and makes those who fear to die realize clearly that there is something more terrible to human nature than death, for if death is to be feared at all, only that of the spirit should be feared, since in comparison with it that of the body becomes as it were unfelt.[32] □

For Guarini, tragedy induces an acute self-reflection in the spectator and a corresponding desire to reform oneself. He configures this process of self-criticism in Christian terms, suggesting that tragedy can induce a moment of spiritual crisis or self-recognition. Modern critics who advocate an educative reading of *catharsis* generally take the view that *catharsis* may have a more prolonged role in training the emotions and the cognitive faculties.

It should be noted, however, that the educational significance of *catharsis* is not universally accepted among contemporary philosophers. One notable objection has been posed by Lear, who argues that Aristotle's attention to the mimetic nature of tragedy means he cannot have thought that it equips us for real-life experiences of pity and fear. According to this reading, tragedy can prepare us for life only in the most general terms, by improving our emotional condition: the experience of pity and fear inside the theatre does not act as a form of direct preparation for encountering equivalent experiences in real life.[33] As Lear points out, an understanding of *catharsis* as a process of purification rests on an incorrect assumption that Aristotle believes pity and fear to be emotional pollutants, when, in fact, he recognises that they may form an appropriate – and even desirable – response to certain events.[34]

In the twentieth century, one of the most radical commentators on the subject of *catharsis* is Augusto Boal, whose work we touched on in Chapter 3. Boal's account of the 'coercive system of tragedy' – which we will examine shortly – is both radical and traditional in its claim that tragedy functions in such a way as to control and eliminate subversive or undesirable elements in society. For Boal, *catharsis* is central to an understanding of tragedy: 'Tragedy, in all its qualitative and quantitative aspects, exists as a function of the effect it seeks, catharsis. All the unities of tragedy are structured around this concept. It is the center, the essence, the purpose of the tragic system. Unfortunately it is also the most controversial concept.'[35] Boal claims that man has certain objectives relating to wealth, virtue, citizenship and so on, and he suggests that 'When [man] fails in the achievement of those objectives, the art of tragedy intervenes. This correction of man's actions is what Aristotle calls *catharsis*.'[36] Boal argues that tragedy functions as an instrument of political and social control through what he calls its 'coercive system':

> ■ Aristotle's coercive system of tragedy survives to this day, thanks to its great efficacy. It is, in effect, a powerful system of intimidation. The structure of the system may vary in a thousand ways ... but the system will nevertheless be there, working to carry out its basic task: the purgation of all antisocial elements.[37] □

Boal notes that this system can only function during periods of relative stability, and one of its primary aims is to suppress and reform subversive or revolutionary tendencies in the populace. The system operates in order to maintain the status quo: 'This system functions to diminish, placate, satisfy, eliminate all that can break the balance – all, including the revolutionary, transforming impetus'.[38]

Boal summarises the requirements of tragedy's coercive system as follows:

> ■ (a) the creation of a conflict between the character's ethos and the ethos of the society in which he lives; something is not right!
> (b) the establishment of a relationship called empathy, which consists in allowing the spectator to be guided by the character through his experiences; the spectator – feeling as if he himself is acting – enjoys the pleasures and suffers the misfortunes of the character, to the extreme of thinking his thoughts.
> (c) that the spectator experience three changes of a rigorous nature: *peripeteia*, *anagnorisis*, and *catharsis*; he *suffers a blow* with regard to his fate (the action of the play), *recognizes the error* vicariously committed and *is purified of the antisocial characteristic* which he sees in himself.
> This is the essence of the coercive system of tragedy.[39] □

What is distinctive about Boal's account is that he insists on the spectator's close identification with the protagonist of tragedy: here Boal maintains a very different position from that of Hume, which we saw at the beginning of this chapter. Boal takes as an example 'Western' movies in which the spectator feels a natural sympathy for the villain. In showing how the villain dies and how his death is celebrated by the community, Boal argues, films of this genre 'serve the Aristotelian purpose of purging all the spectator's aggressive tendencies'.[40] This interpretation clearly has much in common with the scapegoat theories of tragedy that we considered in Chapter 1.

In twentieth-century accounts of Aristotelian *catharsis*, critics including Gerald Else have suggested that Aristotle is not referring to the purgation of the emotions at all, but rather to events.[41] Else is among a group of critics who suggested that *catharsis* is part of the play, rather than an effect which is experienced at the end of the performance. Else writes:

> ■ Thus the catharsis is not a change or end-product in the spectator's soul, or in the fear and pity (i.e., the dispositions to them) in his soul, but a process carried forward in the emotional material of the play by its structural elements, above all by the recognition ... This interpretation makes catharsis a transitive or operational factor within the tragic structure itself, precedent to the release of pity, and ultimately of the tragic pleasure, rather than the be-all and end-all of tragedy itself.[42] □

More recently, Charles Segal has concurred that *catharsis* can be seen as part of the play itself. He sees tragedy as offering a kind of ritual cleansing from the pollution of death: it is through the performance of funeral rites that the characters on stage experience *catharsis*. Thus the audience is helped towards its own experience of *catharsis* through that which is shown on stage. Segal identifies several Shakespearean tragedies – *Hamlet, Julius Caesar, Romeo and Juliet, Antony and Cleopatra* and *Coriolanus* – as manifesting this kind of cathartic closure.[43]

The tragic emotions: pity, fear, horror

As we have seen from our discussion of *catharsis*, there remains a lack of critical consensus as to what kind of process *catharsis* is, but the interpretative problems do not end there. There is further uncertainty about the emotional objects which it concerns, and this turns on the clause 'of these emotions'. Aristotle is clear on the particular emotions – namely pity and fear – which tragedy arouses and which initiate the process of *catharsis*. But which emotions are actually purged (or purified)? The most common modern interpretation is that pity and fear act self-reflexively. As spectators of tragedy, pity and fear are aroused in us, and then purged. In an alternative reading, pity and fear might act to purge the spectator of a wider category of negative emotions, such as jealousy, anger or guilt, for example. But if this is the case, the parameters of such a category are unspecified by Aristotle and we are required to infer much more than is stated in the text itself. As Nuttall remarks, 'If the pleasure is simply that of eased emotions and the pleasure is in practice initially contested at the conscious level by distressing emotions such as pity and fear, why do we not go for an uncontested discharge – say of emotions like hope or greed?'[44]

In his discussion of *catharsis*, Hegel suggests that we should not place too much emphasis on the emotional effects which tragedy engenders:

■ In this connection Aristotle, as every one knows, laid it down ... that the true effect of tragedy should be to arouse pity and fear and accomplish the catharsis of these emotions. By 'emotions' Aristotle did not mean mere feeling, my subjective sense of something corresponding with me or not, the agreeable or disagreeable, the attractive or the repulsive – this most superficial of all criteria which only recently has been proposed as the principle of dramatic success or failure.[45] □

For Hegel, tragedy directs our faculties towards a response that is of a higher order than the emotions:

■ For the only important thing for a work of art is to present what corresponds with reason and spiritual truth, and if we are to discover the principle of this, we must direct our attention to totally different considerations. Even in the case of Aristotle's dictum we must therefore fix our eyes not on the mere feelings of pity and fear but on the nature of the subject-matter which by its artistic appearance is to purify these feelings.[46] □

Where Hegel does concede that tragedy arouses pity, he places a diminished emphasis on the emotional dimensions of this as a response and instead characterises pity in intellectual terms, suggesting that pity consists in 'sympathy ... with the sufferer's moral justification'.[47]

Hegel argues that tragedy does not involve merely enduring, or even indulging in mere 'spectacles of wretchedness and distress'. Rather, he asserts that tragedy's investigation of issues of human agency and accountability elevates the drama to something far beyond the status of a sad story. He argues:

■ Above mere fear and tragic sympathy there therefore stands that sense of reconciliation which the tragedy affords by the glimpse of eternal justice. In its absolute sway this justice overrides the relative justification of one-sided aims and passions because it cannot suffer the conflict and contradiction of naturally harmonious ethical powers to be victorious and permanent in truth and actuality.[48] □

While Hegel places a diminished emphasis on the role of emotion in our response to tragedy, others have investigated tragedy's capacity to provoke a wide range of intense emotional responses outside the narrow prescriptions of pity and fear. This has led a number of theorists to explore tragedy's engagement with horror and with the grotesque. In his study of the role of 'horrid laughter' in Jacobean tragedy, Nicholas Brooke contends that the familiar opposition that is often drawn between laughter and tears is misleading. Each of these outward expressions, he argues, registers 'a multiplicity of emotional conditions and tones irreducibly different from each other'.[49] In some cases, comic elements might provide 'comic relief' (a term invented by Dryden), but Brooke suggests that it would be a mistake to assume that laughter universally signifies that the tragic tension has been relaxed. He argues that 'Tragedy deals in extreme emotions, not all of the same kind: death, suffering, heroism, torture, cruelty, nobility, horror, and so on. And because they are extreme, they are all *liable* to turn over into laughter.'[50]

Suggesting that Kyd's *The Spanish Tragedy* offers a paradigm for our understanding of the complex relationship between tragedy and laughter, Brooke argues:

> The play is solemn, violent, horrid, grotesque, ironic, tragic, absurd. You may call it all of these, but what you cannot do is to single out any one and suppress the rest. If it is not horrid it is not absurd; and its kind of tragic perception depends on seeing the grotesque ironies. What it certainly is, is stylised ...[51]

Brooke emphasises that the tonal complexities of Kyd's tragedy are not unique but in many ways are typical of the English tragedy of the period: 'It is still common to offer Jacobean tragedy as a sort of amazing decadence from an imaginary condition of "serious" tragedy before, so it is important to stress that never existed in English ... Before Marlowe and Kyd, English tragedy (apart from one isolated academic experiment, *Gorboduc*) was largely violent moral farce.'[52]

Heavily indebted to the spectacles of extreme violence in Jacobean tragedy is an avant-garde movement in the British theatre of the 1990s which has come to be known as 'In-Yer-Face Theatre' or the Theatre of Extremes. During this decade, writers such as Sarah Kane, Mark Ravenhill and Anthony Neilson were producing provocative new drama which tested moral and aesthetic boundaries by staging scenes of graphic sex, mutilation, torture, sexual violence and cannibalism. Relating Sarah Kane's work to the so-called 'New Jacobeans' of the late 1960s and early 1970s, including Edward Bond and Howard Barker, Graham Saunders suggests: 'These dramatists shared an overt sense of theatricality and a number of themes – most notably the depiction of violence and a fascination with the grotesque – which were frequently laced with a mordant black humour.'[53]

In-yer-face theatre is not a subgenre of tragedy, but, in one of the few critical studies which have yet to have been written on the subject,

Aleks Sierz points out that it is a dramatic form that is closely affiliated to classical tragedy:

> ■ On the cover of the playtext of Sarah Kane's *Blasted* is a photograph of a man's face with both eyes gouged out: it could be Oedipus, Gloucester or Hamm ...
> The greatest of the ancient Greek tragedies deal with extreme states of mind: brutal deaths and terrible suicides, agonizing pain and dreadful suffering, human sacrifice and cannibalism, rape and incest, mutilations and humiliations. Thanks to Freud, Oedipus now symbolizes the most familiar taboo – even to people who never go to the theatre.[54] □

Sierz also suggests that there are important parallels between the emotional effects of Greek tragedy and those of in-yer-face theatre:

> ■ ... of all the theories about the purpose of tragedy, the most suggestive is the idea that it was meant to purge the bad feelings of the audience. The idea of putting yourself through hell in order to exorcize your inner demons is at the root of experiential theatre. Yet Greek drama was probably intended not to attack but to heal the audience, to make it better able to face its time. This argues for a kind of utilitarian role for the theatre, making it a form of shock therapy.[55] □

Saunders suggests that Sarah Kane's work has an effect on the audience which is 'visceral':

> ■ Her vision of theatre, in its use of both language and imagery, has been described in similar terms: for instance, attention has been drawn to its qualities which range in intensity [from] 'having your face rammed into an overflowing ashtray ... and then having your whole head held down in a bucket of offal,' to a drama of 'almost unparalleled distilled intensity which is often unbearable to watch.'[56] □

Predictably, the work of Sarah Kane generated intense outrage among journalists and reviewers. Certainly Kane felt that drama failed if it did not provoke intense responses. In one interview, she commented, 'I hate the idea of theatre just being an evening pastime. It should be emotionally and intellectually demanding.'[57] But as critics sympathetic to Kane's work would suggest, her drama does not merely set out to shock. As Natasha Langridge and Heidi Stephenson put it, 'Her plays ... offer us a powerful warning, by showing the tragic but logical conclusion of humanity's escalating, destructive behaviour. Simultaneously they force us to confront our shared responsibility for the brutal reality which already exists.'[58] In the Theatre of the Extremes, we are reminded of Jan Kott's conclusion that 'tragedy brings catharsis, while grotesque offers no consolation whatsoever'.[59] Arguably it is precisely the sense of consolation which the Theatre of the Extremes resists and avoids.

In this chapter we have been thinking once again about audience responses to tragedy. In Chapter 2, we looked at the chorus as the voice of the *polis* in Greek tragedy: the way that the chorus might articulate (and direct) social and political points of view. In this chapter, our focus has been on the emotions. At the same time, we have not entirely set aside a sense of the political. In his account of *catharsis*, Aristotle is aware that tragedy's management of the emotions has political consequences: if citizens are able to discharge negative emotions as spectators of tragedy, this will promote the stability of a well-ordered *polis*.

As we saw early in this chapter, the term 'tragic pleasure' presents us with an apparent paradox in the way that audiences can derive pleasure as spectators of someone else's pain. In tragedy, we watch with pleasure spectacles of suffering which in real life we would want to avoid. Hume tries to resolve this philosophical problem by suggesting we can watch tragedy with pleasure because we know its scenes of suffering are fictional: in other words, we watch at a safe distance. Influenced by Freudian theory, Lionel Trilling suggests that our exposure to tragedy equips us better to cope with the experience of suffering in our own lives.

The subject of *catharsis* has given rise to an extensive body of work. Aristotle's original comments on *catharsis* are ambiguous and it is not clear exactly what kind of process he has in mind. Some critics take *catharsis* to mean 'purgation', that is, the expulsion of negative emotions typically taken to be pity and fear. Others have argued that the meaning of *catharsis* is much closer to 'purification': in this reading, tragedy acts to transfigure our negative emotions rather than to eliminate them. Others have argued that we should see *catharsis* in terms of the insight that is gained, rather than the emotions that are evacuated or quelled. In his account of tragedy as a 'coercive system', Boal argues that tragedy is a potent instrument working for the forces of social conservatism. It works so as to purge the spectator of antisocial characteristics. Unlike Aristotle, who sees emotional effects of tragedy as central to the experience, Hegel argues that we should not place too much emphasis on the role of emotion in tragedy. It is, instead, a matter of aligning ourselves with a particular ethical point of view.

Aristotle's account of *catharsis* mentions, in specific terms, only the emotions of pity and fear. However, in the final stages of this chapter, we looked at the much broader range of emotional responses that tragedy can invite. We noted, in particular, the role of laughter in Jacobean tragedy. We saw how the drama of Sarah Kane, itself heavily influenced by Jacobean tragedy, seeks to provoke shock, horror and disgust as responses which are preferable to indifference or apathy. In her graphic depictions of mental illness, sex and violence, Kane's vision seems distant from the idea of tragic pleasure. But better, in her view, to feel *something* – even the urge to recoil from what is being shown on stage – than to leave the theatre unchanged and untouched. In the next chapter, we move away from our discussion of audience experience to consider tragedy as a form.

CHAPTER SEVEN

Tragedy and Form

Dramatic unity

The so-called dramatic unities of Time, Place and Action are commonly thought to derive from Aristotle's *Poetics*. In fact, Aristotle does not formulate a highly developed theory of dramatic unity; rather, he makes brief references to unity, which subsequent critics have elaborated. The doctrine of the Unity of Time derives from Aristotle's comment that tragedy 'generally endeavours to fall within a single circuit of the sun or thereabouts'.[1] We should note that Aristotle allows a full 24 hours for the action of the play, and even this is reckoned approximately. Thus, in the little Aristotle that does say about the Unity of Time, he is generous in his scope. He does not indicate any requirement for the action of the play to take place in 'real time' corresponding to the duration of the dramatic performance, although some of Aristotle's later disciples – particularly in the French neoclassical school – argued that this is what true Unity of Time should entail. The doctrine of the Unity of Action, meanwhile, comes from Aristotle's observation that, 'The plot must be single rather than double ...'[2] Contrary to popular misconception, Aristotle does not mention the Unity of Place at all.

Commenting on the disparity between Aristotle's own valuation of unity and that of his later commentators, Schlegel says:

■ It is amusing enough to see Aristotle driven perforce to lend his name to these three Unities, whereas the only one of which he speaks with any degree of fulness is the first, the Unity of Action. With respect to the Unity of time, he merely throws out a vague hint; while of the Unity of Place he says not a syllable.[3] □

For English Renaissance writers, the idea of unity came to prominence not so much through Aristotle as through his Roman counterpart, Horace, whose work was more widely read and paraphrased in the period than Aristotle's own. In his *Ars Poetica*, Horace exhorted contemporary Roman dramatists: 'simplex dumtaxat et unum' ('let it be simple and unified', *Ars Poetica* 23). It is from this Horatian dictum that

111

sixteenth-century critics developed a high valuation of dramatic unity. The Italian critic Lodovico Castelvetro first developed a systematic theory of unity, which was influential in the development of Continental thinking on the subject.[4]

During this period, the idea of unity attracted significant controversy, especially in England. There was a fundamental division between writers such as Philip Sidney and Ben Jonson, who were well versed in neoclassical theory and who championed its cause, and popular playwrights (such as Shakespeare), who, for the most part, were not overtly concerned with such precepts.[5] In the *Defence of Poetry*, Philip Sidney complains about the way that contemporary dramatists disregard the unities:

> ■ For where the stage should always represent but one place, and the uttermost time presupposed in it should be, both by Aristotle's precept and common reason, but one day, there is both many days, and many places, inartificially imagined.
>
> But if it be so in *Gorboduc*, how much more in all the rest? where you shall have Asia of the one side and Afric of the other, and so many other under-kingdoms, that the player, when he cometh in, must ever begin with telling where he is, or else the tale will not be conceived. Now ye shall have three ladies walk to gather flowers: and then we must believe the stage to be a garden. By and by we hear news of shipwreck in the same place: and then we are to blame if we accept it not for a rock ...[6] □

In this passage, Sidney suggests that changes of dramatic location also pose a threat to the credibility of the dramatic illusion: such changes render the performance laborious because of the need to indicate in one scene after another where the action is set. Following on from this, he continues to register his objections to breaches of Unity of Time:

> ■ Now, of time they are much more liberal, for ordinary it is that two young princes fall in love; after many traverses, she is got with child, delivered of a fair boy; he is lost, groweth a man, falls in love, and is ready to get another child; and all this in two hours' space ...[7] □

It is not simply on the subject of dramatic unity that Sidney voices his concerns. He also protests about another area of dramatic form, namely the relationship between tragedy and comedy, genres which he believes should be kept strictly separate from one another. In a well-known passage, Sidney writes:

> ■ But besides these gross absurdities, how all their plays be neither right tragedies, not right comedies, mingling kings and clowns, not because the matter so carrieth it, but thrust in the clown by the head and shoulders, to

play a part in majestical matters, with neither decency nor discretion, so as neither the admiration and commiseration, nor the right sportfulness, is by their mongrel tragi-comedy obtained .... I know the ancients have one or two examples of tragi-comedies, as Plautus hath *Amphitruo*. But, if we mark them well, we shall find that they never, or very daintily, match hornpipes and funerals.[8] □

Sidney's reference to tragicomedy as a 'mongrel' reflects his sense that such plays are aesthetically inferior to pure tragedies or pure comedies. Here Sidney appeals to the authority of classical drama, which he suggests (with one or two rare exceptions) does not mix 'hornpipes and funerals' – that is, they do not juxtapose scenes of celebration or hilarity with moments of pathos. Although Sidney's *Defence* was widely known in the period, its precepts largely failed to take hold. Most tragedy of the Elizabethan and Jacobean period is freely inclusive of comic elements. As we saw in Chapter 6, Jacobean tragedy is particularly audacious in experimenting with boundaries between tragedy and the grotesque.

In seventeenth-century France, the influence of neoclassical thinking was more pervasive, perhaps especially in the drama of Racine. Yet Goldmann suggests that rather than being constrained by the Unity of Time in the strict sense, Racine constructs his plays around a principle of atemporality, or what Goldmann calls the 'negation of time'.[9] He argues that there is such a powerful sense of inevitability in Racine's plays that time is of little significance: 'The die has been cast, the future has long been settled, and the past is an ever-present, imminent threat. The three dimensions of temporality are thus contracted into an *atemporal* present which leads only to eternity.'[10]

Richard Parish suggests that Racine's use of space is particularly powerful 'because of the larger reality which it concentrates'.[11] The significance of the stage space can be modified imaginatively rather than through changes of decor. Parish remarks: 'the impact of unity of place is thus achieved by the coexistence with it, and dependence on it, of flexibility and diversity of reference'.[12] In Racine's tragedies, the town or region in which the action is set is always specified but not represented.

Among the most important French neoclassical writers is Pierre Corneille, sometimes referred to as 'the father of French tragedy'.[13] But this appellation does not reflect the rather more problematic status of some of Corneille's work. Critics habitually refer to him as a tragic dramatist, while maintaining a much more equivocal position about the plays themselves, several of which (e.g., *Horace*) are often called melodramas. During Corneille's life, critics argued that his plays could not be considered tragedies because they did not generate pity and fear in the spectators. Furthermore, Leonard Wang contends that Corneille's emphasis on man's absolute liberty mitigates against any critical attempt to classify the plays as tragedies.[14] Wang goes on to conclude: 'Corneille is not a writer of tragedies but of heroic comedies. ... [T]here is no definition of tragedy, however broad and comprehensive, that will fit his work.'[15]

One of the chief controversies during Corneille's lifetime concerned his play *Le Cid* (1637), a controversy that has subsequently become known as the 'Querelle du Cid'. Critics led by Cardinal Richlieu, founder of the Académie française, objected to the play because it did not conform to the Aristotelian unities. In defence of his play, Corneille went on to formulate his theoretical ideas in *Three Discourses on Dramatic Poetry* (published in 1660). In this text, Corneille articulates a respectful but flexible approach to the neoclassical unities. He states, 'It is necessary to observe unity of action, place, and time; that no one doubts. But there is no small difficulty in knowing what unity of action is, or how far one can extend this unity of time and place.'[16] Pursuing his case for flexibility, Corneille continues: 'I should willingly grant that everything taking place in the same city possessed unity of place. Not that I should wish the stage to represent the entire city – that would be rather too large – but only two or three particular places enclosed within the compass of its walls.'[17]

Corneille had a vital influence on the dramatic theory of Dryden. In *An Essay of Dramatic Poesy* (1668; revised 1684), Dryden follows Corneille in suggesting that a play should represent period of 24 hours. Dryden cites the expository prologue of ancient drama as a device which can assist in enabling the play to conform to the Unity of Time. Events spanning a wide chronological period can be summed up, allowing the play to focus on just one phase of a larger narrative. On the Unity of Time, Dryden concurs with Corneille that it is not necessary for the action to take place in precisely the same location: 'it still carries the greater likelihood of truth, if those places be supposed so near each other as in the same town or city, which may all be comprehended under the larger denomination of one place'.[18]

One of the most vigorous challenges to French neoclassicism comes from the German aestheticists, whose work we touched on in Chapter 2. Schlegel complains that French dramatists have, on the one hand, excised the chorus (which both Schlegel and Schiller see as a vital constituent of tragedy), while on the other, they slavishly pursue an idea of unity that is essentially anachronistic to classical conceptions of tragedy. Schlegel particularly complains that French dramatists have replaced the chorus with what he terms 'intrigue', mostly in the form of commentary by minor characters. While Schiller does not attach any importance to naturalism in drama (quite the reverse), Schlegel takes a different view and construes the French attitude to unity as an offence against naturalism. He argues that in life, events develop slowly. If one were to take the murder of Duncan by Macbeth, Schlegel suggests, this would unfold over a considerable period of time. In French tragedy, however, the action is artificially accelerated. Schlegel compares the pace of action to a comet hurtling through the sky.

Schlegel suggests that the strict adherence to the Unity of Place which we find in French drama has a limiting effect on the emotional range of the play:

> ■ In a princely palace no strong emotion, no breach of social etiquette is allowable; and as in a tragedy, affairs cannot always proceed with pure courtesy, every bolder deed, therefore, every act of violence, every thing startling and calculated strongly to impress the senses is transacted behind the scenes, and related merely by confidants or other messengers.[19] □

In conforming so rigorously to the idea of dramatic unity, Schlegel suggests that French tragedy is forced to rely too heavily on the reporting of action that takes place elsewhere: 'In many French tragedies the spectator might well entertain a feeling that great actions were actually taking place, but that he had chosen a bad place to be witness of them.'[20]

In his account of the French neoclassical tragedians and their observation of the unities, George Steiner suggests that Racine is simply not interested in dramatic realism. He argues that Racine sought to set his action at a distance from the experience of the spectators, and, in doing so, anticipates Brecht's technique of alienation. While Steiner clearly admires the economy of Racine's dramatic construction, he notes that others have been less favourably disposed and he concedes that the drama of Corneille and Racine is now more often performed 'as museum pieces rather than living theatre'.[21]

Schiller argues that the French tragedians placed an unduly heightened emphasis on the value of dramatic unity, while at the same time discarding other conventions of Greek tragedy such as the chorus:

> ■ Thus the French, having completely misunderstood the spirit of the ancients, introduced a unity of place and time upon the stage in the most vulgar empirical sense, as though there were a different place from purely ideal space and a different time from the purely consistent line of action.[22] □

Steiner suggests that the eighteenth-century German dramatist Gotthold Ephraim Lessing saw unity as not about narrow technicalities, but about a work of art's inner coherence. This attitude marks a departure from critics writing in the Aristotelian tradition who urged a narrowly rule-bound approach to the writing and performance of tragedy. As the next section will show, this broadening of horizons gave rise to new questions about relationships between tragedy and form.

Tragedy and non-dramatic forms

For the most part, Western tragedy has been interpreted as a dramatic form. To what extent, however, are the ideas of tragedy and drama necessarily linked? It is a question which has become increasingly pertinent with the rise of the novel. But, even in the centuries before this, writers were exploring the idea that tragedy could be realised in non-dramatic forms. In the *Poetics*, Aristotle suggests that hearing the report of a tragic narrative would affect an auditor in much the same way that the performance of a tragedy would affect a spectator: 'For the plot ought to be so composed that even without seeing the action, a man who just hears what is going on shudders and feels pity because of what happens; this one would feel on hearing the plot of the *Oedipus*, for instance.'[23]

The idea that it is possible to write tragedy in a non-dramatic context is important for Milton's conception of his prose poem, *Samson Agonistes* (published 1671). In the austere Puritan culture of the mid-seventeenth century, theatre had become associated with frivolity and decadence, a view that led to the closure of the theatres in 1642. *Samson Agonistes* – rather like Milton's *Paradise Lost* – reveals an ambivalent rather than hostile view of drama. The text has many of the features of a dramatic text (for example in monologue, dialogue and choral odes) but it was not written for the stage. In his prose preface to the poem, Milton argues:

> ■ Tragedy, as it was anciently composed, hath been ever held the gravest, moralest, and most profitable of all other poems: therefore said by Aristotle to be of power by raising pity and fear, to purge the mind of those and such-like passions, that is to temper and reduce them to just measure with a kind of delight, stirred up by reading or seeing those passions well imitated.[24] □

This statement not only reflects the high esteem in which Milton holds tragedy as a genre; the reference to Aristotelian *catharsis* suggests that Milton also has in mind Aristotle's acknowledgement that a person does not need to *see* tragedy being performed in order to experience its effects. Thus Milton is able to claim the highest classical authority for identifying his text as a tragedy. We should remember that even before Milton was writing, other writers (particularly women) wrote tragedies that were designed for private reading. These closet dramas, as they are known, were often read aloud in a form of private performance.[25] Among important examples of this kind of drama are Mary Sidney's *The Tragedie of Antonie* (1595) and Elizabeth Cary's *The Tragedie of Mariam* (1613). But even much earlier than this, as A. C. Bradley notes, 'To the medieval mind a tragedy meant a narrative rather than a play', a view which is reflected in Chaucer.[26]

In spite of these scattered precedents, the emergence of the novel in the eighteenth and nineteenth centuries as a major literary form posed a challenge to the way that tragedy, as a dramatic form, had traditionally predominated. As Eagleton explains, the concerns of the novel were largely bourgeois rather than aristocratic, private rather than public, and this was clearly at odds with the aesthetic priorities with which tragedy had traditionally been associated. As Eagleton observes: 'Work and home, not court, church and state, become the primary settings, and high politics yields to the intrigues of everyday life. It is a shift from the martial to the marital – the former being part of the problem, the latter of a solution.'[27]

In his account of the 'death of tragedy' (discussed in detail in Chapter 8), Steiner argues that the dominance of the prose novel fatally undermined the terms on which tragedy had traditionally been scripted and performed. Like Eagleton, Steiner notes – in amplified and ironic terms – the way that the novel's quotidian concerns contrast sharply with the higher dramatic register of tragedy: 'In prose fiction, as D. H. Lawrence remarked, "you know there is a watercloset on the premises." We are not called upon to envisage such facilities at Mycenae and Elsinore. If there are bathrooms in the houses of tragedy, they are for Agamemnon to be murdered in.'[28] Whereas Steiner believes the rise of the novel permanently eroded the conditions in which tragedy could continue to thrive, Eagleton suggests that the crisis associated with the emergence of a major new literary form is only temporary. By the nineteenth century, Eagleton suggests, the novel has assimilated the concerns of tragedy; and tragedy, 'having been overtaken by the novel, catches up with it again'.[29]

Jeanette King's book *Tragedy in the Victorian Novel* (1978) is an important landmark in the study of tragedy and the novel.[30] King begins by addressing a sense of transition that was emerging in the late eighteenth century between tragedy as a form which had traditionally been dominant and the novel as a form which was newly emerging. As King notes, as early as 1748, in the Postscript to *Clarissa*, Samuel Richardson likens the novel to tragedy.[31]

The publication of *Clarissa* set an important precedent, and, as King shows, by the nineteenth century reviewers were readily and regularly building on analogies between the tragedies of the Greeks and Shakespeare, and the novel. King therefore frames the relationship between tragic drama and the tragic novel in chronological terms: not in a steady, linear evolution but as a moment of crisis in which modernity was reflecting on and consciously reworking revered traditions of the past. As she says, 'the later genre was attempting to do, in a new and often controversial way, many of the things that the older genre had done'.[32] This brought into focus the question of whether drama was unique in its ability to explore particular themes of tragedy, or whether the novel could achieve the same effects, but by using different tools.

King argues that British drama was in decline in the nineteenth century and she suggests that this was instrumental in creating a division between highbrow and lowbrow forms of entertainment, examples of the latter being found in pantomime and melodrama. Peter Brooks has robustly challenged the idea that melodrama should be characterised as an inferior or degraded form of tragedy:

> ■ Melodrama does not simply represent a 'fall' from tragedy, but a response to the loss of the tragic vision. It comes into being in a world where the traditional imperatives of truth and ethics have been violently thrown into question, yet where the promulgation of truth and ethics, their instauration as a way of life, is of immediate, daily, political concern.[33] □

While King emphasises points of continuity between the dramatic tradition and the nineteenth-century novel, Brooks sees the melodrama as a response to a particular historical moment, born out of the French Revolution. While tragedy and comedy, he argues, reflect a secure view of social hierarchy, these forms were no longer viable at a time when social hierarchies were vulnerable to collapse. Thus, Brooks argues, the form of melodrama emerges to interrogate new ethical struggles; it insistently returns to stage the struggle between good and evil. Steiner, Brooks notes, sees the Romantic movement as a catalyst in the decline of tragedy and regards melodrama as its inferior successor.[34] Brooks suggests that melodrama is instead a serious, urgent and topical alternative to tragedy in its own right.

As King observes, most important nineteenth-century poets wrote poetic tragedy; among notable examples of this trend is Shelley's five-act verse drama *The Cenci* (1819). In some cases, King suggests, the poetic tragedies of the period were rather stilted, narrowly imitative and amounting to pastiche. A renewed vogue for closet drama undermined the claims that the theatre was the natural vehicle for the production and performance of tragedy. King writes:

> ■ The novel obviously presented itself as a more satisfactory vehicle for modern tragedy than the drama had become. When serious drama was itself reduced to a form for private reading, the novel was a formidable

rival. It combined its serious reflections on life with the popular appeal it shared with the theatre, healing – for a time – the breach between 'literature' and 'entertainment'. In the novel was also realised that ideal of interaction, of combining the dramatic and the narrative, the poetic and the contemporary reality, that critics of drama and the novel alike were demanding.[35] ☐

As we saw in Chapter 3, the novel typically takes characters of relatively humble status as its subject. This gave rise to a concern that the fall of the ordinary man did not carry wide enough significance to be considered tragic. When novelists wrote about characters of low or middling social status, some critics objected that this was contrary to Aristotle's precepts in the *Poetics*, and therefore had a limiting effect on the idea that the novel can engage successfully with tragedy. As King suggests, many nineteenth-century critics tended to refer – often rather inflexibly – to Greek tragedy, and, even more unhelpfully, to the *Poetics*. A particular point of contention was the ending of the novel, and the question of whether it could deliver *catharsis*. Novelists such as Henry James preferred to resist a sense of resolution at the end, and this seemed to militate against the more decisive – and therefore, it was thought, potentially cathartic – ending of Greek drama, which conventionally ended with the hero's death. Rather than turning to the *Poetics*, King argues, it would have been more fruitful to understand the role of Shakespearean tragedy as a source for what nineteenth-century novelists were attempting to explore in their work.

We noted in Chapter 5 the importance of Darwinian theory in shaping the narratives of the nineteenth-century novel. King explores the importance of heredity as a determining influence on character in George Eliot's novels, *Felix Holt* (1866) and *The Mill on the Floss* (1860), and she suggests that George Eliot, Henry James and Thomas Hardy show a particular preoccupation with the themes of family influence and wider social pressure. Hardy's novels investigate a conflict between man's natural instincts and the social conventions of the time. For example, in *Jude the Obscure* (1895), Jude's desire for learning (an inherited trait) brings him into conflict with a social and educational establishment which will never accept him as a self-made man. King suggests that Jude is at the centre of additional conflicts in the realm of sex and marriage: his obligations to Sue and the institution of marriage, on the one hand, and his desire for Arabella on the other. In the context of these themes, King suggests, the nineteenth-century novel is able to take up the philosophical enquiries of tragedy into questions of individual freedom and external constraint. For our earlier discussion of tragic agency, see Chapter 3.

Among nineteenth-century novelists, George Eliot had an intimate familiarity with Greek tragedy: as we saw in Chapter 4, Sophocles'

Antigone is known to have made a particular impression on her. George Eliot was familiar with Aristotle: her journal testifies to her reading the *Poetics* in 1865 (an entry in which she refers to having read the text on a previous occasion) and again in 1873.[36] In his study of George Eliot and tragedy, Darrel Mansell Jr traces Aristotelian influence in George Eliot's fiction in the device of the *peripeteia* (reversal of fortune). He argues that George Eliot presents us with the idea of an 'inexorable law of consequences': he says that 'George Eliot's tragic heroes and heroines ... are intellectually incapable of perceiving what will be the inexorable consequences of what they do'.[37] Mansell argues that Eliot's works of fiction are tragedies of character rather than plot, and he cites George Eliot's own criticism of her contemporary, Wilkie Collins, for not caring 'to interest us in his personages, but only in what happens to them'.[38]

In his essay 'Tragedy and the Whole Truth' (1931), Aldous Huxley argues that the novel tells what he describes as the 'Whole Truth'.[39] As an early precursor to this, he gives the example of Homer's *Odyssey*, Book XII, in which Odysseus and his men eat their supper after some of their companions have been brutally devoured by the monster Scylla. This detail, Huxley argues, gives us the 'Whole Truth' in recognising that even those who are grieving carry on with basic activities such as eating. Huxley argues that a tragic writer would treat the same episode very differently: there would be an exclusive focus on lamentation, and the realities of cooking and eating would be glossed over. In another example, Huxley looks at the moment in Henry Fielding's novel *Tom Jones* (1749), when the innkeeper lifts Sophia from her horse and collapses beneath her weight. Huxley observes 'that brief and pearly gleam of Sophia's charming posterior was sufficient to scare the Muse of Tragedy out of *Tom Jones*'.[40] Huxley argues that the Whole Truth – the incidental, potentially unseemly details of real life – is incompatible with tragedy. Tragedy does not aim to offer a comprehensive view of life. Rather, Huxley claims:

> ■ To make a tragedy the artist must isolate a single element out of the totality of human experience and use that exclusively as his material. Tragedy is something that is separated out from the Whole Truth, distilled from it, so to speak, as an essence is distilled from the living flower. Tragedy is chemically pure. Hence its power to act quickly and intensely on our feelings.[41] □

Huxley contrasts this with the effect of Wholly Truthful literature, which does not act as immediately, but which affects its readers in a more lasting fashion. Huxley suggests that the effect of tragedy is to induce 'temporary inebriations', whereas Wholly Truthful literature promotes a more profound sense of resignation.[42]

In its amplitude and its detail, the novel does not afford the distilled sense of crisis in which tragic drama deals. Responding to this claim, Eagleton asks whether the short story might lend itself more readily to tragic treatment than the novel. Yet Eagleton contends that this view of tragedy (and the novel) comes from 'an exaggerated respect for the classical doctrine that tragedy is always a question of crisis'.[43] He comments that tragedy can exist as 'quite as much a condition as an event'.[44] Viewed in this way, the novel is remarkably well suited as a form in which to construct tragic narratives.

We saw in Chapter 2 that several critics have recognised the way that Thomas Hardy adapts the Greek tragic device of the chorus and converts it into a form which is embodied in the various rustic Wessex figures who appear in his novels. In his account of Hardy, Ted Spivey focuses on the tragic hero: 'Hardy saw man beaten down by forces within and without himself and sought to record man's eternal struggle with fate.'[45] Spivey suggests that the form of Hardy's writing is to some extent incidental and that he was 'a tragic poet, if you will, who did his work in prose'.[46] Spivey notes that Hardy does register a sense of social optimism at times in *Jude* – a sense that there is the possibility for society to evolve for the better – but he argues that this does not qualify or compromise the essential tragic outlook which Hardy projects in the novel. Instead of bringing a formal definition of tragedy to bear on Hardy's novels, and seeing if they match up to it, Spivey's method is to scrutinise the novels themselves and see what kind of tragedy they present. Like Sidney Zink, he believes that an analysis of the tragic hero is crucial to this process: 'for without the tragic hero there can be no tragedy'.[47] For Spivey, Hardy's tragic hero exhibits a complex mixture of defiance and acceptance. In an Aristotelian reading of the novels, he suggests that all of Hardy's tragic heroes (the word that Spivey uses to include female characters as well) exhibit some form of tragic flaw. In some cases, this can be easily pinpointed, for example in Jude's weakness for drink. For some of the other characters, Spivey's argument is less exact. He says that Henchard 'has the devil within', and that Tess's tragic flaw is that she turns again to Alec. Here, Spivey elides characteristics and actions; however, it is integral to his argument that Hardy's heroes are destroyed by internal and external forces. Indeed, Hardy himself is fond of quoting the maxim, 'Character is fate.' According to Spivey, we sympathise with Hardy's tragic heroes because they are nobler than the forces which bring about their destruction. He describes them as characters 'whose desires are never fulfilled, but whose spirits, in the best traditions of tragedy, are never crushed'.[48] As Spivey concludes,

'Tragedy for Hardy is the defeat of the romantic hero's desire to reach a higher spiritual state.'[49]

In a detailed character study of Sue Bridehead in *Jude the Obscure*, Robert Heilman argues:

> ■ The split that creates the coquette is not unlike the tragic split; the latter, of course, implies deeper emotional commitments and more momentous situations. Yet one might entitle an essay on Sue 'The Coquette as Tragic Heroine.' Because she has a stronger personality than Jude, has more initiative, and endeavours more to impose her will, she is closer to tragic stature than he. Like traditional tragic heroes, she believes that she can dictate terms and clothe herself in special immunities; like them, she has finally to reckon with neglected elements in herself and in the order of life.[50] □

Although Heilman frequently uses the term 'tragic' in relation to Sue, he pauses to question his critical approach:

> ■ The problem is, then, whether the story of Sue merely touches on tragedy, with its characteristic reordering of a chaotic moral world, or becomes mainly a case history of clinical disorder ... As always, the problem of illness is its representativeness: have we a special case, interesting for its own sake, pitiable, shocking, but limited in its relevance, or is the illness symbolic, containing a human truth that transcends its immediate terms?[51] □

Heilman concludes by asserting not only that Hardy's portrayal of Sue does indeed offer us insights into one particular manifestation of neurosis, but that his characterisation of her 'gives us, in dramatic terms, an essential revelation about human well-being'.[52]

As we have seen in this chapter, the idea of the dramatic unities of Time, Place and Action originates in Aristotle's *Poetics*. However, Aristotle does not attach much importance to these ideas in the text as it stands, nor does he work up a highly systematic account of unity. Subsequent generations of critics invested in Aristotle's account a heightened reverence for the idea of dramatic unity. In the sixteenth and seventeenth centuries and beyond, debate rages about the extent to which dramatists should conform to the principles of unity. In his critique of French neoclassicism, Schlegel points out that observing the unities comes at a cost to other aesthetic considerations such as dramatic realism.

The debate about unity is specifically a concern for tragic drama. In the second part of this chapter, our discussion moved on to consider other aspects of tragic form. Here, we considered much wider questions about whether tragedy is, by definition, a dramatic form; and to what extent tragedy takes shape in other forms, such as the novel. Huxley argues that tragedy (as a dramatic form) and the novel have very different aims: while tragedy is pared down and distilled, the novel takes a much more comprehensive view of life's experiences. Huxley hereby suggests that there is a quintessential antipathy between tragedy and the novel. Conversely, in the work of Jeanette King, we saw that eighteenth- and nineteenth-century novelists are experimenting with the concept of tragedy and often explicitly situating themselves within the tragic tradition. The novel, as we have seen, put new pressure on conceptions of tragedy as a form exclusively concerned with royal personages and those of high rank. In the following chapter, we consider whether – in the light of these and other re-evaluations of tragedy's scope and subject matter in the modern era – tragedy is a form in crisis.

CHAPTER EIGHT

Modern Tragedy

Culture and ideology

In 1955, Albert Camus posed the question, 'Is modern tragedy possible?'[1] It is a question which has profoundly divided critics over the last few decades. Some critics such as George Steiner, whose work receives detailed consideration in this chapter, argue that the conditions of modernity are inhospitable to a tragic view of life; others, most notably Raymond Williams, contend that the experience of the modern and postmodern world is endowing tragedy with a new sense of relevance and urgency. This chapter considers this major area of critical debate from both sides, and looks at how the debate is developing in the twenty-first century.

But first, how *does* modernity pose a challenge to the production and performance of tragedy? In the 1930s, several critics (who are known collectively as members of the Frankfurt School) argued that art itself is under threat in the modern era. In his essay 'The Work of Art in the Age of Mechanical Reproduction' (1936), Walter Benjamin claims that technology is robbing art of its distinctive mystical 'aura' because of the potential for mass reproduction.[2] He defines aura as 'a unique manifestation of a remoteness, however close [the work of art] may be'.[3] Whereas it has always been possible to reproduce works of art manually, Benjamin suggests that art loses its authority when it is reproduced by means of technology since it removes art from the realm of tradition into the realm of the marketplace. In this context, objects of art no longer have cultic (or ritual) value; they have political and commercial value. Benjamin expresses particular concerns about the new media of photography and cinema: these do not even reproduce a prior manual work of art but dispense with manual art altogether. In the form of cinema, Benjamin identifies a direct challenge to the values of the theatre: the film actor plays to the camera, and no longer to an audience. Benjamin thus compares the experience of watching *Macbeth* in the theatre with watching it on film:

■ The aura surrounding Macbeth onstage cannot, for the live audience, be detached from the aura that surrounds the actor playing him. But what is peculiar about filming in the studio is that in the latter situation the audience is replaced by a piece of equipment. The aura surrounding the player must thus be lost – and with it, at the same time, the aura around the character played.[4] □

Also affiliated to the Frankfurt School is the critic Theodor Adorno, who proposes a view of mass culture as symptomatic of social decline. Like Benjamin, Adorno argues that the spread of industrialisation and technology has fundamentally debased art. In the *Dialectic of Enlightenment* (1947), Adorno and Max Horkheimer coin the term 'culture industry' to refer to a process of standardisation by which mass culture was coming to replace art itself.[5] The culture industry manifested a tendency to homogenise and mass produce images in the media. Culture was no longer spontaneous or true but had instead become a commodity, its images formulaic and repetitive. Whereas Marx had anticipated that a rise in economic production would be conducive to revolution, Adorno and Horkheimer argue that it achieved the opposite effect: that it was turning the population into undiscerning consumers. The culture industry tended to suppress anything suggestive of conflict. As a casualty of this process, tragedy was inevitably falling into neglect.

It is a view echoed by Bertolt Brecht, who argues in his 'Short Organum for Theatre' that the experience of being in the theatre lacks potency and that performances have become anodyne. (This is a perception more recently shared by Sarah Kane; for discussion of her turn to provocative forms of drama, see Chapter 6.) Brecht refers to the audience as a 'cowed, credulous, hypnotized mass'.[6] Brecht's concern is not with technology (as in the case of Benjamin) or mass media (in the case of Adorno); Brecht argues much more comprehensively that science has had a pernicious effect on the production of art. In attaching supreme importance to empirical truth, science has inculcated an undesirable emphasis on accuracy as an aesthetic value. Brecht wants to recover an emphasis on theatre as a form of entertainment and argues that we should not attribute to it a higher purpose. For Brecht, illusion matters more than accuracy. The fact that we still turn to the drama of the past suggests that contemporary theatre is failing to fulfil our needs. As he writes, 'Our theatres no longer have either the capacity or the wish to tell these stories, even the relatively recent ones of the great Shakespeare, at all clearly.'[7]

According to Brecht, science has profoundly altered man's relationships with his surroundings. On the one hand, man's ability to exploit natural resources such as fuel has given him unprecedented power. On the other hand, Brecht argues, the mood of enlightenment which gave impetus to scientific discoveries stalled, and failed to permeate society as a whole. Science brought about the industrial revolution, but instead of liberating man, it has brought profit to a minority and servitude to the majority. Brecht sees the theatre as a mechanism for empowering workers, to enable them to understand and change their role in society.

The death of tragedy

Camus takes the view that tragedy has only flourished at specific moments in time, a position which George Steiner also later adopts. Camus himself identifies Greek tragedy, and the flowering of tragedy across Western Europe from Shakespeare to Racine, as instances of this kind of flourishing. He explores the possibility that the mid-twentieth century might provide conditions conducive to the production of tragedy, though he notes in reference to the world wars of 1914–18 and 1939–45 that 'the most monstrous wars have not inspired a single tragic poet'.[8] Camus goes on to consider what might bring about a resurgence of tragedy:

> ■ our only reason for hope lies in the visible transformation of individualism, and in the slow recognition by the individual, under the pressure of history, that he does have limits. The world which the individual of the eighteenth century thought he could conquer and transform by reason and science has in fact taken shape, but this is a monstrous one. ... [A]t this degree of *hubris*, history has put on the mask of destiny. Man doubts whether he can conquer history, all he can do is struggle within it. By a curious fatality, humanity has refashioned itself a hostile destiny with the very same weapons that it used to reject fatality. After having deified the human reign, man is once more turning against this god. He is struggling, at the same time both a warrior and a refugee, torn between absolute hope and final doubt. Thus he lives in a tragic climate. Perhaps this explains why tragedy is seeking to be reborn. Today, man is proclaiming his revolt while knowing that this revolt has limits, is demanding liberty and undergoing necessity, and this contradictory man, torn apart, conscious henceforth of human and historical ambiguity, is the essentially tragic man.[9] □

Writing in *The Birth of Tragedy*, first published in 1872, Friedrich Nietzsche claims in uncompromising terms not only that there is no real tragedy after the Greeks, but still further, that there is no real tragedy after Aeschylus and Sophocles. He claims that it is Euripides who brings about the death of tragedy:

> ■ Greek tragedy met an end different from that of her older sister-arts: she died by suicide, in consequence of an irreconcilable conflict; she died tragically, while all the others passed away calmly and beautifully at a ripe old age ...

> It was *Euripides* who fought this death struggle of tragedy; the later artistic genre is known as *New Attic Comedy*. In it the degenerate form of tragedy lived on as a monument of its exceedingly painful and violent death.[10]

In likening Euripidean drama to New Attic Comedy, Nietzsche is implicitly referring to Euripidean happy-ending drama (discussed in Chapter 6). He continues:

> ▪ Euripides brought the *spectator* onto the stage. He who has perceived the material out of which the Promethean tragic writers prior to Euripides formed their heroes, and how remote from their purpose it was to bring the faithful mask of reality onto the stage, will also be aware of the utterly opposite tendency of Euripides. Through him the everyday man forced his way from the spectators' seats onto the stage; the mirror in which formerly only grand and bold traits were represented now showed the painful fidelity that conscientiously reproduces even the botched outlines of nature.[11]

Nietzsche's reference to the intrusion of the spectator onto the stage is a reference to the tentative steps which Euripides starts to make in the direction of dramatic realism. For example, in his *Electra*, Euripides allows Electra to reject the conventional tokens (the cloak, the footprints and the lock of hair) by which she might recognise her brother. For Nietzsche, such a scene diminishes tragedy by making it accountable to everyday standards of reasoning and scepticism which, for Nietzsche, are only applicable outside the theatre. Nietzsche characterises this new rational element as the 'Socratic'. Thus Nietzsche argues that the tension between the Apollonian and the Dionysian (discussed in Chapter 5) is permanently disrupted by the new perspective which Euripides introduces into tragedy: 'This is the new opposition: the Dionysian and the Socratic – and the art of Greek tragedy was wrecked on this'.[12]

In questioning whether moderns can write tragedy, Alfred Cary Schlesinger echoes Nietzsche's identification of Euripidean tragedy as a turning point in the evolution of tragedy towards a more rational basis.[13] Schlesinger suggests that Euripides is sympathetic to the scientific outlook because of his interest in depicting the domination of man by nature. Building on Brechtian theory discussed earlier in this chapter, Schlesinger suggests that science has posed a challenge to tragedy. One of the main effects of the rise of science is to inculcate a belief that the universe is knowable: tragedy and science share a common methodology of working from the evidence towards generalisations.

In his essay, Schlesinger also reflects on the question of Christian tradition and its prescriptions for ethical conduct. He suggests that Scripture provides a general outline and the individual must still bear responsibility for interpreting these precepts according to particular circumstances; here is the potential for tragedy to flourish. Schlesinger points out that the modern era is historically minded, and he suggests that this is inimical to the production of tragedy. The Athenians believed in the truth of myths. Following the Frankfurt School, Schlesinger contends that we demand accuracy in a way that the ancient world did not, and this is potentially a hindrance to the flourishing of tragic art.

Taking a very different position on this question, Søren Kierkegaard argues that there is an essential continuity between ancient and modern tragedy and here he draws on the idea that suffering is a universal condition. Kierkegaard suggests that one of the key differences between ancient and modern tragedy is that ancient tragedy does not proceed from character. He argues: 'in the ancient world subjectivity was not fully conscious and reflective. Even though the individual moved freely, he still depended on substantial categories, on state, family, and destiny.' [14] According to Kierkegaard, 'In ancient tragedy the sorrow is deeper, the pain less; in modern tragedy, the pain is greater, the sorrow less.'[15] He suggests that the relationship between sorrow and pain which we witness in Greek tragedy is like a child watching an older person suffering: the child feels sorrow, but cannot feel pain because he does not understand. In modern tragedy, Kierkegaard suggests, the pain is greater because of a stronger conception of guilt. When modern tragedy dramatises guilt in the form of remorse, it can no longer be regarded as tragic.

In a wide-ranging transhistorical study of European drama, Steiner suggests that Shakespeare's rejection of the neoclassical unities (discussed in Chapter 7) precipitates a fundamental crisis in the evolution of tragedy as a form. He points out that while in the sixteenth century Calvinism had emphasised man's depravity and his impotence in a determinist universe, Rousseauism in the eighteenth century promoted the idea that man can be redeemed during his own lifetime (not simply after death) since his faults are not his own. Steiner argues that this conception is fundamentally non-tragic. In the world of tragedy, the tragic hero must take responsibility regardless of fault. Steiner refers to the drama which grows out of this philosophical outlook as the drama of remorse, or 'near-tragedy', which he concedes is in itself a byword for melodrama.[16] (For previous discussion of Steiner's situating melodrama as tragedy's successor, see Chapter 7.) In the eighteenth century, Romanticism explained human misery in terms of social injustice rather than man's own errors and this current of thought posed a further challenge to the viability of tragedy as a form.

Steiner considers the possibility that opera embodies the legacy of the tragic tradition more fully than twentieth-century drama. As Wagner argues, tragedy was born out of music and dance and, in opera, it could claim to have come full circle. Of modern dramatists who have turned explicitly to Greek tragedy as a literary model, Steiner is almost universally dismissive.[17] He sees this as a way of lazily capitalising on the cultural value which tragedy has traditionally been thought to enjoy. Steiner sees allusions to Greek tragedy as crass shorthand for claims to profundity and meaning. Drama of this kind, he suggests, lacks the very intellectual and aesthetic energy which characterises Greek tragedy.

Although Steiner takes a chronological approach to his subject, he does not offer any sense of a continuum from the Greeks to modernity. Rather, he is interested in moments of crisis and change, both at what he sees as those rare moments when tragedy emerges and at other times, when its premises are radically challenged or undermined. Steiner thinks simultaneously in terms of gradual evolution and abrupt shifts at specific moments in intellectual history. It is in this latter vein that he pinpoints (perhaps too specifically for some) Ibsen's *Pillars of Society* (1877) as the moment at which modern drama begins. He situates Ibsen as being on the cusp of social and cultural changes which make tragedy impossible. For tragedy to flourish, Steiner argues, there needs to be a shared 'context of mythological, symbolic, and ritual reference': a higher ideological plane to which tragedy refers.[18] This shared context is more vital to the production of tragedy than much narrower structural definitions of tragedy as a dramatic form which ends sadly. Ibsen, Steiner suggests, is able to harness the last vestiges of this shared frame of reference. There is still a degree of homogeneity in Ibsen's audiences; or rather, where that homogeneity is beginning to fragment, Ibsen is able to show his tragic protagonists as internalising the symptoms of the social crisis which threatens the future of tragic drama. So Ibsen's tragedy is essentially self-reflexive: 'Ibsen turned his deprivations to advantage. He made the precariousness of modern beliefs and the absence of an imaginative world order his starting point.'[19]

Steiner takes a dispiriting view not only about the demise of tragedy, but the degradation of language generally: 'Many of the habits of language in our culture are no longer fresh or creative responses to reality, but stylized gestures which the intellect still performs efficiently, but with a diminishing return of new insight and new feeling. Our words seem tired and shopworn.'[20] He suggests that tragedy is not possible without a language appropriate to it. Thus, in Steiner's account, the impoverished status of language itself is both a symptom of cultural decline and, at the same time, a contributing factor.

Raymond Williams poses a powerful counter-argument to Steiner. What the two critics have in common, however, is an inclination to see tragedy as existing in a state of flux, rather than as a static, historical form. As Williams remarks, 'Tragedy is then not a single and permanent kind of fact, but a series of experiences and conventions and institutions.'[21] Crucially, Williams challenges the view that suffering that occurs as part of everyday life cannot be regarded as tragic. As we have seen, Steiner and others maintain that in the context of modernity and an agnostic or secular age, events are no longer explicable in terms of a wider frame of reference. Steiner argues that a shared mythological and cultural framework is needed as either an explicit or implied interpretative framework for tragedy. Without it, he suggests, audiences splinter into their manifold perspectives and tragedy cannot speak to such heterogeneity.

Williams rejects this and argues that wherever there is suffering, this is at least potentially within the compass of tragedy. He asks whether the existence of a particular philosophical 'order' is necessary as a precondition of tragedy. He suggests that this order does not precede tragedy but rather that the relationship is more dynamic. Tragedy represents and so helps to *construct* the order to which a particular culture subscribes. It is a reciprocal process rather than a linear one. In a later reading, Georg Lukács was to suggest an even more radical relationship between tragedy and the cultural and ideological order, suggesting that 'Tragedy destroys the hierarchy of the higher worlds; in it there is no God and no demon, for the outside world is only the occasion for the soul to find itself, for the hero to become a hero ...'[22]

Williams argues with critics who have tried to describe various kinds of social and religious ideology in order to understand tragedy; rather, he suggests, this order is inseparable from the very fabric of tragedy itself. You can only apprehend order through tragedy, not in isolation from it. Like Huxley, Williams uses a chemical analogy to suggest the way in which order permeates tragedy: 'The ideas of order matter, critically, only when they are in solution in particular works; as precipitates they are of only documentary interest.'[23] Williams develops this image by suggesting that in modern times, the order is still in solution and so we cannot perceive it: the implication is that it is only retrospectively that one can see how culture inscribes its ideologies, its sense of order, in tragedy. It is interesting to see critics like Williams and Huxley employing scientific metaphors in their discussions of tragedy, in the light of claims advanced by Brecht that science has contributed to the creation of a climate that is hostile to the production of tragedy. In Williams, Huxley and Rabkin, the language of science is reclaimed as a resource for literary analysis.

Examining claims that tragedy is no longer possible in a secular society, Williams argues that while the majority may no longer have faith, they do have beliefs; for Williams, we cannot discriminate between secular beliefs and religious faith. Nor, according to Williams, do these beliefs need to be stable. He points out that Elizabethan and Jacobean

England was a period of great religious division, but that it was tremendously generative of tragedy. As he argues:

> ■ Important tragedy seems to occur, neither in periods of real stability, nor in periods of open and decisive conflict. Its most common historical setting is the period preceding the substantial breakdown and transformation of an important culture. Its condition is the real tension between old and new: between received beliefs, embodied in institutions and responses, and newly and vividly experienced contradictions and possibilities.[24] □

Williams says that in the modern era we prefer to think in terms of a 'crisis of personal belief' and we pay insufficient attention to the fact that the major determinants of human suffering lie in external conditions such as war, poverty, torture, famine and so on.[25] As a Marxist study, *Modern Tragedy* does not just reflect on literary texts but builds an argument in favour of revolution. Williams emphasises that while revolution often entails violence and disorder, it is directed towards the production of a better order. He argues that what is tragic is the state of the world, and the continuing presence of evils which are not inevitable but the result of human choices.

Like Williams, Terry Eagleton takes the view that the conditions of modernity are highly conducive to the production of tragedy. He argues that 'What happens to tragedy in the twentieth century is not that it dies, but that it mutates into modernism.' Modernism generates new mythologies in the form of 'vast, anonymous forces – language, Will, power, history, production, desire …'[26]

Rita Felski deliberates about 'the vernacular use of "tragedy" and "tragic," ubiquitously applied to car accidents, the death of children, and most recently to events such as 9/11'.[27] Arthur Miller explores this very question in an essay in which he attempts to differentiate between the tragic and the pathetic. He says:

> ■ Let me put it this way. When Mr. B., while walking down the street, is struck on the head by a falling piano, the newspapers call this a tragedy. In fact, of course, this is only the pathetic end of Mr. B. Not only because of the accidental nature of his death; that is elementary. It is pathetic because it merely arouses our feelings of sympathy, sadness, and possibly of identification. What the death of Mr. B. does not arouse is the tragic feeling.
>
> To my mind the essential difference, and the precise difference, between tragedy and pathos is that tragedy brings us not only sadness, sympathy, identification and even fear; it also, unlike pathos, brings us knowledge or enlightenment.

But what sort of knowledge? In the largest sense, it is knowledge pertaining to the right way of living in the world. The manner of Mr. B.'s death was not such as to illustrate any principle of living. In short, there was no illumination of the ethical in it.[28] ☐

Similarly, Adrian Poole contemplates the modern journalistic appropriation of the term 'tragic':

■ Open the paper, turn on the news, and sooner or later you'll meet the words 'tragic' and 'tragedy'. Even as I write, 19 Chinese cockle-pickers are reported drowned in Morecambe Bay, Lancashire. 'The gangs behind the tragedy are on the run,' one headline assures us. The story attracts no fewer than ten or more 'tragedies' across two reports and a leader in the *Guardian* (7 February 2004). Tragedy: how many more times, of how many more disasters, before you read *this*? Even as this goes to press, the number of lives lost to the Asian tsunami and its aftermath appears literally countless.

It's easy to feel overwhelmed by the word.[29] ☐

In her introduction to an important recent collection of essays, Rita Felski argues that the time is ripe for a re-evaluation of tragedy. She says that there was a monolithic emphasis on political readings of tragedy in the 1980s and 1990s – even where these political readings tended in different directions, this represented a uniformity of approach which was damaging to the critical climate as a whole. Felski suggests that new thinking about agency in the wake of poststructuralist theory has helped to create conditions for a re-evaluation of tragedy, that tragedy provides a mode for exploring contemporary crisis concerning 'the impossibility of gauging to what extent individuals can be held accountable for actions that wreak catastrophe on themselves and the world'.[30]

Felski suggests that it is more helpful to think about tragedy as a mode than as a genre:

■ A more elastic term than 'genre,' 'mode' lends itself especially well to the complicated history and vicissitudes of tragic art. Modes are adjectival, remarks Alistair Fowler, denoting a selective group of features rather than a text's overall defining structure; the term thus draws our attention to the hybrid, mixed qualities of genres. This adjectival usage can emancipate us from prescriptive taxonomies in literary criticism that persist in equating the tragic with a now virtually defunct form of poetic drama ... Conceiving of the tragic as a mode also gives us a more selective rubric than its everyday use to mean 'very sad'; it directs our attention to the formal particulars that render sadness tragic – details of plot and structure, characterization and language, what I have called the shape of suffering – while still allowing us to enfold multiple media and forms within its purview.[31] ☐

Like Felski, Peter Szondi prefers to think in terms of the tragic mode as an expression of his own radical view that 'There is no such thing as the tragic, at least not as an essence. Rather, the tragic is a mode, a particular manner of destruction that is threatening or already completed: the dialectical manner.'[32]

In this chapter, we have considered the highly contested question of whether tragedy is possible in the modern world. One of the most important voices in this debate, George Steiner, proclaimed the death of tragedy in an influential book of that name in 1961. For Steiner, the loss of a shared religious, mythological or philosophical frame of reference in Western culture has proved profoundly detrimental to the production of tragedy. In a powerful counter-argument to Steiner, Raymond Williams refuses to discriminate between certain images of suffering as 'tragic' and others that are not. For Williams, all suffering is potentially tragic. He argues that tragedy does not reflect a prior intellectual and cultural order, as Steiner suggests, but rather that it *constructs* such an order. Moreover, Williams argues, the lack of widely shared belief systems in the Western world (particularly in terms of the rise of agnosticism or atheism) is not a condition which militates against the production of tragedy. On the contrary, Williams points out, tragedy thrives in cultures in which belief systems are being challenged or are in crisis.

Critics such as Arthur Miller have argued that modern tragedy can legitimately explore everyday experience. Can the experiences of suffering that we read about on a daily basis in international news media, therefore, be properly described as 'tragic'? The modal adjective 'tragic' provides some critics with a way of sidestepping the more monolithic noun 'tragedy'. But this strategy brings with it its own risks, suggests Adrian Poole, of journalistic appropriation and over-usage.

In the following chapter we will look at the question of modern tragedy from a fresh angle, focusing in particular on reworkings of Greek tragedy in Africa, America and Ireland, and the role these are playing in postcolonial critical discourses. We will finish by looking – as we did in Chapter 1 – at Yoruba drama and reflecting on the vitality of tragedy in cultures outside the Western tradition.

CHAPTER NINE

Postcolonial and Multiethnic Tragedy

Postcolonial tragedy

This chapter is concerned with postcolonial readings of tragedy, starting with Shakespeare and moving on to the large body of translations and adaptations of Greek tragedy in Irish, African, African American and diaspora across the world. In her introduction to an important collection of essays, Lorna Hardwick asks whether classical inheritance is a tool of Western colonising power, or whether it is a mechanism by which independent nations express their identity in the postcolonial world.[1] Historically, processes of colonisation have involved not only acts of violence but the imposition of a cultural base on the colonised land. As Kevin Wetmore says, 'The classics can and have been used as weapons of cultural imperialism, forced upon persons of African descent as the model of culture, and used to supplant indigenous literature ....'[2] In the final part of the chapter, we turn to the subject of indigenous literature: through Wole Soyinka's theoretical work on Yoruba drama, we explore interpretations of tragedy outside the European and Anglophone world.

While the two parts of the chapter may seem to engage with very different areas of critical interest (tragedy in translation on the one hand, and African tragedy on the other), it is important to emphasise that there are important points of contact between these two bodies of work. Take, for example, Soyinka's *The Bacchae of Euripides: A Communion Rite* (performed at the Old Vic in 1973), in which praise-verses from Yoruba rituals of the god Ogun are interpolated in Soyinka's version of the Greek text. As this chapter will explore, many postcolonial critics argue that African and Greek forms of drama and culture readily accommodate one another; and writers from across the African continent have repeatedly turned to Greek tragedy as an important source. As John Djisenu has remarked: 'For us in Africa, and Ghana in particular, there exists a number of cross-cultural bonds that facilitate our ready acceptance and appreciation of ancient Greek drama.'[3] He notes the significance of myth and polytheism as key elements in this cross-cultural dialogue. Indeed, Djisenu cites Soyinka's *The Bacchae of Euripides* as an example of this kind of organic fusion between ancient Greek and African culture. Commenting on Soyinka's play, Djisenu writes that 'even though a Greek flavour wafts in the background of [Soyinka's] play, what is generally perceived is a mastery in the use of verse that decorates cross-cultural elements, such as dances, songs, processions, libation-pouring, and marriage ceremonies, whose ingredients are essentially African.'[4]

One of the distinctive features of this recent body of work on the reception of Greek tragedy in African, Irish and other cultures is its heterogeneity. Postcolonial critics are, for the most part, resistant to the formulation of overarching theories; they widely recognise the need in this area of work to interrogate ideological constructions, rather than to affirm them. As Lorna Hardwick notes, many postcolonial critics want to preserve specificities of national and ethnic identity, and to resist generalisations which suppress the very questions of identity and national difference in which the texts themselves are involved.

Much of the work discussed in this chapter is politically highly nuanced; while there are analogies to be drawn between the treatment of Sophocles' *Antigone* in South Africa or in Ireland, the differences are as important and revealing as the similarities. Thus many of the postcolonial studies discussed in this chapter are concerned with individual rather than groups of plays. However, while it is important to reflect the diversity in postcolonial critical practice, we can also recognise that many of these critics share a common interest in features of performance (in terms of date, location, language, casting, audience) in order to explore political meaning.

Before exploring the production of tragedy outside European and Anglophone contexts, we should take note of some of the important postcolonial work which is being produced in the field of Shakespeare studies. Ania Loomba, an important voice in the current generation of postcolonial critics of Shakespeare, highlights the way in which the concept of English nationhood was being forged in the sixteenth and seventeenth centuries; this, she argues, brings a new urgency to the way in which racial difference was being explored on the stage. She notes:

> ■ It has also been suggested that it may be particularly anachronistic to speak of racial difference in that period because whereas today the term 'race' carries overwhelming connotations of skin colour, in early modern Europe the bitterest conflicts between European Christians and others had to do with religion. As we begin to historicize these ideas, the question also arises whether our contemporary vocabularies are at all adequate for analysing the past. Are words such as 'race' or 'racism', 'xenophobia', 'ethnicity', or even 'nation' useful for looking at community

identities in early modern Europe? Some of these words were coined only later and others, such as 'race', did not necessarily carry the meanings they now do.[5] ☐

Loomba notes that it is precisely the visible signs of race (such as skin colour) which are the most vulnerable to change or eradication through reproduction. Her readings of *Othello* and *Titus Andronicus* explore anxieties about the way that procreation can cause skin colour to change or vanish. In an historicist reading, Loomba draws attention to the volume of migration in early modern London. She notes that there were some 10,000 'strangers' (including Africans and Jews) in London at about the time Shakespeare wrote *Othello*.[6] With this contextual evidence in mind, Loomba shows that the play touches on themes which are highly topical for the play's original audiences. Like Callaghan (whose work we discussed in Chapter 4), Loomba emphasises the interdependence of discourses concerning gender and race:

■ The strangeness of foreign lands and people was also expressed in terms of a departure from normative gender roles and sexual behaviour. ... Such inversions haunt Shakespeare's Egypt in *Antony and Cleopatra*, where Antony is seen to be unmanned by Cleopatra. Muslims and Africans were also imagined as hyper-sexual and as given to same-sex practices.[7] ☐

Loomba continues:

■ during the early modern period, gender and sexuality provided a language for expressing and developing ideas about religious, geographic, and ultimately *racial* difference. European, Christian identity is increasingly expressed in terms of masculinity, its superiority and power are described and comprehended as the penetration, rape, or husbanding of an inferior and feminized race.[8] ☐

Greek tragedy and Ireland

Loomba is interested in showing how Shakespeare's plays interrogate questions of race and identity. Other critics, meanwhile, have shown how dramatists have turned away from Shakespearean tragedy as a potential model for their own plays because, as they see it, Shakespeare has come to stand as an icon of English cultural imperialism. As Marianne McDonald notes, many Irish dramatists have turned to Greek as a way of resisting English cultural authority.[9] Greek tragedy, she says, provides an important mechanism for Ireland's construction of political and cultural identity. She notes the long history of classical scholarship in Ireland which has cultivated fertile ground for the modern reception of classical texts.

McDonald notes that four versions of the *Antigone* were performed in Ireland in 1984: these were plays by Tom Paulin, Brendan Kennelly and Aidan Carl Mathews as well as Pat Murphy's film *Anne Devlin*. She further notes that this was an important year for women's rights in Ireland: the divorce referendum had just been rejected and a proposal to legalise abortion had also been rejected.

During the performance of Aidan Carl Mathews' *Antigone: A Version* at the Dublin Project Arts Centre, members of the audience were handed copies of the Criminal Justice Bill that proposed to extend police powers to arrest and hold suspects without charge. The text of the bill was read at the end of Act I and during the interval 'so the lines between past and present, audience and stage, were purposefully blurred'.[10]

McDonald argues that Ireland's history is one in which the dead inspire the living to fight for their cause and here she notes in particular Ireland's collective memory of those who died in the famine of the mid-nineteenth century. McDonald also mentions the importance of Catholic rituals for remembering the dead, and suggests that Greek tragedy has particular resonance in a culture which remembers, honours and remains connected with its dead in the way that Ireland does. Catholicism echoes through the translation in the use of religious imagery and litanies. While in Chapter 1 we explored the many difficulties inherent in the notion of Christian tragedy, McDonald suggests that Irish Catholicism assimilates pagan elements relatively easily, so that 'God' can be substituted for 'gods' without sounding incongruous. McDonald situates her reading of Irish tragedy in relation to the Troubles.[11] In the context of this bloody history, McDonald suggests, Irish audiences have a heightened interest in tragedy's exploration of the destructive consequences of revenge.

In a study we touched on in Chapter 6, Fiona Macintosh draws attention to a number of similarities between the death speeches of Greek tragedy and those of modern Irish tragedy. While she acknowledges that the basis for this comparison might seem surprising, she points out that the mythical material on which tragedy of the Irish Literary Revival is based shares some of its perspectives with Greek.[12] She argues that several writers, notably Yeats and Synge, 'explicitly turned to the Greek tragedians as exempla in their attempt to found a national theatre'.[13] The Irish hero Cuchulain, for example, was often compared to Greek heroes such as Heracles and Achilles. Like McDonald, Macintosh suggests that both ancient Greek and twentieth-century Irish cultures manifest a highly demonstrative culture of mourning and lamentation.

Macintosh argues that in death speeches, the dying protagonist occupies a liminal space between death and life:

■ The process of the characters' death begins early in the tragedies – indeed, it could be maintained that the cost of tragic status is exclusion from the full process of living. During the course of the big speech, it becomes clear that the dying characters have only the most tenuous of links with their immediate surroundings; it is as if they already occupied the liminal world beyond the world of the living that the chief mourners themselves are understood to occupy during the course of the burial rites.[14] □

Macintosh continues:

■ The dying characters in both the Greek and Irish plays frequently turn away from their immediate surroundings in order to address the environment ... That the characters occupy a liminal space is clearly evidenced by the imagined audience: it is the dead themselves to whom their words are commonly addressed, not their living auditors.[15] □

In Chapter 3 we noted the prominence of the first-person pronoun. However, Macintosh says that this is more typically absent in the death speeches of ancient Greek and modern Irish tragedy, suggesting that this delineates a point of separation between *psuche* (the Greek word often translated as 'soul') and body and arguing that 'The hyperconsciousness of self that the characters display on the threshold of death in the plays of Synge and Yeats is clearly related to the attainment of full mythical status that comes with death.'[16] From this she concludes:

■ Therefore, what is most distinctive (and indeed most noteworthy) about the last words in general is not their uniqueness, but their highly stylized nature, both in terms of form and content. The stylization of the big speech and the lament, I suggest, grants the speakers access to a shared inheritance that is recognized by the members of the audience no less than by the dramatic characters themselves. It is not simply that particular pains have been absorbed into the generality of human suffering, but that the audience respond to the repetitions and allusions with pleasure.[17] □

Stephen E. Wilmer argues that Heaney's *Burial at Thebes* (2004) participates in anti-American as well as anti-British discourse.[18] Heaney wrote the play for the centennial year of the opening of the Irish National Theatre, also known as the Abbey Theatre, in Dublin. In a question and answer session at the Abbey Theatre on 27 April 2004, Heaney recalled the death of a hunger striker, Francis Hughes, whose body remained in the custody of the Royal Ulster Constabulary while his family appealed for the right to arrange a burial. For Heaney, this sense of a profound urge to conduct a proper burial connects Irish culture and Sophocles' *Antigone*, and it was in order to emphasise this that Heaney changed the title of his play to reflect the importance of burial as the play's central concern. Wilmer goes on to argue that the play engages not just with Irish political contexts but with the wider international context too:

> ■ Heaney uses the aggressive dictatorial policies of Creon not only as a metaphor for British colonial attitudes in Ireland but also for American imperialism. Creon's language starts to resemble the rhetoric of George Bush in his war on terror. By emphasizing such words as 'patriot,' 'patriotic duty,' 'patriots in life and death,' as well as 'safety' and 'security,' Creon's phraseology calls to mind the post-9/11 climate of fear, loyalty (to the government), and vengefulness, which was encouraged by the US president through the adoption of the USA Patriot Act, the creation of the Department of Homeland Security and the invasion of Afghanistan and Iraq.[19] □

Greek tragedy and Africa

At first sight, the reception of Greek tragedy in Africa might seem a long way from the Irish contexts which we have been considering. As McDonald and Walton suggest, in their introduction to Athol Fugard's essay, '*Antigone* in Africa', the play's exploration of tyranny is pertinent to Irish and African contexts. McDonald and Walton go on to explore parallels between the political theatre of South Africa and the work of the Field Day Theatre Company in Ireland.

In his essay, Athol Fugard considers the resonance which his play, *The Island*, has had outside the place of its first performance in Cape Town in 1973. The play was televised in Ireland in the 1980s and staged at the Gate Theatre in Dublin in 1986, and Fugard himself directed the play in Cork and Listowel in 1999. Fugard retraces the genesis of *The Island* to his experience of living in black townships around Port Elizabeth during apartheid; he notes that this was reputed to be 'the most highly politicized black area in South Africa' and was the area from which figures such as Nelson Mandela and Steve Biko came.[20] Fugard's experience of living in the area at this time shaped his reading of the *Antigone* as 'the greatest political play of all time'. As he read this play with a group of actors, he says, 'The story of that one lone voice raised in protest against what was considered an unjust law struck to the hearts of every member of the group.'[21]

Fugard reports that the police harassed and intimidated the group throughout the rehearsal period. Eventually, one of the cast members, Sharkie (Sipho Mguqulwa), was taken into police custody, accused of political offences and eventually sent to prison on Robben Island where Mandela and other members of the African National Congress were serving sentences. In spite of police opposition, Fugard managed to stage the play in New Brighton. He concluded from the audience reaction that 'our young theatre group had in fact become the Antigone of New Brighton. It was speaking out against and defying the edicts of the apartheid Creon.'[22]

Fugard reports that Sharkie went on to stage a heavily condensed version of the *Antigone* while in prison. His fellow inmate Mandela was not allowed to witness that performance but, years later (still in prison but under less restrictive conditions), Mandela went on to organise another staging of *Antigone*, in which he played the part of Creon.

Highly apparent throughout Fugard's essay is his identification of Antigone as a figurehead for black resistance. In an essay on Femi Osofisan's *Tegonni: an African Antigone*, first performed in 1994, Barbara Goff discusses this construction of Antigone and urges the need for caution in approaching the text too straightforwardly as an endorsement of political resistance:

> ■ Within African rewritings, the story of Antigone has proved very popular and the reasons for this presumably include the fact that the story involves a confrontation with overweening power, which can readily be adapted to various situations. In Western rewritings, a play based on *Antigone* often figures resistance against an arrogant state, as with Anouilh and Brecht. In African *Antigones*, one might expect Creon to be identified with the colonial occupiers, but in fact, this is rarely the case in any straightforward way. In *The Island* (1973) by Fugard, Kani, and Ntshona, it is clearly the white apartheid system that throws up its Creons, but there is also a power struggle in the cell, between Winston and John ... This muddying of the political waters is linked to an aspect of the character, Antigone, that makes it difficult to recuperate her simply as a figure for African resistance: since she is part and parcel of the cultural equipment that the colonizers drew on to explain the success of their inroads into other cultures, she presumably only comes to Africa by way of colonial Europe.[23] □

Other theorists have explored the relationship between Greek tragedy and Africa not in terms of its more recent reception, but in terms of ethnic migration. In a series of controversial books, Martin Bernal has argued that Greek culture originally derives from African (particularly Egyptian) culture.[24] This claim (though one that has not been widely accepted) radically inverts any sense that Africa is indebted to Greece for its literary models, and instead posits Africa (not Athens) as the very wellspring of the tragic tradition. In his own account of Greek tragedy and African American theatre, Kevin Wetmore offers a more moderate position, observing that it is probably unhelpful to try to quantify Egyptian influence on Greece.

In a useful analysis of these complex processes of reception, Wetmore posits three models for understanding the place of Greek tragedy in cultures of the African diaspora:

■ The first, 'Black Orpheus' is a model that is rooted in parallel and overlay. The works in this category tend to be 'straightforward' adaptations with direct, one-to-one correspondences, or not even adaptations, but referential works, pieces that use Greek culture as a metaphor for African culture. 'Black Orpheus' is a model of equation; the African material is the equivalent of this aspect of Greek culture.

The second model, 'Black Athena', is a reappropriation of material that is already African in origin. Under this model, the Greeks received their myths, their religion, their culture, etc. from the Egyptians. Therefore, all Greek material is really all African in the first place. The use of Greek material is not cultural colonialism and an expression of western superiority, but rather a corrective, returning the culture to its rightful African context.

The third paradigm is 'Black Dionysus,' which considers adaptation of Greek tragedy within the context of the African diaspora as a creative and constructive system of complex intertextuality designed to critique the very cultures that prioritize ancient Greek culture. It seeks to uncover the historical reality behind both Greek and African cultures, respecting both within their own contexts.[25] ☐

Wetmore urges wariness about the idea that Greek tragedy has been widely performed and imitated because of its putative 'universality'. He argues that Greek tragedy:

■ is the product of a culture that itself resulted from many different influences. Universality is a western conceit that would place western culture at the center and above all others ... 'universality' can only be achieved through violent change, either to the tragedy or to the culture to which the tragedy is being adapted. Adaptation, in one sense, is a form of violence. In another sense, it is a kind of transformation that allows the audience to perceive something new in something old.[26] ☐

Wetmore's study of 'Black Medea' looks at the story of a young African American slave, Margaret Garner. In 1856, Margaret Garner escaped slavery with her children and fled from Kentucky to Cincinnati. When Margaret was caught by US marshals, she killed one of her children and attempted to kill the other three: she would rather they faced death than a life of slavery. Some ten years later, an image of Margaret being captured by guards was painted by Thomas Satterwhite Noble and entitled *Margaret Garner, or the Modern Medea*. One of the distinctive features of the painting is that it shows two dead children (rather than one) at the feet of their mother, in what Wetmore argues is an attempt to align this act of infanticide with Medea's killing of her own two children in Euripides' play. He observes that this was perhaps the earliest appropriation of Greek tragedy to frame African American experience. The story was later fictionalised as the basis of Toni Morrison's Pulitzer Prize-winning novel, *Beloved* (1987).

The fourth stage

In the final part of this Guide, we come back to the point at which we began: the subject of tragedy and ritual. Wole Soyinka's essay, 'The Fourth Stage: *Through the Mysteries of Ogun* to the Origin of Yoruba Tragedy' (1976), is a seminal account of Yoruba tragedy.[27] The Yoruba are an ethnic group in West Africa; although the population is dispersed widely across several countries in that region, there is a concentration of Yoruba in Nigeria. As another pioneering critic, Joel Adedeji, has shown, Yoruba drama is intimately connected with ritual.[28] Adedeji traces it to the ritual drama of the Egungun, the cult of the ancestors. Like Greek tragedy, performers in Yoruba tragedy wear masks. Unlike Greek tragedy, however, the form of Yoruba drama is non-narrative: the performance (which is partially scripted and partially improvised) consists of episodes and tableaux, and, as Adedeji remarks, 'There is no continuous story.'[29] For the Yoruba, theatre is a fusion of many different aesthetic and cultural elements: 'theatrical pleasure can be derived only when the essence of the total performance is meaningful ... The creative arts combine with religion, politics, psychology, and medical practice to construct a complete system. It is the fusion of all these elements that forms the Yoruba aesthetic system.'[30]

Soyinka takes Nietzsche's *The Birth of Tragedy* as a paradigm for his own explication of divinity in Yoruba drama. As Soyinka explains, at the heart of Yoruba tragedy is the god Ogun. He is a divinity associated with many different areas including creativity, metal and war. Soyinka situates his account of Yoruban tragedy in terms of a relationship between Ogun and Obatala, the sculptural god. It is a paradigm which, as Soyinka acknowledges, is reminiscent of the Nietzschean model of Dionysus–Apollo. For this reason, he is careful to register differences between his account and that of Nietzsche. To take one example, Soyinka suggests that Ogun alone embodies the qualities which Nietzsche attributes to two deities: 'Ogun, for his part, is best understood in Hellenic values as a totality of the Dionysian, Apollonian and Promethean virtues.'[31] While Nietzsche's account of Greek tragedy focuses on the Olympian gods (those of the upper world), Soyinka suggests that Yoruba tragedy is also concerned with the chthonic world (which is associated with the rites and deities of the Underworld): 'Yoruba tragedy plunges straight into the "chthonic realm", the seething cauldron of the dark world of will and psyche, the transitional yet inchoate matrix of death and becoming.'[32]

According to Soyinka, Yoruba ritual is directed towards overcoming the gulf between man and deities, man and his ancestors, man and the unborn. This strongly recalls Nietzsche's discussion of the *principium individuationis*, man's painful separation from fellow man and from nature at large. Soyinka suggests that psychic pain originates in a sense of man's severance from this realm of being: 'man is grieved by a consciousness of the loss of the eternal essence of his being and must indulge in symbolic transactions to recover his totality of being'.[33] For the Yoruba, tragedy does not exist in order to bridge this gulf but in order to dramatise it:

> ■ Tragedy, in Yoruba traditional drama, is the anguish of this severance, the fragmentation of essence from self. Its music is the stricken cry of man's blind soul as he flounders in the void and crashes through a deep abyss of a-spirituality and cosmic rejection. Tragic music is an echo from that void; the celebrant speaks, sings and dances in authentic archetypal images from within the abyss. All understand and respond, for it is the language of the world.[34] □

Here, too, Soyinka's emphasis on the importance of music recalls Nietzsche's insistence on the role of choral music as a vital constituent and expression of the Dionysian. Soyinka explains the role of the singer in reference to the Yoruban belief that there are three stages of existence: the dead/ancestors, the present and the future/the unborn. The singer is not a mouthpiece for particular moments in time,

> ■ but of the no-man's-land of transition between and around these temporal definitions of experience. The past is the ancestor's, the present belongs to the living, and the future to the unborn. The deities stand in the same situation to the living as do the ancestors and the unborn, obeying the same laws, suffering the same agonies and uncertainties, employing the same masonic intelligence of rituals for the perilous plunge into the fourth area of experience, the immeasurable gulf of transition. Its dialogue is liturgy, its music takes form from man's uncomprehending immersion in this area of existence, buried wholly from rational recognition. The source of the possessed lyricist, chanting hitherto unknown mythopoetic strains whose

antiphonal refrain is, however, instantly caught and thrust with all its terror and awesomeness into the night by swaying votaries, this source is residual in the numinous area of transition.
This is the fourth stage, the vortex of archetypes and home of the tragic spirit.[35] ☐

The passage reflects Soyinka's emphasis on tragedy as a non-rational form, once again echoing Nietzsche's insistence that tragedy is an aesthetic rather than a rational or interrogative form. From a sense of this non-rational basis, Soyinka suggests that Yoruba tragedy achieves and enacts a sense of being outside temporal dimensions.

This chapter has sought to extend Chapter 8's enquiry into the status of tragedy in the modern world. It has shown that one form in which tragedy is surviving and flourishing is in the form of translation and adaptation. To that end, we have been looking in particular at adaptations of Greek tragedy in Ireland, America and outside the Western world. We have also engaged with the work of postcolonial critics who have sought to understand the relevance of these reworkings of classical texts in the modern world. As we have seen, Greek tragedy has resonated with modern dramatists in cultures as various as Ireland, South Africa and America as a way of articulating political concerns and of posing political resistance.

While much of this Guide has been concerned with tragedy in the Western tradition, in the final part of the chapter we turned to the work of the Yoruba writer, Wole Soyinka. Yoruba drama has emerged independently of the Western tradition; at the same time, Soyinka is sensitive to affinities between Yoruba tragedy and Western (particularly Greek) tragedy. Whereas many of the texts discussed in this chapter manifest a high degree of relevance to contemporary political situations, Soyinka shows how Yoruba tragedy seeks to transcend the immediate moment of performance and instead to enter an atemporal plane.

In the Conclusion, we will refocus our attention on temporal relationships between past and present as we consider possible future directions for tragic theory, and for tragedy itself as a form.

Conclusion: Recent and Future Directions

This Guide has explored some of the most important and influential discussions of tragedy from Aristotle in the fourth century BC to the most exciting criticism of the present day. The critical field is dynamic and interdisciplinary. As we have seen, the task of theorising tragedy is the provenance not just of the literary critic, but of philosophers, historians and others too. And among literary scholars, tragic theory engages the Renaissance critic as much as the postcolonial theorist and is relevant to students of ancient Greek literature, English, French, German, Russian, Norwegian, to name but a few. It is doubtful that many other art forms can claim to have this kind of longevity and relevance across time and space. There is already an extensive critical tradition: now we must ask, where does tragic theory go from here?

In Chapter 8, we considered arguments that tragedy, as a form, has had its day. Yet many prominent classicists of the present generation stress the continuing – even heightened – relevance of Greek tragedy in the modern world. Rush Rehm suggests that Greek tragedy is itself Janus-like, looking back and looking forward at the same time. He contends that for ancient Greek audiences, the past provided a lens through which to contemplate the present and the future:

> ■ The priority of the past in Greek tragedy is not about nostalgia, or the desire to escape to an easier time, or a psychological fear of the unknown. On the contrary, as the plays demonstrate, tragic characters turn to the past in order to influence – 'flow into' – the future ... The complex interplay between then and now vitalized the audience's sense of the choices that lay before them.[1] □

Rehm goes on to argue that 'by its manifold untimeliness, therefore, Greek tragedy offers (minimally) some "perspective by incongruity" (as Kenneth Burke puts it), its temporal "otherness" refracting our parochial, market-driven sense of time'.[2] Here Rehm is suggesting that Greek tragedy is fundamentally resistant to the kind of Marxist constructions which we have intermittently encountered in this Guide: for Rehm, Greek tragedy is not (just) of its moment in time; it transcends the historical conditions of its own production and, in doing so, allows us to see our own experience and our own historical moment through new eyes.

Like Rehm, Rebecca Bushnell emphasises the relevance of the tragedies we have inherited from the past, but she reinstates a sense that each text is historically situated: 'tragedies will speak to us in our own moment, even though they cannot be detached from the time of their making'.[3] She speculates about the form which tragic drama will take in the century ahead, and notes that just as the cinema supplanted the theatre in the twentieth century as a medium of mass entertainment, now other forms of entertainment media are supplanting live cinema. She argues:

> ■ But the global market in film and image and the internet do enable a new cultural communality. Paradoxically, the same technologies that have increased cultural fragmentation through the proliferation of unimaginably diverse kinds of music, art, and film have also produced new ways of sharing art: an image or text can be instantly downloaded by people around the world. The power of this technology has mostly lent itself to the circulation of the cheap fragment of horror, comedy, or scandal, but it does hold great potential for the future of a new democratic art and thus the art of tragedy. In the developed world, it may appear that a large percentage of the population is locked away into the private world channeled through their headphones, cell phones or ipods. But at the same time, artists and writers are producing new forms of narrative and screen art, for a global audience. Who can say what sort of tragic art will emerge?[4] □

Thus, as Bushnell argues, tragedy itself is evolving in ways we cannot predict, as our culture is increasingly shaped by new technologies. For Bushnell, these rival forms of entertainment are posing a threat to the communal experience of sitting together in the theatre. It is an argument which recalls the debate surrounding the emergence of the novel in the nineteenth century (discussed in Chapter 7). At the time, the shift from public to private consumption of literary narratives posed a challenge to the survival of tragedy as a form.

As we have seen, the questions that tragedy and its critics pose are characteristically challenging. It is unsurprising, therefore, that many of the key questions have invited and sustained prolonged debate. Some of the major questions about tragedy (for example, what is meant by *catharsis*?) are so far unsolved or insoluble and will continue to provoke critical debate. On the subject of *catharsis*, the medical humanities is an area emerging as one of the fastest-growing areas of interdisciplinary enquiry, drawing on expertise from literary criticism, psychology and the history of medicine, among other fields. From this emerging scholarly base there will be new critical tools to address this ancient question and there will be continuing interest in attempts to theorise responses to tragedy in relation to physiological and affective models. We have seen, at different moments in the Guide, the argument that science is inimical to tragedy (see discussions of Brecht and Schlesinger in Chapter 8). We have also seen how some critics have drawn on analogies with science in their account of tragedy (see Huxley in Chapter 7 and Williams in Chapter 8). In the coming decades, the separation of literary questions from scientific ones will be less distinct, as collaborations between scientists, literary critics and others will create a new scholarly agenda.

It is likely that work in the medical humanities will not just turn its attention to the task of elucidating audience experience, but will also further enrich our understanding of the relationship between mind and body in the ancient and the early modern world. As we saw earlier in this Guide, critics such as Padel, Hillman and Paster have amassed crucial evidence to suggest how intimately premodern conceptions of the self were realised and expressed not just through philosophical concepts but also – perhaps even more importantly – via bodily experience. This is likely to be a stimulus for further debate.

One of the other major emerging fields shaping the agenda of contemporary literary studies is ecocriticism. This began as a fringe movement of literary criticism in the 1970s, but is now taking its place in more mainstream critical consciousness. The first decade of the twenty-first century has seen a steady stream of ecocritical studies, particularly of Shakespeare, coming into print.[5] Ecocriticism is a broad theoretical umbrella term and its practitioners are interested in pursuing a diverse range of critical concerns. From this critical school has emerged a distinctive stance on the subject of tragedy. Joseph Meeker, whose work we encountered in Chapter 5, argues that tragedy reflects and inculcates a dangerously anthropocentric view of the world:

■ Prerequisite to tragedy is the belief that the universe cares about the lives of human beings. There must be a faith that some superior order exists and that man will be punished if he transgresses against it. It matters little whether this principle takes the form of fate, the gods, or impersonal moral law, for all are symbols of the world's interest in human actions and evidence that the welfare of all creation somehow depends upon what humans do. Corollary to this is the assumption that man is essentially superior to animal, vegetable, and mineral nature and is destined to exercise mastery over all natural processes, including those of his own body.[6] □

Meeker argues that in pitting man against great forces (such as nature, the gods, moral law), tragedy does not depict man's vulnerability but rather his greatness since man is deemed worthy of such a fight: 'Tragic literature and philosophy, then, undertake to demonstrate that man is equal to or superior to his conflict. The tragic man takes his conflict seriously, and feels compelled to affirm his mastery and greatness in the face of his own destruction. He is a triumphant image of what man can be.'[7]

Meeker believes that this is not only wrong but has had catastrophic implications for the ecological management of the world: 'The tragic view of man, for all its flattering optimism, has led to cultural and biological disasters, and it is time to look for alternatives which might encourage better the survival of our own and other species.'[8] This is not so much a claim – *pace* Steiner – that tragedy *has* died but a claim that it *should* die. While Meeker may represent a minority view, it is clear that wider questions of social and ecological responsibility and bioethics will continue to shape the critical agenda in the decades ahead.

It is not just new critical schools which are emerging. The literary canon itself is expanding, and our sense of the range of texts that demand critical attention has never been greater. One of the most important areas of activity is now postcolonial literature. As we saw in Chapter 9, many of the most innovative performances and adaptations of Greek tragedy in English in the last few decades have been situated outside Europe, or outside the Western world. It is likely that this will continue to be an important area of scholarly debate. Postcolonial critics will carry on exploring the work of contemporary writers, and revisiting older, canonical texts (such as Shakespeare's *Othello*) with an informed sense of the colonial and imperial narratives in which they are implicated. Meanwhile (with the exception of Yoruba drama, which we discussed in Chapter 9), relatively little is known about forms of tragedy, or drama that is analogous to tragedy, outside the Western tradition. Here, there are new discoveries to be made and fresh comparative work to be done.

Feminist criticism will continue to pose questions about female agency and the representation of women in tragedy. Attention will focus not just on female characters in drama, but on the work of female writers too. As we have seen, tragedy is often considered to be a form of drama written about men, by men and for men. But this is a paradigm that is far from secure. In this Guide, we have briefly touched on the work of Mary Sidney and Elizabeth Cary (in Chapter 7) and on the work of Sarah Kane (in Chapter 6). There remains much more to be done on the way that these and other female writers have engaged with the tragic tradition.

Performance studies and film studies will continue to flourish, both in the work of postcolonial critics and others. This academic discipline will thrive not only as a specialist area in its own right; increasingly (as we have seen in this Guide), traditional forms of literary and textual criticism are taking account of the performative dimensions of the text. As Rebecca Bushnell has suggested, modern technology continually offers new media for performance and entertainment and these will pose both opportunities and challenges for tragedy as a form.

Let us leave the last word, for now, to Aldous Huxley whose essay on 'Wholly Truthful' art we looked at in Chapter 7. Confronting his own doubts about the capacity of tragedy to survive the challenges of modern culture, Huxley concludes by reflecting that there is, indeed, an assured future for tragedy's 'chemically pure' art:

■ I have sometimes wondered whether tragedy, as a form of art, may not be doomed. But the fact that we are still profoundly moved by the tragic masterpieces of the past – that we can be moved, against our better judgment, even by the bad tragedies of the contemporary stage and film – makes me think that the day of chemically pure art is not over. Tragedy happens to be passing through a period of eclipse, because all the significant writers of our age are too busy exploring the newly discovered, or re-discovered, world of the Whole Truth to be able to pay any attention to it. But there is no good reason to believe that this state of things will last forever. Tragedy is too valuable to be allowed to die.[9] □

Notes

INTRODUCTION

1. A. Miller, 'The Nature of Tragedy', from *The Theater Essays of Arthur Miller*, ed. R. A. Martin (Viking Press: New York, 1978), pp. 8–11 (p. 8).
2. T. Eagleton, *Sweet Violence: The Idea of the Tragic* (Oxford: Blackwell, 2003), p. 3.
3. Eagleton, *Sweet Violence*, p. 3.
4. K. Muir, *Shakespeare's Tragic Sequence* (London: Hutchinson, 1972), p. 12.
5. As, for example, in *Tragedy and the Tragic: Greek Theatre and Beyond*, ed. M. S. Silk (Oxford: Clarendon Press, 1996).
6. G. Steiner, *The Death of Tragedy* (first published 1961; London: Faber, 1963).
7. R. Williams, *Modern Tragedy* (London: Chatto & Windus, 1966).

CHAPTER ONE: THE GODS

1. For discussion of this etymology, see A. Lesky, *Greek Tragedy*, trans. H. A. Frankfort (London: Ernest Benn, 1978), p. 34. On the etymology of the word 'tragedy' and a hypothesis on its sacrificial origins, see W. Burkert, 'Greek Tragedy and Sacrificial Ritual', *Greek, Roman and Byzantine Studies* 7 (1966), 87–121.
2. Aristotle, *Poetics in Classical Literary Criticism*, ed. D. A. Russell and M. Winterbottom (Oxford: Oxford University Press, 1991), p. 55. All subsequent quotations from Aristotle are taken from this edition unless otherwise stated.
3. See G. Murray, 'Excursus on the Ritual Forms in Greek Tragedy', in J. E. Harrison, *Themis: A Study of the Social Origins of Greek Religion* (London: Merlin Press, 1963).
4. Murray, 'Excursus', p. 341.
5. Murray, 'Excursus', p. 342.
6. A. W. Pickard-Cambridge, *Dithyramb, Tragedy and Comedy* (Oxford: Clarendon Press, 1927).
7. Pickard-Cambridge, *Dithyramb, Tragedy and Comedy*, p. 187.
8. Pickard-Cambridge, *Dithyramb, Tragedy and Comedy*, p. 188.
9. L. Woodbridge and E. Berry, eds, *True Rites and Maimed Rites: Ritual and Anti-ritual in Shakespeare and His Age* (Urbana and Chicago: University of Illinois Press, 1992), p. 3. The anthropologist to whom Woodbridge and Berry refer is Sir James Frazer, author of *The Golden Bough* (1890).
10. R. Friedrich, 'Everything to Do with Dionysos? Ritualism, the Dionysiac, and the Tragic', in *Tragedy and the Tragic: Greek Theatre and Beyond*, ed. M. S. Silk (Oxford: Clarendon Press, 1996), pp. 257–83 (p. 265).
11. Friedrich, 'Everything to Do with Dionysos?', p. 260.
12. C. Segal, *Dionysiac Poetics and Euripides' Bacchae* (Princeton, NJ: Princeton University Press, 1982), p. 16.
13. See, for example, S. Scullion, '"Nothing to Do with Dionysus": Tragedy Misconceived as Ritual', *Classical Quarterly* 52 (2002), 102–37; Friedrich, 'Everything to do with Dionysos?'; and an important collection of essays by J. Winkler and F. Zeitlin, eds, *Nothing to Do with Dionysos? Athenian Drama in its Social Context* (Princeton: Princeton University Press, 1990).
14. S. Goldhill, 'The Great Dionysia and Civic Ideology', *Journal of Hellenic Studies* 107 (1987), 56–76.
15. Goldhill, 'The Great Dionysia', p. 74.

16. O. Taplin, *Greek Tragedy in Action* (London: Taylor & Francis, 1978), p. 162, and Scullion, '"Nothing to Do with Dionysus"'.
17. B. Brecht, *Brecht on Theatre: The Development of an Aesthetic*, ed. and trans. J. Willett (London: Eyre Methuen, 1974), p. 181.
18. Friedrich, 'Everything to do with Dionysos?', p. 271.
19. Friedrich, 'Everything to do with Dionysos?', p. 272.
20. P. E. Easterling, 'Tragedy and Ritual: "Cry 'Woe, woe', but may the good prevail!"' *Métis* 3 (1988), 87–109.
21. Woodbridge and Berry, *True Rites and Maimed Rites*, p. 9.
22. L. Gernet, *Anthropologie de la Grèce antique*, ed. J.-P. Vernant (Paris: F. Maspéro, 1968); W. Burkert, *Greek Religion: Archaic and Classical* (first published 1977; Oxford: Blackwell, 1985), pp. 82–4. For a recent analysis of the historical evidence, see J. Bremmer, 'Scapegoat Rituals in Ancient Greece', *Harvard Studies in Classical Philology* 87 (1983), 299–320.
23. Burkert, *Greek Religion*, p. 82.
24. Burkert, *Greek Religion*, p. 84.
25. R. Girard, *Violence and the Sacred*, trans. P. Gregory (Baltimore: Johns Hopkins University Press, 1977). For a sceptical approach to the authority of Girard, see Woodbridge and Berry, *True Rites and Maimed Rites*, pp. 11–12.
26. Girard, *Violence and the Sacred*, p. 96.
27. C. Segal, 'Greek Tragedy and Society: A Structuralist Perspective', in *Greek Tragedy and Political Theory*, ed. J. P. Euben (Berkeley and Los Angeles: University of California Press, 1986), pp. 43–75 (p. 50).
28. Girard, *Violence and the Sacred*, p. 1.
29. Girard, *Violence and the Sacred*, p. 2.
30. Girard, *Violence and the Sacred*, pp. 9–10.
31. Girard, *Violence and the Sacred*, p. 95.
32. Girard, *Violence and the Sacred*, p. 4.
33. Girard, *Violence and the Sacred*, p. 95.
34. J. Kott, *The Eating of the Gods: An Interpretation of Greek Tragedy*, trans. B. Taborksi and E. J. Czerwinski (Evanston: Northwestern University Press, 1987), p. 193.
35. J. Derrida, 'Plato's Pharmacy', in *Dissemination*, trans. B. Johnson (London: Athlone Press, 1981), pp. 61–171.
36. Derrida, 'Plato's Pharmacy', p. 133.
37. Derrida, 'Plato's Pharmacy', p. 133.
38. J. Holloway, *The Story of the Night: Studies in Shakespeare's Major Tragedies*. (London: Routledge & Kegan Paul, 1961).
39. N. C. Liebler, *Shakespeare's Festive Tragedy: The Ritual Foundations of Genre* (London and New York: Routledge, 1995). The term 'festive tragedy' which Liebler adopts, and indeed the title of her book, are explicit gestures towards the work of C. L. Barber's *Shakespeare's Festive Comedy: A Study of Dramatic Form and Its Relation to Social Custom* (Princeton: Princeton University Press, 1959).
40. Liebler, *Shakespeare's Festive Tragedy*, pp. 12–13.
41. Liebler, *Shakespeare's Festive Tragedy*, p. 54.
42. Liebler, *Shakespeare's Festive Tragedy*, p. 85.
43. Liebler, *Shakespeare's Festive Tragedy*, p. 85.
44. W. Soyinka, *Myth, Literature and the African World* (Cambridge: Cambridge University Press, 1976), pp. 1–2.
45. Soyinka, *Myth, Literature and the African World*, p. 7.
46. Williams, *Modern Tragedy*, p. 30.
47. G. Lukács, *The Theory of the Novel* (London: Merlin Press, 1971), p. 88.
48. S. Sontag, 'The Death of Tragedy', in *Against Interpretation and Other Essays* (New York: Farrar, Straus and Giroux, 1966), p. 137.
49. A. Camus, 'Lecture Given in Athens on the Future of Tragedy', in *Selected Essays and Notebooks*, ed. and trans. P. Thody (Harmondsworth: Penguin, 1970), p. 199.

50. Camus, 'Lecture Given in Athens', pp. 197–8.
51. W. R. Elton, *King Lear and the Gods* (San Marino, CA: Huntington Library, 1966).
52. C. Leech, *Shakespeare's Tragedies: and Other Studies in Seventeenth-Century Drama* (London: Chatto & Windus, 1950), p. 18.
53. G. Steiner, '"Tragedy," Reconsidered', in *Rethinking Tragedy*, ed. R. Felski (Baltimore and London: Johns Hopkins University Press, 2008), 29–44, p. 41.
54. J. T. Shawcross, *The Uncertain World of 'Samson Agonistes'* (Cambridge: D. S. Brewer, 2001), p. 39.
55. This reading of the play has been notably challenged by Joseph Wittreich, who sees the play as a critique of the code of violence. See J. Wittreich, *Interpreting 'Samson Agonistes'* (Princeton: Princeton University Press, 1986).
56. Shawcross, *Uncertain World*, p. 41.
57. L. Michel, 'The Possibility of a Christian Tragedy', *Thought* 31 (1956), 403–28.
58. S. Kierkegaard, 'Ancient Tragedy's Reflection in the Modern', in *Either/Or*, (Harmondsworth: Penguin Books, 1992), p. 149.
59. J. C. Maxwell, 'The Technique of Invocation in *King Lear*', *Modern Language Review* 45 (1950), 142–7.
60. Williams, *Modern Tragedy*, p. 30.
61. E. O'Neill, 'Working Notes and Extracts from a Fragmentary Work Diary', in *American Playwrights on Drama*, ed. H. Frenz (New York: Hill & Wang, 1965), p. 9.
62. L. Goldmann, *Racine*, trans. A. Hamilton (Cambridge: Rivers Press, 1972), p. 5.
63. Goldmann, *Racine*, p. 7.
64. W. H. Auden, 'The Christian Tragic Hero', *New York Times*, 16 December 1945. Quoted in D. D. Waters, *Christian Settings in Shakespeare's Tragedies* (London: Associated University Presses, 1994), p. 74.
65. K. Jaspers, *Tragedy Is Not Enough* (London: Victor Gollancz, 1953), pp. 38–9.
66. E. Zanin, 'Early Modern Oedipus: A Literary Approach to Christian Tragedy', in *The Locus of Tragedy*, ed. A. Cools, T. Crombez, R. Slegers and J. Taels (Leiden: Brill, 2008), pp. 65–80.
67. Zanin, 'Early Modern Oedipus', p. 76.
68. A. C. Bradley, *Shakespearean Tragedy* (Harmondsworth: Penguin, 1991), p. 262.
69. J. Kott, *Shakespeare Our Contemporary*, trans. B. Taborski (London: Methuen, 1967), p. 103.
70. Kott, *Shakespeare Our Contemporary*, p. 103.
71. Kott, *Shakespeare Our Contemporary*, p. 104.
72. Kott, *Shakespeare Our Contemporary*, p. 105.
73. Kott, *Shakespeare Our Contemporary*, p. 105.
74. Kott, *Shakespeare Our Contemporary*, p. 105.
75. Kott, *Shakespeare Our Contemporary*, p. 108.
76. Kott, *Shakespeare Our Contemporary*, p. 112.
77. Kott, *Shakespeare Our Contemporary*, p. 112.
78. Elton, *King Lear and the Gods*, p. 337.
79. The classic account of this is E. Duffy, *The Stripping of the Altars: Traditional Religion in England 1400–1580* (New Haven and London: Yale University Press, 1992).
80. S. Greenblatt, *Hamlet in Purgatory* (Princeton: Princeton University Press, 2001), pp. 18–19.
81. M. Neill, *Issues of Death: Mortality and Identity in English Renaissance Tragedy* (Oxford: Clarendon Press, 1997), pp. 245ff.
82. R. N. Watson, *The Rest Is Silence: Death as Annihilation in the English Renaissance* (Berkeley: University of California Press, 1994).
83. Models from Greek tragedy include Darius in Aeschylus' *The Persians*, Clytaemnestra in Aeschylus' *Eumenides* and Polydorus in Euripides' *Hecuba*.
84. Greenblatt, *Hamlet in Purgatory*, p. 208.
85. Greenblatt, *Hamlet in Purgatory*, p. 245.

CHAPTER TWO: THE CHORUS
1. G. Steiner, *Antigones* (Oxford: Oxford University Press, 1984), p. 166.
2. H. P. Foley, 'Envisioning the Tragic Chorus on the Modern Stage', in *Drama, Myth, and Ritual in Greek Art and Literature*, ed. C. Kraus, S. Goldhill, H. P. Foley and J. Elsner (Oxford: Oxford University Press, 2007), p. 355.
3. J. Gould, 'Tragedy and Collective Experience', in *Tragedy and the Tragic: Greek Theatre and Beyond*, ed. M. S. Silk (Oxford: Clarendon Press, 1996), p. 225.
4. Gould, 'Tragedy and Collective Experience', p. 223.
5. Steiner, *Antigones*, p. 166.
6. E. Hall, *Inventing the Barbarian: Greek Self-Definition through Tragedy* (Oxford: Clarendon Press, 1989), p. 115.
7. G. Lukács, *The Theory of the Novel* (London: Merlin Press, 1971), p. 42f.
8. C. Meier, *The Political Art of Greek Tragedy*, trans. A. Webber (Cambridge: Polity Press, 1993).
9. J. P. Euben, ed., *Greek Tragedy and Political Theory* (Berkeley and Los Angeles: University of California Press, 1986), p. 23.
10. Euben, (1986), *Greek Tragedy and Political Theory*, p. 29.
11. J.-P.Vernant, *Tragedy and Myth in Ancient Greece* (Brighton: Harvester Press, 1981), p. 9.
12. Vernant, *Tragedy and Myth in Ancient Greece*, pp. 9 and 10.
13. S. Goldhill, 'Collectivity and Otherness – The Authority of the Tragic Chorus', in *Tragedy and the Tragic: Greek Theatre and Beyond*, ed. M. S. Silk (Oxford: Clarendon Press, 1996), p. 247.
14. O. Longo, 'The Theater of the Polis', in *Nothing to Do with Dionysos? Athenian Drama in its Social Context*, ed. J. Winkler and F. Zeitlin (Princeton: Princeton University Press, 1990), pp. 12–19 (p. 15).
15. Longo, 'The Theater of the Polis', pp. 16–17.
16. Gould, 'Tragedy and Collective Experience'.
17. Goldhill, 'Collectivity and Otherness'.
18. H. P. Foley, 'Choral Identity in Greek Tragedy', *Classical Philology* 98 (2003), 1–30 (p. 1).
19. Foley, 'Choral Identity in Greek Tragedy', p. 7.
20. Foley, 'Choral Identity in Greek Tragedy', p. 17.
21. Foley, 'Choral Identity in Greek Tragedy', p. 24.
22. J. Lacan, *The Ethics of Psychoanalysis 1959–1960*, ed. J.-A. Miller, Book VII, trans. D. Porter (London: Routledge, 1992), in *Tragedy*, ed. J. Drakakis and N. C. Liebler (London and New York: Longman, 1998), pp. 184–95 (p. 193).
23. F. Schiller, 'On the Use of the Chorus in Tragedy', in *The Bride of Messina, William Tell and Demetrius*, trans. C. E. Passage (New York: Ungar, 1962), p. 6.
24. L. Goldmann, *Racine*, trans. A. Hamilton (Cambridge: Rivers Press, 1972), p. 13.
25. Schiller, 'On the Use of the Chorus in Tragedy', p. 7.
26. Schiller, 'On the Use of the Chorus in Tragedy', p. 7.
27. Schiller, 'On the Use of the Chorus in Tragedy', p. 7.
28. Schiller, 'On the Use of the Chorus in Tragedy', p. 8.
29. Schiller, 'On the Use of the Chorus in Tragedy', pp. 10–11.
30. Schiller, 'On the Use of the Chorus in Tragedy', p. 9.
31. A. W. Schlegel, *A Course of Lectures on Dramatic Art and Literature* (London: Henry G. Bohn, 1846), p. 70.
32. Schlegel, *A Course of Lectures*, p. 69f.
33. Schlegel, *A Course of Lectures*, p. 70.
34. Schlegel, *A Course of Lectures*, p. 70.
35. F. Nietzsche, *The Birth of Tragedy*, trans., with commentary, by W. Kaufmann (New York: Random House, 1967), p. 59.
36. Nietzsche, *The Birth of Tragedy*, p. 57.
37. Nietzsche, *The Birth of Tragedy*, p. 57.
38. Nietzsche, *The Birth of Tragedy*, p. 58.
39. Schlegel, *A Course of Lectures*, p. 70.

40. Schlegel, *A Course of Lectures*, p. 70f.
41. Schlegel, *A Course of Lectures*, p. 71.
42. Schlegel, *A Course of Lectures*, p. 71.
43. Foley, 'Envisioning the Tragic Chorus', p. 353.
44. Foley, 'Envisioning the Tragic Chorus', p. 354.
45. Foley, 'Envisioning the Tragic Chorus', p. 359.
46. Foley, 'Envisioning the Tragic Chorus', p. 358.
47. Foley, 'Envisioning the Tragic Chorus', pp. 358–9.
48. Foley, 'Envisioning the Tragic Chorus', p. 359.
49. Foley, 'Envisioning the Tragic Chorus', p. 360.
50. Foley, 'Envisioning the Tragic Chorus', p. 361.
51. Foley, 'Envisioning the Tragic Chorus', p. 363.
52. V. Lambropoulos, 'Greek Chorus in 09', *Journal of Modern Greek Studies*, 28.2 (2010), 277–84.
53. H. C. Montgomery, 'Some Later Uses of the Greek Tragic Chorus', *The Classical Journal* 38.3 (1942), 148–60.
54. T. Ferguson, 'Bonfire Night in Thomas Hardy's *The Return of the Native*', *Nineteenth-Century Literature* 67.1 (2012), 87–107 (p. 100).
55. C. Reed Anderson, 'Time, Space, and Perspective in Thomas Hardy', *Nineteenth-Century Fiction* 9.3 (1954), 192–208 (p. 206).
56. C. M. Jackson-Houlston, 'Thomas Hardy's Use of Traditional Song', *Nineteenth-Century Literature* 44.3 (1989), 301–34 (p. 332).

CHAPTER THREE: THE TRAGIC HERO

1. Aristotle, *Poetics in Classical Literary Criticism*, ed. D. A. Russell and M. Winterbottom (Oxford: Oxford University Press, 1991), p. 59.
2. S. Zink, 'The Novel as a Medium of Modern Tragedy', *The Journal of Aesthetics and Art Criticism* 17.2 (1958), 169–73 (p. 169).
3. A. C. Bradley, *Shakespearean Tragedy* (Harmondsworth: Penguin, 1991), pp. 24–5.
4. Bradley, *Shakespearean Tragedy*, p. 29.
5. Bradley, *Shakespearean Tragedy*, p. 25.
6. R. Felski, ed., *Rethinking Tragedy* (Baltimore and London: Johns Hopkins University Press, 2008), p. 7.
7. B. M. W. Knox, *The Heroic Temper: Studies in Sophoclean Tragedy* (Berkeley and Los Angeles: University of California Press, 1964), p. 1.
8. Knox, *The Heroic Temper*, p. 3.
9. Knox, *The Heroic Temper*, p. 5.
10. M. Gellrich, *Tragedy and Theory: The Problem of Conflict since Aristotle* (Princeton: Princeton University Press 1988), p. 256.
11. Gellrich, *Tragedy and Theory*, p. 246.
12. Knox, *The Heroic Temper*, p. 33.
13. Knox, *The Heroic Temper*, p. 36.
14. G. Braden, *Renaissance Tragedy and the Senecan Tradition: Anger's Privilege* (New Haven and London: Yale University Press, 1985), p. 28.
15. Braden, *Renaissance Tragedy*, p. 39.
16. L. Bamber, *Comic Women, Tragic Men: A Study of Gender and Genre in Shakespeare* (Stanford: Stanford University Press, 1982), pp. 22–23.
17. R. Williams, *Modern Tragedy* (London: Chatto & Windus, 1966), p. 55.
18. C. Segal, 'Greek Tragedy and Society: A Structuralist Perspective', in *Greek Tragedy and Political Theory*, ed. J. P. Euben (Berkeley and Los Angeles: University of California Press, 1986), p. 47f.
19. J. Dollimore, *Radical Tragedy: Religion, Ideology and Power in the Drama of Shakespeare and His Contemporaries* (first publ. 1984; Hemel Hempstead: Harvester Wheatsheaf, 1989), p. 269.

20. C. Belsey, *The Subject of Tragedy: Identity and Difference in Renaissance Drama* (London and New York: Methuen, 1985), p. 223.
21. Belsey, *Subject of Tragedy*, p. 40.
22. Belsey, *Subject of Tragedy*, p. 42.
23. Belsey, *Subject of Tragedy*, p. 42.
24. Belsey, *Subject of Tragedy*, p. 164.
25. Belsey, *Subject of Tragedy*, p. 56.
26. Segal, 'Greek Tragedy and Society', p. 51.
27. Belsey, *Subject of Tragedy*, p. 43.
28. Braden, *Renaissance Tragedy*, p. 33.
29. Belsey, *Subject of Tragedy*, p. 35.
30. J. Gould, 'Tragedy and Collective Experience', in *Tragedy and the Tragic: Greek Theatre and Beyond*, ed. M. S. Silk (Oxford: Clarendon Press, 1996), p. 222.
31. F. Macintosh, 'Tragic Last Words: The Big Speech and the Lament in Ancient Greek and Modern Irish Tragic Drama', in *Tragedy and the Tragic: Greek Theatre and Beyond*, ed. M. S. Silk (Oxford: Clarendon Press, 1996), p. 419.
32. T. S. Eliot, 'Shakespeare and the Stoicism of Seneca', *Selected Essays 1917–1932* (London: Faber, 1991), pp. 126–40 (p. 129).
33. Eliot, 'Shakespeare and the Stoicism of Seneca', pp. 130–1.
34. R. Padel, *In and Out of the Mind: Greek Images of the Tragic Self* (Princeton: Princeton University Press, 1992), p. 12.
35. Padel, *In and Out of the Mind*, pp. 48–9.
36. Other scholars, such as David Hillman, have been interested in classical constructions of mind and body as interconnected, and in the significance of this idea for our reading of early modern English drama. See D. Hillman, *Shakespeare's Entrails: Belief, Scepticism and the Interior of the Body* (Basingstoke: Palgrave Macmillan, 2007).
37. G. Steiner, '"Tragedy," Reconsidered', in *Rethinking Tragedy*, ed. R. Felski (Baltimore and London: Johns Hopkins University Press, 2008), p. 37.
38. Aristotle, *Poetics*, pp. 52–3, 56.
39. For discussion of the ambiguity of these terms in the Greek, see H. A. Kelly, *Ideas and Forms of Tragedy from Aristotle to the Middle Ages* (Cambridge: Cambridge University Press, 1993), pp. 1–5.
40. Donatus, 'De Fabula: Excerpta De Comoedia', IV. ii, in *Aeli Donati Commentum Terenti*, ed. P. Wessner (Stuttgart: Teubner, 1967) (translation mine).
41. P. Sidney, 'The Defence of Poetry', in *English Renaissance Literary Criticism*, ed. B. Vickers (Oxford: Oxford University Press, 1999), p. 383.
42. Bradley, *Shakespearean Tragedy*, p. 26.
43. R. Nevo, 'Tragic Form in *Romeo and Juliet*', *Studies in English Literature, 1500–1900* 9.2 (1969), 241–58 (p. 243).
44. Bradley, *Shakespearean Tragedy*, p. 35.
45. G. W. F. Hegel, *Aesthetics: Lectures on Fine Art*, trans. T. M. Knox (Oxford: Clarendon Press, 1975), vol. 2, pp. 1194–5. All further quotations are taken from this edition unless otherwise stated.
46. G. Lukács, *The Theory of the Novel* (London: Merlin Press, 1971), p. 67.
47. J. King, *Tragedy in the Victorian Novel: Theory and Practice in the Novels of George Eliot, Thomas Hardy and Henry James* (Cambridge: Cambridge University Press, 1978), p. 3.
48. G. Steiner, *The Death of Tragedy* (London: Faber, 1963), p. 274.
49. W. Benjamin, *The Origin of German Tragic Drama*, trans. J. Osborne (London: Verso, 1985). Excerpted in *Tragedy*, ed. J. Drakakis and N. C. Liebler (London and New York: Longman, 1998), p. 112. For further discussion of Benjamin's project in this text, see P. Szondi, *An Essay on the Tragic* (Stanford: Stanford University Press, 2002), pp. 49–51.
50. Benjamin, *Origin of German Tragic Drama*, p. 113.
51. Benjamin, *Origin of German Tragic Drama*, p. 113.

52. Williams, *Modern Tragedy*, p. 49.
53. Williams, *Modern Tragedy*, p. 50.
54. A. Miller, 'Tragedy and the Common Man', in *The Theater Essays of Arthur Miller*, ed. R. A. Martin (Viking Press: New York, 1978), pp. 3–7 (p. 5). The essay was first published in the *New York Times*, 27 February 1949. Martin notes (p. 3) that the essay appeared shortly after the opening of Miller's *Death of a Salesman* at the Morosco Theatre on 10 February 1949.
55. Miller, 'Common Man', p. 3.
56. Felski, *Rethinking Tragedy*, p. 9.
57. Miller, 'Common Man', p. 4.
58. Miller, 'Common Man', pp. 4–5.
59. Miller, 'Common Man', pp. 5–6.
60. Miller, 'Common Man', p. 6.
61. Bradley, *Shakespearean Tragedy*, p. 28.
62. Aristotle, *Poetics*, p. 66.
63. L. T. Fitz, 'Egyptian Queens and Male Reviewers: Sexist Attitudes in *Antony and Cleopatra* Criticism', *Shakespeare Quarterly* 28.3 (1977), 297–316 (p. 313).
64. Bradley, *Shakespearean Tragedy*, p. 28.
65. Bradley, *Shakespearean Tragedy*, p. 36.
66. S. Kierkegaard, *Either/Or*, trans. A. Hannay (Harmondsworth: Penguin Books, 1992), p. 143. Pelagius, active in the fourth century AD, advocated a doctrine of free will which asserted that man was capable of goodness independent of God's grace.
67. Kierkegaard, *Either/Or*, p. 143.
68. G. W. F. Hegel, 'Tragedy as a Dramatic Art', in *Tragedy*, ed. J. Drakakis and N. C. Liebler (London and New York: Longman, 1998), pp. 23–52 (pp. 40–1).
69. Hegel, 'Tragedy as a Dramatic Art', p. 41.
70. K. Jaspers, *Tragedy Is Not Enough* (London: Victor Gollancz, 1953), p. 52.
71. Jaspers, *Tragedy Is Not Enough*, p. 52.
72. Jaspers, *Tragedy Is Not Enough*, p. 53.
73. Jaspers, *Tragedy Is Not Enough*, p. 53.
74. Jaspers, *Tragedy Is Not Enough*, p. 54.
75. Jaspers, *Tragedy Is Not Enough*, p. 55.
76. Jaspers, *Tragedy Is Not Enough*, p. 56.
77. Steiner, '"Tragedy," Reconsidered', p. 33.
78. Steiner, '"Tragedy," Reconsidered', pp. 30–1.
79. P. Hammond, *The Strangeness of Tragedy* (Oxford: Oxford University Press, 2009).
80. S. Freud, 'The "Uncanny"', in *The Standard Edition of the Complete Psychological Works of Sigmund Freud*, ed. J. Strachey et al., 24 vols (London: Hogarth Press, 1953–74), vol. 17, pp. 220–6.
81. A. Boal, *Theater of the Oppressed*, trans. C. A. and M.-O. Leal McBride (London: Pluto Press, 1979), 28.
82. Boal, *Theater of the Oppressed*, p. 19.
83. M. Nussbaum, *The Fragility of Goodness: Luck and Ethics in Greek Tragedy and Philosophy* (Cambridge: Cambridge University Press, 2001), p. 387.

CHAPTER FOUR: TRAGIC WOMEN

1. C. Belsey, *The Subject of Tragedy: Identity and Difference in Renaissance Drama* (London and New York: Methuen, 1985), p. ix.
2. H. P. Foley, *Female Acts in Greek Tragedy* (Princeton: Princeton University Press, 2001), p. 3.
3. M. Shaw, 'The Female Intruder: Women in Fifth Century Drama', *Classical Philology* 70.4 (1975), 255–66 (p. 256).

4. R. Rehm, '"If You are a Woman": Theatrical Womanizing in Sophocles' *Antigone* and Fugard, Kani, and Ntshona's *The Island*', in *Classics in Post-Colonial Worlds*, ed. L. Hardwick and C. Gillespie (Oxford: Oxford University Press, 2007), pp. 211–27 (p. 212).
5. See, for example, J. Butler, *Gender Trouble: Feminism and the Subversion of Identity* (New York and London: Routledge, 1990).
6. Foley, *Female Acts*, pp. 335–6.
7. Foley, *Female* Acts, p. 336.
8. F. I. Zeitlin, 'Playing the Other: Theater, Theatricality, and the Feminine in Greek Drama', in *Nothing to Do with Dionysos? Athenian Drama in Its Social Context*, ed. J. Winkler and F. Zeitlin (Princeton: Princeton University Press, 1990), p. 69 (note 13).
9. Zeitlin, 'Other', p. 67.
10. Zeitlin, 'Other', p. 64.
11. Zeitlin 'Other', p. 67.
12. Zeitlin 'Other', p. 69.
13. Zeitlin 'Other', p. 77. For one of the best studies of entrances and exits in Greek tragedy, and the way that figures such as Clytaemnestra exert control over the dramatic space, see O. Taplin, *The Stagecraft of Aeschylus: The Dramatic Use of Entrances and Exits in Greek Tragedy* (Oxford: Clarendon Press, 1977).
14. L. Hopkins, *The Female Hero in English Renaissance Tragedy* (Basingstoke: Palgrave Macmillan, 2002), p. 3.
15. J. Dollimore, *Radical Tragedy: Religion, Ideology and Power in the Drama of Shakespeare and His Contemporaries* (Hemel Hempstead: Harvester Wheatsheaf, 1989), p. 240.
16. A. C. Bradley, *Shakespearean Tragedy* (Harmondsworth: Penguin, 1991), p. 186.
17. Bradley, *Shakespearean Tragedy*, p. 191.
18. L. T. Fitz, 'Egyptian Queens and Male Reviewers: Sexist Attitudes in *Antony and Cleopatra* Criticism', *Shakespeare Quarterly* 28.3 (1977), 297–316 (p. 297).
19. Fitz, 'Egyptian Queens', p. 307.
20. Fitz, 'Egyptian Queens', p. 298.
21. D. Callaghan, *Shakespeare without Women: Representing Gender and Race on the Renaissance Stage* (London: Routledge, 2000), p. 11f.
22. L. Bamber, *Comic Women, Tragic Men: A Study of Gender and Genre in Shakespeare* (Stanford: Stanford University Press, 1982), p. 6.
23. Bamber, *Comic Women, Tragic Men*, p. 8.
24. Bamber, *Comic Women, Tragic Men*, p. 2.
25. Bamber, *Comic Women, Tragic Men*, p. 15.
26. Bamber, *Comic Women, Tragic Men*, p. 19.
27. E. Showalter, 'Representing Ophelia: Women, Madness, and the Responsibilities of Feminist Criticism', in *Shakespeare and the Question of Theory*, ed. P. Parker and G. Hartman (London: Methuen, 1985). Showalter is responding to J. Lacan, 'Desire and the Interpretation of Desire in *Hamlet*', in *Literature and Psychoanalysis: The Question of Reading: Otherwise*, ed. S. Felman (Baltimore: Johns Hopkins University Press, 1982). Showalter points out that etymology of Ophelia is incorrect.
28. Showalter, 'Representing Ophelia', p. 78.
29. Showalter, 'Representing Ophelia', p. 79.
30. Here Showalter is referring to G. Bachelard, *L'Eau et les rêves* (Paris: José Corti, 1942), pp. 109–25.
31. Showalter, 'Representing Ophelia', p. 82.
32. P. Berry, *Shakespeare's Feminine Endings: Disfiguring Death in the Tragedies* (London and New York: Routledge, 1999). For our earlier discussion of Neill's work, see Chapter 1.
33. Berry, *Shakespeare's Feminine Endings*, p. 5.
34. Berry, *Shakespeare's Feminine Endings*, pp. 6–7. For further discussion of the religious and intellectual crisis to which Berry refers, see Chapter 1.
35. Berry, *Shakespeare's Feminine Endings*, pp. 26, 27.

36. Berry, *Shakespeare's Feminine Endings*, p. 28.
37. J. Gould, 'Tragedy and Collective Experience', in *Tragedy and the Tragic: Greek Theatre and Beyond*, ed. M. S. Silk (Oxford: Clarendon Press, 1996), p. 222.
38. Foley, *Female Acts*, p. 334.
39. Foley, *Female Acts*, p. 4.
40. Foley, *Female Acts*, p. 337.
41. N. Loraux, *Tragic Ways of Killing a Woman*, trans. A. Forster (Cambridge, MA: Harvard University Press, 1987).
42. Loraux, *Tragic Ways*, p. 3.
43. Loraux, *Tragic Ways*, p. 8.
44. Loraux, *Tragic Ways*, p. 13.
45. Loraux, *Tragic Ways*, p. 23.
46. Loraux, *Tragic Ways*, p. 47.
47. Loraux, *Tragic Ways*, p. 48.
48. Hopkins, *The Female Hero*, p. 2.
49. Hopkins, *The Female Hero*, p. 3.
50. N. C. Liebler, ed., *The Female Tragic Hero in English Renaissance Drama* (Basingstoke: Palgrave, 2002), p. 2.
51. Liebler, *The Female Tragic Hero*, p. 11.
52. Liebler, *The Female Tragic Hero*, p. 11.
53. G. Steiner, *Antigones* (Oxford: Oxford University Press, 1984), p. 199.
54. B. Honig, *Antigone, Interrupted* (Cambridge: Cambridge University Press, 2013), p. 6.
55. M. Arnold, *The Poems of Matthew Arnold*, ed. K. Allott (London: Longmans, Green and Co., 1965), p. 603.
56. G. Joseph, 'The *Antigone* as Cultural Touchstone: Matthew Arnold, Hegel, George Eliot, Virginia Woolf, and Margaret Drabble', *Proceedings of the Modern Language Association* 96.1 (1981), 22–35 (p. 23).
57. Joseph, 'The *Antigone* as Cultural Touchstone', p. 32. The term 'Doing as One Likes' is a reference taken from Arnold's *Culture and Anarchy* (1869).
58. G. Eliot, 'The *Antigone* and Its Moral', *Selected Critical Writings*, ed. R. Ashton (Oxford: Oxford University Press, 1992), p. 243.
59. Eliot, 'The *Antigone* and Its Moral', p. 244.
60. Eliot, 'The *Antigone* and Its Moral', p. 245.
61. Joseph, 'The *Antigone* as Cultural Touchstone', p. 28.
62. V. Woolf, 'Three Guineas', in *A Room of One's Own and Three Guineas*, ed. M. Siach (Oxford: Oxford University Press, 1992), p. 272. In the Greek text, the line from *Antigone* consists of five words.
63. Steiner, *Antigones*, p. 10.
64. B. M.W. Knox, *The Heroic Temper: Studies in Sophoclean Tragedy* (Berkeley and Los Angeles: University of California Press, 1964), p. 62.
65. Knox, *The Heroic Temper*, p. 85.
66. H. Foley, 'Antigone as Moral Agent', in *Tragedy and the Tragic: Greek Theatre and Beyond*, ed. M. S. Silk (Oxford: Clarendon Press, 1996), pp. 49–73 (p. 49).
67. Foley, 'Antigone as Moral Agent', p. 57.
68. Foley, 'Antigone as Moral Agent', p. 57.
69. Foley, 'Antigone as Moral Agent', p. 58.
70. C. Sourvinou-Inwood, 'Assumptions and the Creation of Meaning: Reading Sophocles' *Antigone*', *The Journal of Hellenic Studies* 109 (1989), 134–48.
71. Sourvinou-Inwood, 'Assumptions', p. 148.
72. P. Holt, '*Polis* and Tragedy in the *Antigone*', *Mnemosyne*, Fourth Series, vol. 52, fasc. 6 (1999), 658–90 (p. 658).
73. J. Butler, *Antigone's Claim: Kinship Between Life and Death* (New York: Columbia University Press, 2000).

74. Butler, *Antigone's Claim*, p. 6.
75. Butler, *Antigone's Claim*, p. 24.
76. Honig, *Antigone, Interrupted*, p. 23f.
77. S. Freud, 'Mourning and Melancholia', in *The Standard Edition of the Complete Psychological Works of Sigmund Freud*, ed. J. Strachey et al., 24 vols (London: Hogarth Press, 1953–74), vol. 14, pp. 243–60.
78. M. Sanders, 'Ambiguities of Mourning: Law, Custom, and Testimony of Women before South Africa's Truth and Reconciliation Commission', in *Loss: The Politics of Mourning*, ed. D. L. Eng and D. Kazanjian (Berkeley and Los Angeles: University of California Press, 2003), pp. 77–98.
79. Honig, *Antigone, Interrupted*, p. 90.

CHAPTER FIVE: TRAGIC DUALITIES

1. J. W. Goethe, Letter of 6 June 1824 to Chancellor Müller. Cited in A. Lesky, *Greek Tragedy*, trans. H. A. Frankfort (London: Ernest Benn, 1978), p. 8.
2. R. Williams, *Modern Tragedy* (London: Chatto & Windus, 1966), p. 189.
3. C. Segal, 'Greek Tragedy and Society: A Structuralist Perspective', in *Greek Tragedy and Political Theory*, ed. J. P. Euben (Berkeley and Los Angeles: University of California Press, 1986), p. 57.
4. J.-P. Vernant, *Tragedy and Myth in Ancient Greece* (Brighton: Harvester Press, 1981), p. 10.
5. S. Goldhill, 'Collectivity and Otherness – The Authority of the Tragic Chorus', in *Tragedy and the Tragic: Greek Theatre and Beyond*, ed. M. S. Silk (Oxford: Clarendon Press, 1996), pp. 248–51.
6. M. Gellrich, *Tragedy and Theory: The Problem of Conflict since Aristotle* (Princeton: Princeton University Press, 1988).
7. Gellrich, *Tragedy and Theory*, p. 10.
8. Gellrich, *Tragedy and Theory*, p. 244.
9. Evanthius, IV.ii (translation mine).
10. J. W. Meeker, 'The Comic Mode', in *The Ecocriticism Reader: Landmarks in Literary Ecology*, ed. C. Glotfelty and H. Fromm (Athens, GA: University of Georgia Press, 1996).
11. G. Steiner, *Antigones* (Oxford: Oxford University Press, 1984), p. 231.
12. Steiner, *Antigones*, p. 232.
13. L. Bamber, *Comic Women, Tragic Men: A Study of Gender and Genre in Shakespeare* (Stanford: Stanford University Press, 1982), p. 5.
14. M. Shaw, 'The Female Intruder: Women in Fifth-Century Drama', *Classical Philology* 70.4 (1975), 255–66 (pp. 256–7).
15. Shaw, 'The Female Intruder', pp. 265–6.
16. H. P. Foley, 'The "Female Intruder" Reconsidered: Women in Aristophanes *Lysistrata* and *Ecclesiazusae*', *Classical Philology* 77.1 (1982), 1–21 (p. 2).
17. Foley, 'The "Female Intruder" Reconsidered', p. 3.
18. F. I. Zeitlin, 'Thebes: Theater of Self and Society in Athenian Drama', in *Nothing to Do with Dionysos? Athenian Drama in its Social Context*, ed. J. Winkler and F. Zeitlin (Princeton: Princeton University Press, 1990), pp. 130–67 (p. 131).
19. Zeitlin, 'Thebes', pp. 144–5.
20. Zeitlin, 'Thebes', p. 131.
21. E. Hall, *Inventing the Barbarian: Greek Self-Definition through Tragedy* (Oxford: Clarendon Press, 1989), p. 4.
22. Hall, *Inventing the Barbarian*, p. 1.
23. Hall, *Inventing the Barbarian*, p. 57.
24. Hall, *Inventing the Barbarian*, p. 71.
25. N. Rabkin, *Shakespeare and the Common Understanding* (Chicago: University of Chicago Press, 1984).

26. Rabkin, *Common Understanding*, p. 22.
27. Rabkin, *Common Understanding*, p. 27.
28. Rabkin, *Common Understanding*, p. 30.
29. B. McElroy, *Shakespeare's Mature Tragedies* (Princeton: Princeton University Press, 1973).
30. McElroy, *Shakespeare's Mature Tragedies*, p. 10.
31. McElroy, *Shakespeare's Mature Tragedies* p. 12.
32. McElroy, *Shakespeare's Mature Tragedies* p. 13.
33. T. McAlindon, *Shakespeare's Tragic Cosmos* (Cambridge: Cambridge University Press, 1991), p. 6.
34. McAlindon, *Shakespeare's Tragic Cosmos*, p. 134.
35. McAlindon, *Shakespeare's Tragic Cosmos*, p. xiii.
36. McAlindon, *Shakespeare's Tragic Cosmos*, p. 3.
37. E. M. W. Tillyard formulated an influential account of a cosmic Chain of Being in *The Elizabethan World Picture* (London: Chatto & Windus, 1943).
38. N. Grene, *Shakespeare's Tragic Imagination* (Basingstoke: Macmillan, 1992), p. ix.
39. Grene, *Shakespeare's Tragic Imagination*, p. 12.
40. Grene, *Shakespeare's Tragic Imagination*, p. 62.
41. Grene, *Shakespeare's Tragic Imagination*, p. 63.
42. Grene, *Shakespeare's Tragic Imagination*, p. 63.
43. On the influence of Darwin on the nineteenth-century novel, see G. Beer, *Darwin's Plots: Evolutionary Narrative in Darwin, George Eliot and Nineteenth-Century Fiction* (London: Routledge & Kegan Paul, 1983).
44. Meeker, 'The Comic Mode', p. 164.
45. A. Strindberg, 'Preface to *Miss Julie*', in *Plays: One*, trans. and introduced by M. Meyer (London: Methuen Drama, 1989), p. 92.
46. Strindberg, 'Preface', p. 97.
47. Strindberg, 'Preface', p. 97.
48. Strindberg, 'Preface', p. 96.
49. Strindberg, 'Preface', p. 96.
50. G. W. F. Hegel, *Aesthetics: Lectures on Fine Art*, trans. T. M. Knox (Oxford: Clarendon Press, 1975), vol. 2, p. 1196.
51. Hegel, *Aesthetics*, p. 1197.
52. Hegel, *Aesthetics*, p. 1197.
53. Hegel, 'Tragedy as a Dramatic Art', in *Tragedy*, ed. J. Drakakis and N. C. Liebler (London and New York: Longman, 1998), p. 41.
54. Hegel, *Aesthetics*, p. 1217.
55. Hegel, *Aesthetics*, pp. 1217–18.
56. F. Nietzsche, *The Birth of Tragedy*, trans., with commentary, by W. Kaufmann (New York: Random House, 1967), p. 42.
57. M. S. Silk and J. P. Stern, *Nietzsche on Tragedy* (Cambridge: Cambridge University Press, 1981), p. 266.
58. Silk and Stern, *Nietzsche on Tragedy*, p. 270.
59. Nietzsche, *Birth of Tragedy*, p. 55.
60. Nietzsche, *Birth of Tragedy*, p. 36.
61. Nietzsche, *Birth of Tragedy*, p. 37.
62. Silk and Stern, *Nietzsche on Tragedy*, p. 267.
63. C. Segal, *Dionysiac Poetics and Euripides' Bacchae* (Princeton: Princeton University Press, 1982), p. 8.
64. Segal, *Dionysiac Poetics*, p. 12.
65. Segal, *Dionysiac Poetics*, p. 13.
66. Segal, *Dionysiac Poetics*, p. 14.
67. Segal, *Dionysiac Poetics*, p. 160, p.165.
68. The principal work on which Segal draws is P. Vidal-Naquet, 'The Black Hunter and the Origin of the Athenian Ephebeia', *Proceedings of the Cambridge Philological Society* 194 (1968), 49–64.

NOTES 161

CHAPTER SIX: TRAGIC PLEASURE
1. T. Eagleton, *Sweet Violence: The Idea of the Tragic* (Oxford: Blackwell, 2003), pp. 168–9.
2. A. D. Nuttall, *Why Does Tragedy Give Pleasure?* (Oxford: Clarendon Press, 1996), p. 6.
3. Eagleton, *Sweet Violence*, pp. 153–4.
4. See B. Weinberg, *A History of Literary Criticism in the Italian Renaissance*, 2 vols (Chicago: Chicago University Press, 1961), vol. 1, pp. 521, 543, 316.
5. P. Sidney, 'The Defence of Poetry', in *English Renaissance Literary Criticism*, ed. B. Vickers (Oxford: Oxford University Press, 1999), p. 363.
6. Aristotle, *Poetics in Classical Literary Criticism*, ed. D. A. Russell and M. Winterbottom (Oxford: Oxford University Press, 1991), p. 67 (translation mine).
7. For discussion of Euripidean happy-ending tragedy, see A. Pippin Burnett, *Catastrophe Survived: Euripides' Plays of Mixed Reversal* (Oxford: Clarendon Press, 1971), and B. Knox, 'Euripidean Comedy', *Word and Action: Essays on the Ancient Theater* (Baltimore: Johns Hopkins University Press, 1979), pp. 250–74.
8. Nuttall, *Why Does Tragedy Give Pleasure?*, p. 1.
9. D. Hume, 'Of Tragedy', *Essays Moral, Political, and Literary*, ed. E. F. Miller (Indianapolis: Liberty Classics, 1987), pp. 217–18.
10. Eagleton, *Sweet Violence*, p. 169.
11. Hume, 'Of Tragedy', p. 220.
12. Hume, 'Of Tragedy', p. 221.
13. Hume, 'Of Tragedy', p. 222.
14. F. Schiller, 'On the Art of Tragedy', *Essays*, ed. W. Hinderer and D. O. Dahlstrom (New York: Continuum, 1993) (translation mine).
15. For discussion of Freud's reading of Greek tragedy and Shakespeare, see N. Ray, *Tragedy and Otherness: Sophocles, Shakespeare, Psychoanalysis* (Bern: Peter Lang, 2009). Ray is particularly concerned in this book with Jean Laplanche's reformulation of Freud's seduction theory, something which Freud abandoned in 1897.
16. S. Freud, 'Beyond the Pleasure Principle', in *On Metapsychology: The Theory of Psychoanalysis*, ed. A. Richards and J. Strachey (Harmondsworth: Penguin, 1984).
17. The term 'Mithridatic' refers to Mithridates VI, King of Pontus, who was said to have developed an immunity to poison by deliberately ingesting small quantities of it on a regular basis. On the Mithridatic account of tragedy, see L. Trilling, 'Freud and Literature', in *The Liberal Imagination: Essays on Literature and Society* (Harmondsworth: Penguin, 1970), pp. 47–68.
18. F. Macintosh, 'Tragic Last Words: The Big Speech and the Lament in Ancient Greek and Modern Irish Tragic Drama', in *Tragedy and the Tragic: Greek Theatre and Beyond*, ed. M. S. Silk (Oxford: Clarendon Press, 1996), pp. 414–25 (p. 423).
19. Aristotle, *Poetics*, p. 57.
20. Nuttall, *Why Does Tragedy Give Pleasure?*, pp. 5–15.
21. Nuttall, *Why Does Tragedy Give Pleasure?*, p. 36.
22. M. Nussbaum, *The Fragility of Goodness: Luck and Ethics in Greek Tragedy and Philosophy* (Cambridge: Cambridge University Press, 2001), p. 389.
23. Nussbaum, *Fragility of Goodness*, p. 389.
24. Nuttall, *Why Does Tragedy Give Pleasure?*, p. 14.
25. Nuttall, *Why Does Tragedy Give Pleasure?*, p. 6.
26. Nussbaum, *Fragility of Goodness*, pp. 388–91. See L. Golden, 'Catharsis', *Transactions and Proceedings of the Philological Association of America* 93 (1962), 51–60 (pp. 56–7).
27. Golden, 'Catharsis', p. 58.
28. Nussbaum, *Fragility of Goodness*, p. 391.
29. J. Lear, 'Katharsis', in *Essays on Aristotle's Poetics*, ed. A. O. Rorty (Princeton: Princeton University Press, 1992), pp. 315–40 (pp. 320–1).
30. E. Schaper, 'Aristotle's Catharsis and Aesthetic Pleasure', *The Philosophical Quarterly* 18 (1968), 131–43 (p. 135).
31. S. Halliwell, *Aristotle's Poetics* (London: Duckworth, 1998), pp. 198–9.

162 NOTES

32. G. Guarini, 'The Compendium of Tragicomic Poetry', in *Literary Criticism: Plato to Dryden*, ed. A. H. Gilbert (Detroit: Wayne State University Press, 1962), p. 518.
33. Lear, 'Katharsis', pp. 320–1.
34. Lear, 'Katharsis', p. 334.
35. A. Boal, *Theater of the Oppressed*, trans. C. A. and M.-O. Leal McBride (London: Pluto Press, 1979), p. 27.
36. Boal, *Theater of the Oppressed*, p. 27.
37. Boal, *Theater of the Oppressed*, p. 46.
38. Boal, *Theater of the Oppressed*, p. 47.
39. Boal, *Theater of the Oppressed*, p. 40.
40. Boal, *Theater of the Oppressed*, p. 47.
41. G. F. Else, *Aristotle's Poetics: The Argument* (Cambridge, MA: Harvard University Press, 1957), p. 299.
42. Else, *Aristotle's Poetics*, p. 439.
43. C. Segal, 'Catharsis, Audience, and Closure in Greek Tragedy', in *Tragedy and the Tragic: Greek Theatre and Beyond*, ed. M. S. Silk (Oxford: Clarendon Press, 1996), pp. 149–81 (p. 163).
44. Nuttall, *Why Does Tragedy Give Pleasure?*, p. 39.
45. G. W. F. Hegel, *Aesthetics: Lectures on Fine Art*, trans. T. M. Knox (Oxford: Clarendon Press, 1975), p. 1197.
46. Hegel, *Aesthetics*, p. 1197.
47. Hegel, *Aesthetics*, p. 1198.
48. Hegel, *Aesthetics*, p. 1198.
49. N. Brooke, *Horrid Laughter in Jacobean Tragedy* (London: Open Books, 1979), p. 3.
50. Brooke, *Horrid Laughter*, p. 3.
51. Brooke, *Horrid Laughter*, p. 5.
52. Brooke, *Horrid Laughter*, p. 7. *Gorboduc* is the earliest English tragedy in blank verse. It was written by Thomas Sackville and Thomas Norton and performed in 1561. See also Sidney's reference to the play in the discussion of dramatic unity in Chapter 7.
53. G. Saunders, *'Love me or kill me': Sarah Kane and the Theatre of Extremes* (Manchester and New York: Manchester University Press, 2002), p. 19.
54. A. Sierz, *In-Yer-Face Theatre: British Drama Today* (London: Faber & Faber Ltd, 2000), p. 10.
55. Sierz, *In-Yer-Face Theatre*, p. 10.
56. Saunders, *'Love me or kill me'*, p. 15. Saunders is quoting reviews of Kane's work by P. Taylor, *Independent*, 20 January 1995 and D. Benedict, *Independent*, 9 May 1998.
57. Quoted in Saunders, *'Love me or kill me'*, p. 15.
58. Quoted in Saunders, *'Love me or kill me'*, p. 29.
59. J. Kott, *Shakespeare Our Contemporary*, trans. B. Taborski (London: Methuen, 1967), p. 104.

CHAPTER SEVEN: TRAGEDY AND FORM

1. Aristotle, *Poetics in Classical Literary Criticism*, ed. D. A. Russell and M. Winterbottom (Oxford: Oxford University Press, 1991), p. 57 (translation mine).
2. Aristotle, *Poetics*, p. 66 (translation mine).
3. A. W. Schlegel, *A Course of Lectures on Dramatic Art and Literature.* (London: Henry G. Bohn, 1846), p. 237.
4. On Castelvetro's role in formalising the doctrine of the unities, see H. B. Charlton, *Castelvetro's Theory of Poetry* (Manchester: Manchester University Press, 1913) and B. Weinberg, 'Castelvetro's Theory of Poetics', in *Critics and Criticism*, ed. R. S. Crane (Chicago: University of Chicago Press, 1952).
5. Shakespeare alludes to the doctrine of the unities in several passages in his plays, most notably in *The Winter's Tale* (IV.i. 4–7), where Time playfully apologises for the play's breach

of dramatic unity. Shakespeare is clearly aware of the doctrine of the unities, but – with the exception of *The Comedy of Errors* and *The Tempest* – he chooses not to subscribe to it.
6. P. Sidney, 'The Defence of Poetry', in *English Renaissance Literary Criticism*, ed. B. Vickers (Oxford: Oxford University Press, 1999), p. 381. On *Gorboduc*, see also Brooke's discussion of tragic pleasure and dramatic decorum in Chapter 6. Sidney evidently admires the play, in spite of its failure to conform to dramatic unity.
7. Sidney, Defence of Poetry', p. 382.
8. Sidney, Defence of Poetry', p. 383. Plautus' *Amphitryo* is not generally recognised as a tragicomedy, although Plautus refers to the play as a 'tragicommedia' (apparently a Plautine coinage) in the prologue.
9. L. Goldmann, *Racine*, trans. A. Hamilton (Cambridge: Rivers Press, 1972), p. 19.
10. Goldmann, *Racine*, p. 18.
11. R. Parish, *Racine: The Limits of Tragedy* (Paris, Seattle and Tübingen: Biblio 17: Papers on French Seventeenth Century Literature, 1993), p. 73.
12. Parish, *Racine*, p. 73.
13. L. Wang, 'The "Tragic" Theatre of Corneille', *The French Review* 25.3 (1952), 182–91.
14. Wang, '"Tragic" Theatre of Corneille', p. 190.
15. Wang, '"Tragic" Theatre of Corneille', p. 191.
16. P. Corneille, *Discourse I*, in *Literary Criticism: Plato to Dryden*, ed. A. H. Gilbert (Detroit: Wayne State University Press, 1962), pp. 575–6.
17. Corneille, *Discourse III*, in Gilbert, ed., p. 579.
18. J. Dryden, *An Essay of Dramatic Poesy*, *Literary Criticism: Plato to Dryden*, ed. A. H. Gilbert (Detroit: Wayne State University Press, 1962), p. 607.
19. Schlegel, *A Course of Lectures*, p. 256.
20. Schlegel, *A Course of Lectures*, p. 257.
21. G. Steiner, *The Death of Tragedy* (London: Faber, 1963), p. 46.
22. F. Schiller, 'On the Use of the Chorus in Tragedy', *The Bride of Messina, William Tell and Demetrius*, trans. C. E. Passage (New York: Ungar, 1962), pp. 6–7.
23. Aristotle, *Poetics*, p. 67.
24. J. Milton, *Milton: Complete Shorter Poems*, ed. J. Carey (London: Longman, 1997).
25. One of the best recent studies of closet drama, in this case focusing on that written by women, is M. Straznicky, *Privacy, Playreading, and Women's Closet Drama 1550-1700* (Cambridge: Cambridge University Press, 2004).
26. A. C. Bradley, *Shakespearean Tragedy* (Harmondsworth: Penguin, 1991), p. 25.
27. T. Eagleton, *Sweet Violence: The Idea of the Tragic* (Oxford: Blackwell, 2003), p. 178.
28. Steiner, *Death of Tragedy*, p. 243.
29. Eagleton, *Sweet Violence*, p. 179.
30. J. King, *Tragedy in the Victorian Novel: Theory and Practice in the Novels of George Eliot, Thomas Hardy and Henry James* (Cambridge: Cambridge University Press, 1978).
31. King, p.1. Eagleton, *Sweet Violence*, p. 202, also regards *Clarissa* as a crucial development in the emergence of the tragic novel.
32. King, *Tragedy in the Victorian Novel*, p. 2.
33. P. Brooks, *The Melodramatic Imagination: Balzac, Henry James, Melodrama, and the Mode of Excess* (New Haven and London: Yale University Press, 1976), p. 15.
34. Brooks, *Melodramatic Imagination*, p. 81.
35. King, *Tragedy in the Victorian Novel*, p. 39.
36. D. Mansell, Jr, 'George Eliot's Conception of Tragedy', *Nineteenth-Century Fiction* 22.2 (1967), 155–71.
37. Mansell, 'Eliot's Conception of Tragedy', p. 165.
38. Mansell, 'Eliot's Conception of Tragedy', p. 164.
39. A. Huxley, 'Tragedy and the Whole Truth', *Music at Night, and Other Essays* (London: Chatto & Windus, 1931).
40. Huxley, 'Tragedy and the Whole Truth', p. 10.

164 NOTES

41. Huxley, 'Tragedy and the Whole Truth', pp. 12–13.
42. Huxley, 'Tragedy and the Whole Truth', p. 16.
43. Eagleton, *Sweet Violence*, p. 201.
44. Eagleton, *Sweet Violence*, p. 201.
45. T. R. Spivey, 'Thomas Hardy's Tragic Hero', *Nineteenth-Century Fiction* 9.3 (1954), 179–91 (p. 181).
46. Spivey, 'Hardy's Tragic Hero', p. 181.
47. Spivey, 'Hardy's Tragic Hero', p. 182.
48. Spivey, 'Hardy's Tragic Hero', pp. 185–6.
49. Spivey, 'Hardy's Tragic Hero', p. 188.
50. R. B. Heilman, 'Hardy's Sue Bridehead', *Nineteenth-Century Fiction* 20.4 (1966), 307–23 (p. 315).
51. Heilman, 'Hardy's Sue Bridehead', pp. 316–17.
52. Heilman, 'Hardy's Sue Bridehead', p. 327.

CHAPTER EIGHT: MODERN TRAGEDY

1. A. Camus, 'Lecture Given in Athens on the Future of Tragedy', *Selected Essays and Notebooks*, ed. and trans. P. Thody (Harmondsworth: Penguin, 1970), p. 192.
2. W. Benjamin, *The Work of Art in the Age of Mechanical Reproduction*, trans. J. A. Underwood (Harmondsworth: Penguin, 2008).
3. Benjamin, *Work of Art*, p. 9.
4. Benjamin, *Work of Art*, p. 19.
5. T. W. Adorno and M. Horkheimer, *Dialectic of Enlightenment*, trans. J. Cumming (London and New York: Verso, 1997).
6. B. Brecht, *Brecht on Theatre: The Development of an Aesthetic*, ed. and trans. J. Willett (London: Eyre Methuen, 1974), p. 188.
7. Brecht, *Brecht on Theatre*, p. 183.
8. Camus, 'Lecture', p. 200.
9. Camus, 'Lecture', p. 200.
10. F. Nietzsche, *The Birth of Tragedy*, trans., with commentary, by W. Kaufmann (New York: Random House, 1967), p. 76.
11. Nietzsche, *Birth of Tragedy*, p. 77.
12. Nietzsche, *Birth of Tragedy*, p. 82.
13. A. C. Schlesinger, 'Can We Moderns Write Tragedy?', *Transactions and Proceedings of the American Philological Association* 77 (1946), 1–21.
14. S. Kierkegaard, *Either/Or*, trans. A. Hannay (Harmondsworth: Penguin Books, 1992), p. 142.
15. Kierkegaard, *Either/Or*, p. 146.
16. G. Steiner, *The Death of Tragedy* (London: Faber, 1963), p. 133.
17. One example of this self-conscious form of imitation is Eugene O'Neill's play, *Mourning Becomes Electra* (1931), an adaptation of Aeschylus' *Oresteia*.
18. Steiner, *Death of Tragedy*, p. 292.
19. Steiner, *Death of Tragedy*, p. 293.
20. Steiner, *Death of Tragedy*, p. 314.
21. R. Williams, *Modern Tragedy* (London: Chatto & Windus, 1966), p. 45f.
22. G. Lukács, *The Theory of the Novel* (London: Merlin Press, 1971), p. 87.
23. Williams, *Modern Tragedy*, p. 53.
24. Williams, *Modern Tragedy*, p. 54.
25. Williams, *Modern Tragedy*, p. 62.
26. T. Eagleton, *Sweet Violence: The Idea of the Tragic* (Oxford: Blackwell, 2003), p. 206.
27. R. Felski, *Rethinking Tragedy* (Baltimore and London: Johns Hopkins University Press, 2008), p. 3.
28. A. Miller, 'The Nature of Tragedy', from *The Theater Essays of Arthur Miller*, ed. R. A. Martin (Viking Press: New York, 1978), p. 9.

29. A. Poole, *Tragedy: A Very Short Introduction* (Oxford: Oxford University Press, 2005), p. 3.
30. Felski, *Rethinking Tragedy*, p. 11.
31. Felski, *Rethinking Tragedy*, p. 14.
32. P. Szondi, *An Essay on the Tragic* (Stanford: Stanford University Press, 2002), p. 55.

CHAPTER NINE: POSTCOLONIAL AND MULTIETHNIC TRAGEDY

1. L. Hardwick and C. Gillespie, eds, *Classics in Post-Colonial Worlds* (Oxford: Oxford University Press, 2007).
2. K. Wetmore, Jr, *Black Dionysus: Greek Tragedy and African American Theatre* (Jefferson, NC and London: McFarland, 2003), p. 7.
3. J. Djisenu, 'Cross-Cultural Bonds Between Ancient Greece and Africa: Implications for Contemporary Staging Practices', in *Classics in Post-Colonial Worlds*, ed. L. Hardwick and C. Gillespie (Oxford: Oxford University Press, 2007), pp. 72–85 (p. 73).
4. Djisenu, 'Cross-Cultural Bonds', p. 79.
5. A. Loomba, *Shakespeare, Race, and Colonialism* (Oxford: Oxford University Press, 2002), p. 2.
6. Loomba, *Shakespeare*, p. 15.
7. Loomba, *Shakespeare*, p. 31.
8. Loomba, *Shakespeare*, p. 31.
9. M. McDonald, 'The Irish and Greek Tragedy', in *Amid Our Troubles: Irish Versions of Greek Tragedy*, ed. M. McDonald and J. M. Walton (London: Methuen, 2002), pp. 37–86.
10. McDonald, 'Irish and Greek Tragedy', p. 58.
11. 'The Troubles' is the name given to a period of conflict in Northern Ireland's history concerning the region's constitutional status and its relationship with the United Kingdom. Violence arising from this conflict was at its height from the 1960s until a political settlement was reached in 1998.
12. F. Macintosh, 'Tragic Last Words: The Big Speech and the Lament in Ancient Greek and Modern Irish Tragic Drama', in *Tragedy and the Tragic: Greek Theatre and Beyond*, ed. M. S. Silk (Oxford: Clarendon Press, 1996), p. 414.
13. Macintosh, 'Tragic Last Words', p. 414.
14. Macintosh, 'Tragic Last Words', p. 415.
15. Macintosh, 'Tragic Last Words', pp. 418–19.
16. Macintosh, 'Tragic Last Words', p. 419.
17. Macintosh, 'Tragic Last Words', p. 423.
18. S. E. Wilmer, 'Finding a Post-Colonial Voice for Antigone: Seamus Heaney's *Burial at Thebes*', in *Classics in Post-Colonial Worlds*, ed. L. Hardwick and C. Gillespie (Oxford: Oxford University Press, 2007), pp. 228–42.
19. Wilmer, 'Finding a Post-Colonial Voice', p. 235.
20. A. Fugard, '*Antigone* in Africa', in *Amid Our Troubles: Irish Versions of Greek Tragedy*, ed. M. McDonald and J. M. Walton (London: Methuen, 2002), p. 131.
21. Fugard, '*Antigone* in Africa', p. 132.
22. Fugard, '*Antigone* in Africa', p. 133.
23. B. Goff, 'Antigone's Boat: the Colonial and the Postcolonial in *Tegonni: an African Antigone* by Femi Osofisan', in *Classics in Post-Colonial Worlds*, ed. L. Hardwick and C. Gillespie (Oxford: Oxford University Press, 2007), pp. 40–53 (pp. 40–1).
24. See M. Bernal, *Black Athena: The Afroasiatic Roots of Classical Civilization* (New Brunswick: Rutgers University Press, 1987).
25. Wetmore, *Black Dionysus*, p. 15.
26. Wetmore, *Black Dionysus*, p. 3.
27. W. Soyinka, *Myth, Literature and the African World* (Cambridge: Cambridge University Press, 1976), pp. 140–60.
28. J. Adedeji, 'Traditional Yoruba Theater', *African Arts* 3.1 (Spring 1969), 60–3.
29. Adedeji, 'Traditional Yoruba Theater', p. 61.

30. Adedeji, 'Traditional Yoruba Theater', p. 63.
31. Soyinka, *Myth, Literature and the African World*, p. 141.
32. Soyinka, *Myth, Literature and the African World*, p. 142.
33. Soyinka, *Myth, Literature and the African World*, pp. 144–5.
34. Soyinka, *Myth, Literature and the African World*, p. 145.
35. Soyinka, *Myth, Literature and the African World*, pp. 148–9.

CONCLUSION: RECENT AND FUTURE DIRECTIONS

1. R. Rehm, *Radical Theatre: Greek Tragedy and the Modern World* (London: Duckworth, 2003), p. 138.
2. Rehm, *Radical Theatre*, p. 139.
3. R. Bushnell, *Tragedy: A Short Introduction* (Oxford: Blackwell, 2008), p. 113.
4. Bushnell, *Tragedy*, p. 122.
5. For recent examples of this, see G. Egan, *Green Shakespeare: From Ecopolitics to Ecocriticism* (London: Routledge, 2006); L. Bruckner and D. Brayton, eds, *Ecocritical Shakespeare* (Farnham: Ashgate, 2011); and S. C. Estok, *Ecocriticism and Shakespeare: Reading Ecophobia* (London: Palgrave Macmillan, 2011).
6. J. Meeker, 'The Comic Mode', in *The Ecocriticism Reader: Landmarks in Literary Ecology*, ed. C. Glotfelty and H. Fromm (Athens, GA: University of Georgia Press, 1996), p. 167.
7. Meeker, 'The Comic Mode', p. 157.
8. Meeker, 'The Comic Mode', p. 158.
9. A. Huxley, 'Tragedy and the Whole Truth', *Music at Night, and Other Essays* (London: Chatto & Windus, 1931), pp. 17–18.

Bibliography

GENERAL
Aristotle. *Poetics* in *Classical Literary Criticism*, ed. D. A. Russell and M. Winterbottom. Oxford: Oxford University Press, 1991.
Bradley, A. C. *Shakespearean Tragedy*. Harmondsworth: Penguin, 1991.
Brecht, B. *Brecht on Theatre: The Development of an Aesthetic*, ed. and trans. J. Willett. London: Eyre Methuen, 1974.
Camus, A. *Selected Essays and Notebooks*, ed. and trans. P. Thody. Harmondsworth: Penguin, 1970.
Drakakis, J. and N. C. Liebler, eds. *Tragedy*. London and New York: Longman, 1998.
Eagleton, T. *Sweet Violence: The Idea of the Tragic*. Oxford: Blackwell, 2003.
Felski, R., ed. *Rethinking Tragedy*. Baltimore and London: Johns Hopkins University Press, 2008.
Hegel, G. W. F. *Aesthetics: Lectures on Fine Art*, trans. T. M. Knox. Oxford: Clarendon Press, 1975. 2 vols.
Jaspers, K. *Tragedy Is Not Enough*. London: Victor Gollancz, 1953.
Kierkegaard, S. *Either/Or*, trans. A. Hannay Harmondsworth: Penguin Books, 1992.
Knox, B. M.W. *The Heroic Temper: Studies in Sophoclean Tragedy*. Berkeley and Los Angeles: University of California Press, 1964.
Lukács, G. *The Theory of the Novel*. London: Merlin Press, 1971.
Nietzsche, F. *The Birth of Tragedy*, trans., with commentary, by W. Kaufmann. New York: Random House, 1967.
Nussbaum, M. *The Fragility of Goodness: Luck and Ethics in Greek Tragedy and Philosophy*. Cambridge: Cambridge University Press, 2001.
Silk, M. S., ed. *Tragedy and the Tragic: Greek Theatre and Beyond*. Oxford: Clarendon Press, 1996.
Steiner, G. *The Death of Tragedy*. London: Faber, 1963.
Taplin, O. *Greek Tragedy in Action*. London: Taylor & Francis, 1978.
Williams, R. *Modern Tragedy*. London: Chatto & Windus, 1966.
Winkler, J. and F. Zeitlin, eds. *Nothing to Do with Dionysos? Athenian Drama in Its Social Context*. Princeton: Princeton University Press, 1990.

INTRODUCTION
Miller, A. 'The Nature of Tragedy'. In *The Theater Essays of Arthur Miller*, ed. R. A. Martin. Viking Press: New York, 1978.
Muir, K. *Shakespeare's Tragic Sequence*. London: Hutchinson, 1972.

CHAPTER ONE: THE GODS
Barber, C. L. *Shakespeare's Festive Comedy: A Study of Dramatic Form and Its Relation to Social Custom*. Princeton: Princeton University Press, 1959.
Brecht, B. *Brecht on Theatre: The Development of an Aesthetic*, ed. and trans. J. Willett. London: Eyre Methuen, 1974.
Bremmer, J. 'Scapegoat Rituals in Ancient Greece'. *Harvard Studies in Classical Philology* 87 (1983), 299–320.
Burkert, W. *Greek Religion: Archaic and Classical*. Oxford: Blackwell, 1985.

168 BIBLIOGRAPHY

Burkert, W. 'Greek Tragedy and Sacrificial Ritual'. *Greek, Roman and Byzantine Studies* 7 (1966), 87–121.
Derrida, J. *Dissemination*, trans. B. Johnson. London: Athlone Press, 1981.
Duffy, E. *The Stripping of the Altars: Traditional Religion in England 1400–1580*. New Haven and London: Yale University Press, 1992.
Easterling, P. E. 'Tragedy and Ritual: "Cry 'Woe, woe', but may the good prevail!"'. *Métis* 3 (1988), 87–109.
Elton, W. R. *King Lear and the Gods*. San Marino, CA: Huntington Library, 1966.
Gernet, L. *Anthropologie de la Grèce antique*, ed. J.-P. Vernant. Paris: F. Maspéro, 1968.
Girard, R. *Violence and the Sacred*, trans. P. Gregory Baltimore: Johns Hopkins University Press, 1977.
Goldmann, L. *Racine*, trans. A. Hamilton. Cambridge: Rivers Press, 1972.
Greenblatt, S. *Hamlet in Purgatory*. Princeton: Princeton University Press, 2001.
Harrison, J. E. *Themis: A Study of the Social Origins of Greek Religion*. London: Merlin Press, 1963.
Holloway, J. *The Story of the Night: Studies in Shakespeare's Major Tragedies*. London: Routledge & Kegan Paul, 1961.
Kott, J. *The Eating of the Gods: An Interpretation of Greek Tragedy*, trans. B. Taborksi and E. J. Czerwinski. Evanston: Northwestern University Press, 1987.
Kott, J. *Shakespeare Our Contemporary*, trans. B. Taborski. London: Methuen, 1967.
Leech, C. *Shakespeare's Tragedies: and Other Studies in Seventeenth-Century Drama*. London: Chatto & Windus, 1950.
Lesky, A. *Greek Tragedy*, trans. H. A. Frankfort. London: Ernest Benn, 1978.
Liebler, N. C. *Shakespeare's Festive Tragedy: The Ritual Foundations of Genre*. London and New York: Routledge, 1995.
Maxwell, J. C. 'The Technique of Invocation in *King Lear*'. *Modern Language Review* 45 (1950), 142–7.
Michel, L. 'The Possibility of a Christian Tragedy'. *Thought* 31 (1956), 403–28.
Milton, J. *Milton: Complete Shorter Poems*, ed. J. Carey. London: Longman, 1997.
Neill, M. *Issues of Death: Mortality and Identity in English Renaissance Tragedy*. Oxford: Clarendon Press, 1997.
O'Neill, E. 'Working Notes and Extracts from a Fragmentary Work Diary'. In *American Playwrights on Drama*, ed. H. Frenz. New York: Hill & Wang, 1965.
Pickard-Cambridge, A. W. *Dithyramb, Tragedy and Comedy*. Oxford: Clarendon Press, 1927.
Scullion, S. '"Nothing to Do with Dionysus": Tragedy Misconceived as Ritual'. *Classical Quarterly* 52 (2002), 102–37.
Segal, C. *Dionysiac Poetics and Euripides' Bacchae*. Princeton: Princeton University Press, 1982.
Segal, C. 'Greek Tragedy and Society: A Structuralist Perspective'. In *Greek Tragedy and Political Theory*, ed. J. P. Euben. Berkeley and Los Angeles: University of California Press, 1986.
Shawcross, J. T. *The Uncertain World of 'Samson Agonistes'*. Cambridge: D. S. Brewer, 2001.
Sontag, S. *Against Interpretation and Other Essays*. New York: Farrar, Straus and Giroux, 1966.
Soyinka, W. *Myth, Literature and the African World*. Cambridge: Cambridge University Press, 1976.
Waters, D. D. *Christian Settings in Shakespeare's Tragedies*. London: Associated University Presses, 1994.
Watson, R. N. *The Rest Is Silence: Death as Annihilation in the English Renaissance*. Berkeley: University of California Press, 1994.
Wittreich, J. *Interpreting 'Samson Agonistes'*. Princeton: Princeton University Press, 1986.
Woodbridge, L. and E. Berry, eds. *True Rites and Maimed Rites: Ritual and Anti-ritual in Shakespeare and His Age*. Urbana and Chicago: University of Illinois Press, 1992.
Zanin, E. 'Early Modern Oedipus: A Literary Approach to Christian Tragedy'. In *The Locus of Tragedy*, ed. A. Cools, T. Crombez, R. Slegers and J. Taels. Leiden: Brill, 2008.

CHAPTER TWO: THE CHORUS

Ferguson, T. 'Bonfire Night in Thomas Hardy's *The Return of the Native*'. *Nineteenth-Century Literature* 67.1 (2012), 87–107.

Foley, H. P. 'Choral Identity in Greek Tragedy'. *Classical Philology* 98 (2003), 1–30.

Foley, H. P. 'Envisioning the Tragic Chorus on the Modern Stage'. In *Visualizing the Tragic: Drama, Myth, and Ritual in Greek Art and Literature*, ed. C. Kraus, S. Goldhill, H. P. Foley and J. Elsner. Oxford: Oxford University Press, 2007.

Goldhill, S. 'Collectivity and Otherness – The Authority of the Tragic Chorus'. In *Tragedy and the Tragic: Greek Theatre and Beyond*, ed. M. S. Silk. Oxford: Clarendon Press, 1996.

Goldhill, S. 'The Great Dionysia and Civic Ideology'. *Journal of Hellenic Studies* 107 (1987), 58–76.

Goldmann, L. *Racine*, trans. A. Hamilton. Cambridge: Rivers Press, 1972.

Gould, J. 'Tragedy and Collective Experience'. In *Tragedy and the Tragic: Greek Theatre and Beyond*, ed. M. S. Silk. Oxford: Clarendon Press, 1996.

Hall, E. *Inventing the Barbarian: Greek Self-Definition through Tragedy*. Oxford: Clarendon Press, 1989.

Jackson-Houlston, C. M. 'Thomas Hardy's Use of Traditional Song'. *Nineteenth-Century Literature* 44.3 (1989), 301–34.

Lacan, J. *The Ethics of Psychoanalysis 1959–1960*, ed. J.-A. Miller, Book VII, trans. D. Porter. London: Routledge, 1992. In *Tragedy*, ed. J. Drakakis and N. C. Liebler. London and New York: Longman, 1998.

Lambropoulos, V. 'Greek Chorus in 09'. *Journal of Modern Greek Studies*, 28.2 (2010), 277–84.

Lukács, G. *The Theory of the Novel*. London: Merlin Press, 1971.

Meier, C. *The Political Art of Greek Tragedy*, trans. A. Webber. Cambridge: Polity Press, 1993.

Montgomery, H. C. 'Some Later Uses of the Greek Tragic Chorus'. *The Classical Journal* 38.3 (1942), 148–60.

Reed Anderson, C. 'Time, Space, and Perspective in Thomas Hardy'. *Nineteenth-Century Fiction* 9.3 (1954), 192–208.

Schiller, F. 'On the Use of the Chorus in Tragedy'. In *The Bride of Messina, William Tell and Demetrius*, trans. C. E. Passage. New York: Ungar, 1962.

Schlegel, A. W. *A Course of Lectures on Dramatic Art and Literature*. London: Henry G. Bohn, 1846.

Vernant, J.-P. *Tragedy and Myth in Ancient Greece*. Brighton: Harvester Press, 1981.

CHAPTER THREE: THE TRAGIC HERO

Bamber, L. *Comic Women, Tragic Men: A Study of Gender and Genre in Shakespeare*. Stanford: Stanford University Press, 1982.

Belsey, C. *The Subject of Tragedy: Identity and Difference in Renaissance Drama*. London and New York: Methuen, 1985.

Benjamin, W. *The Origin of German Tragic Drama*, trans. J. Osborne. In *Tragedy*, ed. J. Drakakis and N. C. Liebler. London and New York: Longman, 1998.

Boal, A. *Theater of the Oppressed*, trans. C. A. and M.-O. Leal McBride. London: Pluto Press, 1979.

Braden, G. *Renaissance Tragedy and the Senecan Tradition: Anger's Privilege*. New Haven and London: Yale University Press, 1985.

Dollimore, J. *Radical Tragedy: Religion, Ideology and Power in the Drama of Shakespeare and His Contemporaries*. Hemel Hempstead: Harvester Wheatsheaf, 1989.

Donatus. *Aeli Donati Commentum Terenti*, ed. P. Wessner. Stuttgart: Teubner, 1967.

Eliot, T. S. *Selected Essays 1917–1932*. London: Faber, 1991.

Fitz, L. T. 'Egyptian Queens and Male Reviewers: Sexist Attitudes in *Antony and Cleopatra* Criticism'. *Shakespeare Quarterly* 28.3 (1977), 297–316.

Gellrich, M. *Tragedy and Theory: The Problem of Conflict since Aristotle*. Princeton: Princeton University Press, 1988.

Hammond, P. *The Strangeness of Tragedy*. Oxford: Oxford University Press, 2009.

Hillman, D. *Shakespeare's Entrails: Belief, Scepticism and the Interior of the Body*. Basingstoke: Palgrave Macmillan, 2007.
Kelly, H. A. *Ideas and Forms of Tragedy from Aristotle to the Middle Ages*. Cambridge: Cambridge University Press, 1993.
Macintosh, F. 'Tragic Last Words: The Big Speech and the Lament in Ancient Greek and Modern Irish Tragic Drama'. In *Tragedy and the Tragic: Greek Theatre and Beyond*, ed. M. S. Silk. Oxford: Clarendon Press, 1996.
Miller, A. 'Tragedy and the Common Man'. In *The Theater Essays of Arthur Miller*, ed. R. A. Martin. Viking Press: New York, 1978.
Nevo, R. 'Tragic Form in *Romeo and Juliet*'. *Studies in English Literature, 1500–1900* 9.2 (1969), 241–58.
Padel, R. *In and Out of the Mind: Greek Images of the Tragic Self*. Princeton: Princeton University Press, 1992.
Sidney, P. 'The Defence of Poetry'. In *English Renaissance Literary Criticism*, ed. B. Vickers. Oxford: Oxford University Press, 1999.
Szondi, P. *An Essay on the Tragic*. Stanford: Stanford University Press, 2002.
Zink, S. 'The Novel as a Medium of Modern Tragedy'. *The Journal of Aesthetics and Art Criticism* 17.2 (1958), 169–73.

CHAPTER FOUR: TRAGIC WOMEN

Arnold, M. *The Poems of Matthew Arnold*, ed. K. Allott. London: Longmans, Green and Co., 1965.
Bachelard, G. *L'Eau et les rêves*. Paris: José Corti, 1942.
Bamber, L. *Comic Women, Tragic Men: A Study of Gender and Genre in Shakespeare*. Stanford: Stanford University Press, 1982.
Berry, P. *Shakespeare's Feminine Endings: Disfiguring Death in the Tragedies*. London and New York: Routledge, 1999.
Butler, J. *Antigone's Claim: Kinship Between Life and Death*. New York: Columbia University Press, 2000.
Butler, J. *Gender Trouble: Feminism and the Subversion of Identity*. New York and London: Routledge, 1990.
Callaghan, D. *Shakespeare without Women: Representing Gender and Race on the Renaissance Stage*. London: Routledge, 2000.
Eliot, G. 'The *Antigone* and Its Moral'. *Selected Critical Writings*, ed. R. Ashton. Oxford: Oxford University Press, 1992.
Fitz, L. T. 'Egyptian Queens and Male Reviewers: Sexist Attitudes in *Antony and Cleopatra* Criticism'. *Shakespeare Quarterly* 28.3 (1977), 297–316.
Foley, H. P. 'Antigone as Moral Agent'. In *Tragedy and the Tragic: Greek Theatre and Beyond*, ed. M. S. Silk. Oxford: Clarendon Press, 1996.
Foley, H. P. *Female Acts in Greek Tragedy*. Princeton: Princeton University Press, 2001.
Freud, S. 'Mourning and Melancholia'. In *The Standard Edition of the Complete Psychological Works of Sigmund Freud*, ed. J. Strachey et al., 24 vols. London: Hogarth Press, 1953–74, vol. 14.
Holt, P. '*Polis* and Tragedy in the *Antigone*'. *Mnemosyne*, Fourth Series, vol. 52, fasc. 6 (1999), 658–90.
Honig, B. *Antigone, Interrupted*. Cambridge: Cambridge University Press, 2013.
Hopkins, L. *The Female Hero in English Renaissance Tragedy*. Basingstoke: Palgrave Macmillan, 2002.
Joseph, G. 'The *Antigone* as Cultural Touchstone: Matthew Arnold, Hegel, George Eliot, Virginia Woolf, and Margaret Drabble'. *Proceedings of the Modern Language Association* 96.1 (1981), 22–35.
Lacan, J. 'Desire and the Interpretation of Desire in *Hamlet*'. In *Literature and Psychoanalysis: The Question of Reading: Otherwise*, ed. S. Felman. Baltimore: Johns Hopkins University Press, 1982.

BIBLIOGRAPHY 171

Liebler, N. C., ed. *The Female Tragic Hero in English Renaissance Drama*. Basingstoke: Palgrave Macmillan, 2002.
Loraux, N. *Tragic Ways of Killing a Woman*, trans. A. Forster. Cambridge, MA: Harvard University Press, 1987.
Rehm, R. '"If You Are a Woman": Theatrical Womanizing in Sophocles' *Antigone* and Fugard, Kani, and Ntshona's *The Island*'. In *Classics in Post-Colonial Worlds*, ed. L Hardwick and C. Gillespie. Oxford: Oxford University Press, 2007.
Sanders, M. 'Ambiguities of Mourning: Law, Custom, and Testimony of Women before South Africa's Truth and Reconcilation Commission'. In *Loss: The Politics of Mourning*, ed. D. L. Eng and D. Kazanjian. Berkeley and Los Angeles: University of California Press, 2003.
Shaw, M. 'The Female Intruder: Women in Fifth-Century Drama'. *Classical Philology* 70.4 (1975), 255–66.
Showalter, E. 'Representing Ophelia: Women, Madness, and the Responsibilities of Feminist Criticism'. In *Shakespeare and the Question of Theory*, ed. P. Parker and G. Hartman. London: Methuen, 1985.
Sourvinou-Inwood C. 'Assumptions and the Creation of Meaning: Reading Sophocles' *Antigone*'. *The Journal of Hellenic Studies* 109 (1989), 134–48.
Steiner, G. *Antigones*. Oxford: Oxford University Press, 1984.
Taplin, O. *The Stagecraft of Aeschylus: The Dramatic Use of Entrances and Exits in Greek Tragedy*. Oxford: Clarendon Press, 1977.
Woolf, V. *A Room of One's Own and Three Guineas*, ed. M. Siach. Oxford: Oxford University Press, 1992.
Zeitlin, F. I. 'Playing the Other: Theater, Theatricality, and the Feminine in Greek Drama'. In *Nothing to Do with Dionysos? Athenian Drama in Its Social Context*, ed. J. Winkler and F. Zeitlin. Princeton: Princeton University Press, 1990.

CHAPTER FIVE: TRAGIC DUALITIES

Beer, G. *Darwin's Plots: Evolutionary Narrative in Darwin, George Eliot and Nineteenth-Century Fiction*. London: Routledge & Kegan Paul, 1983.
Foley, H. P. 'The "Female Intruder" Reconsidered: Women in Aristophanes *Lysistrata* and *Ecclesiazusae*'. *Classical Philology* 77.1 (1982), 1–21.
Freud, S. 'The "Uncanny"'. In *The Standard Edition of the Complete Psychological Works of Sigmund Freud*, ed. J. Strachey et al. 24 vols. London: Hogarth Press, 1953–74), vol. 17.
Gellrich, M. *Tragedy and Theory: The Problem of Conflict since Aristotle*. Princeton: Princeton University Press, 1988.
Grene, N. *Shakespeare's Tragic Imagination*. Basingstoke: Macmillan, 1992.
Hall, E. *Inventing the Barbarian: Greek Self-Definition through Tragedy*. Oxford: Clarendon Press, 1989.
McAlindon, T. *Shakespeare's Tragic Cosmos*. Cambridge: Cambridge University Press, 1991.
McElroy, B. *Shakespeare's Mature Tragedies*. Princeton: Princeton University Press, 1973.
Meeker, J. W. 'The Comic Mode'. In *The Ecocriticism Reader: Landmarks in Literary Ecology*, ed. C. Glotfelty and H. Fromm. Athens, GA: University of Georgia Press, 1996.
Rabkin, N. *Shakespeare and the Common Understanding*. Chicago: University of Chicago Press, 1984.
Segal, C. *Dionysiac Poetics and Euripides' Bacchae*. Princeton: Princeton University Press, 1982.
Silk, M. S. and J. P. Stern, *Nietzsche on Tragedy*. Cambridge: Cambridge University Press, 1981.
Strindberg, A. 'Preface to *Miss Julie*'. In *Plays: One*, trans. and introduced by M. Meyer. London: Methuen Drama, 1989.
Tillyard, E. M. W. *The Elizabethan World Picture*. London: Chatto & Windus, 1943.
Vidal-Naquet, P. 'The Black Hunter and the Origin of the Athenian Ephebeia'. *Proceedings of the Cambridge Philological Society* 194 (1968), 49–64.

Zeitlin, F. I. 'Thebes: Theater of Self and Society in Athenian Drama'. In *Nothing to Do with Dionysos? Athenian Drama in Its Social Context*, ed. J. Winkler and F. Zeitlin. Princeton: Princeton University Press, 1990.

CHAPTER SIX: TRAGIC PLEASURE

Boal, A. *Theater of the Oppressed*, trans. C. A. and M.-O. Leal McBride. London: Pluto Press, 1979.
Brooke, N. *Horrid Laughter in Jacobean Tragedy*. London: Open Books, 1979.
Else, G. F. *Aristotle's Poetics: The Argument*. Cambridge, MA: Harvard University Press, 1957.
Freud, S. 'Beyond the Pleasure Principle'. In *On Metapsychology: The Theory of Psychoanalysis*, ed. A. Richards and J. Strachey. Harmondsworth: Penguin, 1984. Golden, L. 'Catharsis'. *Transactions and Proceedings of the Philological Association of America* 93 (1962), 51–60.
Guarini, G. 'The Compendium of Tragicomic Poetry'. In *Literary Criticism: Plato to Dryden*, ed. A. H. Gilbert. Detroit: Wayne State University Press, 1962.
Halliwell, S. *Aristotle's Poetics*. London: Duckworth, 1998.
Hume, D. *Essays Moral, Political, and Literary*, ed. E. F. Miller. Indianapolis: Liberty Classics, 1987.
Knox, B. *Word and Action: Essays on the Ancient Theater*. Baltimore: Johns Hopkins University Press, 1979.
Lear, J. 'Katharsis'. In *Essays on Aristotle's Poetics*, ed. A. O. Rorty. Princeton: Princeton University Press, 1992.
Macintosh, F. 'Tragic Last Words: The Big Speech and the Lament in Ancient Greek and Modern Irish Tragic Drama'. In *Tragedy and the Tragic: Greek Theatre and Beyond*, ed. M. S. Silk. Oxford: Clarendon Press, 1996.
Nuttall, A. D. *Why Does Tragedy Give Pleasure?* Oxford: Clarendon Press, 1996.
Pippin Burnett, A. *Catastrophe Survived: Euripides' Plays of Mixed Reversal*. Oxford: Clarendon Press, 1971.
Ray, N. *Tragedy and Otherness: Sophocles, Shakespeare, Psychoanalysis*. Bern: Peter Lang, 2009.
Saunders, G. *'Love me or kill me': Sarah Kane and the Theatre of Extremes*. Manchester and New York: Manchester University Press, 2002.
Schaper, E. 'Aristotle's Catharsis and Aesthetic Pleasure'. *The Philosophical Quarterly* 18 (1968), 131–43.
Schiller, F. 'On the Art of Tragedy'. In *Essays*, ed. W. Hinderer and D. O. Dahlstrom. New York: Continuum, 1993.
Segal, S. 'Catharsis, Audience, and Closure in Greek Tragedy'. In *Tragedy and the Tragic: Greek Theatre and Beyond*, ed. M. S. Silk. Oxford: Clarendon Press, 1996.
Sierz, A. *In-Yer-Face Theatre: British Drama Today*. London: Faber & Faber, 2000.
Trilling, L. *The Liberal Imagination: Essays on Literature and Society*. Harmondsworth: Penguin, 1970.
Weinberg, B. *A History of Literary Criticism in the Italian Renaissance*. Chicago: Chicago University Press, 1961. 2 vols.

CHAPTER SEVEN: TRAGEDY AND FORM

Brooks, P. *The Melodramatic Imagination: Balzac, Henry James, Melodrama, and the Mode of Excess*. New Haven and London: Yale University Press, 1976.
Charlton, H. B. *Castelvetro's Theory of Poetry*. Manchester: Manchester University Press, 1913.
Corneille, P. 'Discourses on Dramatic Poetry'. In *Literary Criticism: Plato to Dryden*, ed. A. H. Gilbert. Detroit: Wayne State University Press, 1962.
Dryden, J. *An Essay of Dramatic Poesy*. In *Literary Criticism: Plato to Dryden*, ed. A. H. Gilbert. Detroit: Wayne State University Press, 1962.
Heilman, R. B. 'Hardy's Sue Bridehead'. *Nineteenth-Century Fiction* 20.4 (1966), 307–23.

Huxley, A. 'Tragedy and the Whole Truth'. *Music at Night, and Other Essays*. London: Chatto & Windus, 1931.
King, J. *Tragedy in the Victorian Novel: Theory and Practice in the Novels of George Eliot, Thomas Hardy and Henry James*. Cambridge: Cambridge University Press, 1978.
Mansell, Jr, D. 'George Eliot's Conception of Tragedy'. *Nineteenth-Century Fiction* 22.2 (1967), 155–71.
Milton, J. *Milton: Complete Shorter Poems*, ed. J. Carey. London: Longman, 1997.
Parish, R. *Racine: The Limits of Tragedy*. Paris, Seattle and Tübingen: Biblio 17: Papers on French Seventeenth Century Literature, 1993.
Schiller, F. 'On the Use of the Chorus in Tragedy'. In *The Bride of Messina, William Tell and Demetrius*, trans. C. E. Passage. New York: Ungar, 1962.
Schlegel, A. W. *A Course of Lectures on Dramatic Art and Literature*. London: Henry G. Bohn, 1846.
Sidney, P. 'The Defence of Poetry'. In *English Renaissance Literary Criticism*, ed. B. Vickers. Oxford: Oxford University Press, 1999.
Spivey, T. R. 'Thomas Hardy's Tragic Hero'. *Nineteenth-Century Fiction* 9.3 (1954), 179–91.
Straznicky, M. *Privacy, Playreading, and Women's Closet Drama 1550-1700*. Cambridge: Cambridge University Press, 2004.
Wang, L. 'The "Tragic" Theatre of Corneille'. *The French Review* 25.3 (1952), 182–91.
Weinberg, B. 'Castelvetro's Theory of Poetics'. In *Critics and Criticism*, ed. R. S. Crane. Chicago: University of Chicago Press, 1952.
Zink, S. 'The Novel as a Medium of Modern Tragedy'. *The Journal of Aesthetics and Art Criticism* 17.2 (1958), 169–73.

CHAPTER EIGHT: MODERN TRAGEDY

Adorno, T. W. and M. Horkheimer. *Dialectic of Enlightenment*, trans. J. Cumming. London and New York: Verso, 1997.
Benjamin, W. *The Work of Art in the Age of Mechanical Reproduction*, trans. J. A. Underwood. Harmondsworth: Penguin, 2008.
Poole, A. *Tragedy: A Very Short Introduction*. Oxford: Oxford University Press, 2005.
Schlesinger, A. C. 'Can We Moderns Write Tragedy?'. *Transactions and Proceedings of the American Philological Association* 77 (1946), 1–21.
Szondi, P. *An Essay on the Tragic*. Stanford: Stanford University Press, 2002.

CHAPTER NINE: POSTCOLONIAL AND MULTIETHNIC TRAGEDY

Adedeji, J. 'Traditional Yoruba Theater'. *African Arts* 3.1 (1969), 60–3.
Bernal, M. *Black Athena: The Afroasiatic Roots of Classical Civilization*. New Brunswick: Rutgers University Press, 1987.
Djisenu, J. 'Cross-Cultural Bonds between Ancient Greece and Africa: Implications for Contemporary Staging Practices'. In *Classics in Post-Colonial Worlds*, ed. L. Hardwick and C. Gillespie. Oxford: Oxford University Press, 2007.
Fugard, A. '*Antigone* in Africa'. In *Amid Our Troubles: Irish Versions of Greek Tragedy*, ed. M. McDonald and J. M. Walton. London: Methuen, 2002.
Goff, B. 'Antigone's Boat: the Colonial and the Postcolonial in *Tegonni: an African Antigone* by Femi Osofisan'. In *Classics in Post-Colonial Worlds*, ed. L. Hardwick and C. Gillespie. Oxford: Oxford University Press, 2007.
Hardwick, L. and C. Gillespie, eds. *Classics in Post-Colonial Worlds*. Oxford: Oxford University Press, 2007.
Loomba, A. *Shakespeare, Race, and Colonialism*. Oxford: Oxford University Press, 2002.
McDonald, M. 'The Irish and Greek Tragedy'. In *Amid Our Troubles: Irish Versions of Greek Tragedy*, ed. J. M. Walton and M. McDonald. London: Methuen, 2002.
Soyinka, W. *Myth, Literature and the African World*. Cambridge: Cambridge University Press, 1976.

Walton, J. M. and M. McDonald, eds. *Amid Our Troubles: Irish Versions of Greek Tragedy*. London: Methuen, 2002.
Wetmore, K. *Black Dionysus: Greek Tragedy and African American Theatre*. Jefferson, NC and London: McFarland, 2003.
Wilmer, S. E. 'Finding a Post-Colonial Voice for Antigone: Seamus Heaney's *Burial at Thebes*'. In *Classics in Post-Colonial Worlds*, ed. L. Hardwick and C. Gillespie. Oxford: Oxford University Press, 2007.

CONCLUSION: RECENT AND FUTURE DIRECTIONS
Bruckner, L. and D. Brayton, eds. *Ecocritical Shakespeare*. Farnham: Ashgate, 2011.
Bushnell, R. *Tragedy: A Short Introduction*. Oxford: Blackwell, 2008.
Egan, G. *Green Shakespeare: From Ecopolitics to Ecocriticism*. London: Routledge, 2006.
Estok, S. C. *Ecocriticism and Shakespeare: Reading Ecophobia*. London: Palgrave Macmillan, 2011.
Glotfelty, C. and H. Fromm, eds. *The Ecocriticism Reader: Landmarks in Literary Ecology*. Athens, GA: University of Georgia Press, 1996.
Rehm, R. *Radical Theatre: Greek Tragedy and the Modern World*. London: Duckworth, 2003.

Index

Adorno, Theodor, 125
Aeschylus
  Agamemnon, 27, 51, 70
  Agamemnon, 8, 52, 59, 117
    see also *Oresteia*
  Eumenides, 26–7, 152
    see also *Oresteia*
  Oresteia, 19, 164
  Clytaemnestra, 62, 63, 70, 84
  Persians, 86, 152
  Prometheus Bound, 32
  Prometheus, 8
  Suppliants, 84
Aristotle, 3, 5, 7, 26, 41, 48–9, 54–5, 58, 60, 76, 81, 82, 93, 96, 97, 98, 100–6, 109, 111, 112, 116, 119, 120, 122
Arnold, Matthew, 73

Beckett, Samuel, 20, 57
Belsey, Catherine, 3, 45–7, 48, 59, 61
Benjamin, Walter, 51–2, 124–5
Black Medea, 141–2
Boal, Augusto, 58, 60, 103–4, 109
boundaries, 12, 13, 24, 35, 68, 94–5, 107, 113
Bradley, A. C., 2, 3, 20, 41–2, 49–50, 51, 54, 55, 59, 60, 64, 65, 117
Brecht, Bertolt, 5, 9, 90, 115, 125–6, 130, 140, 147
Butler, Judith, 62, 78

Cambridge School, 8, 10
Camus, Albert, 15–16, 124, 126
catharsis, 5, 58, 96, 99, 100–6, 108, 109, 116, 119, 146
chorus, 3, 18, 26–40, 59, 69, 81, 91, 93, 109, 114, 115, 121
Christianity, 15, 16–25
  see also God
class, social, 37, 49, 51–3, 66, 89, 90–1, 95
  see also rank
comedy, 4, 7, 13, 30, 48–9, 51, 54, 82–3, 89, 97, 112–13, 118, 127, 146
Corneille, Pierre, 5, 20, 113–14, 115
culture industry, 125

Darwin, Charles, 4, 89, 95, 119
Dionysus, 7, 8–9, 18, 24, 48, 63, 92–5, 141, 142
Dollimore, Jonathan, 3, 45, 59, 64, 90
Dryden, John, 5, 107, 114

Eagleton, Terry, 1, 6, 90, 96, 98, 117, 121, 131
ecocriticism, 147
Eliot, George, 5, 51, 73–4, 119–20
Euripides, 36, 42, 69, 95, 126–7
  Andromache, 7
  Bacchae, 7, 12, 18, 63, 94, 134, 135
  Agave, 63
  Electra, 127
  Hecuba, 152
  Hecuba, 70
  Helen, 98
  Heracles see *Herakles*
  Herakles, 85
  Hippolytus, 7, 18
  Hippolytos, 8
  Phaedra, 63
  Ion, 98
  Iphigeneia in Tauris, 98
  Medea, 63, 142
  Medea, 8, 11, 63, 70, 84
  Medeia see Medea
    see also Black Medea; Seneca, *Medea*
  Phoenissae, 27
  Suppliant Women, 85
  Trojan Women, 38

fate, 4, 19, 21, 43, 52, 54, 56, 90, 92, 121, 147
film, 1, 124, 137, 146, 148, 149
Foley, Helene, 3, 27, 31–2, 34, 36, 37–8, 40, 61–3, 69–70, 75–6, 84–5
Frankfurt School, 5, 90, 124–5, 128
Freud, Sigmund, 53, 60, 79, 99–100, 108
  Oedipus complex, 53
  pleasure principle, 100
  unheimlich, 58
Fugard, Athol, 139–40

175

176 INDEX

ghosts, 23, 24, 88
Girard, René, 2, 10, 11–12, 14, 24
God, 17, 18–19, 20, 21, 22, 33, 46, 130, 137
  see also Christianity
gods, the, 4, 7, 8, 10–11, 14, 15, 17, 18,
  19, 21, 29, 33, 43, 58, 63, 83, 88,
  91, 94, 134, 137, 142–3, 147
  see also Dionysus
Goethe, Johann von, 81
Goldhill, Simon, 3, 9, 29, 30, 31, 81
Greenblatt, Stephen, 3, 22, 24, 25
grotesque, 5, 20–1, 51, 106, 107, 109, 113
guilt, 4, 11, 12, 19, 20, 21, 54–60, 67, 89,
  91, 105, 128
  see also hamartia

hamartia, 3–4, 20, 54–5, 58–9, 60, 62
  see also guilt
Hardwick, Lorna, 6, 134, 135
Hardy, Thomas, 5, 6, 39, 119, 121–2
Heaney, Seamus, 138–9
Hegel, G. W. F., 4, 5, 40, 46, 50, 51, 55,
  56, 74, 75, 78, 82, 83, 84, 85, 88,
  89, 91–2, 106, 109
heredity, 89, 119
history, 21, 51, 82, 89, 126, 131
Homer, 5, 48, 69, 120
Horkheimer, Max, *see under* Frankfurt
  School
Hume, David, 4, 98–9, 104, 109
Huxley, Aldous, 120–1, 123, 149

Ibsen, Henrik, 129
in-yer-face theatre, *see* Theatre of
  Extremes
isolation, 33, 42, 43, 50, 59

James, Henry, 119

Kane, Sarah, 6, 107–8, 109–10, 125, 148
  see also Theatre of Extremes
Kierkegaard, Søren, 4, 18, 55–6, 58, 60,
  128
Knox, B. M. W., 3, 42–3, 50, 55, 59, 75
Kott, Jan, 12, 20–2, 108–9

Lacan, Jacques, 32, 67
Loraux, Nicole, 4, 70–1, 80
Lukács, Georg, 15, 28–9, 50, 90, 130

Macintosh, Fiona, 6, 47, 100, 137–8
Mandela, Nelson, 139–40
Marx, Karl, 4, 89, 95, 125
Marxism, 21, 89

Marxist criticism, 2, 5, 45, 59, 89–90, 131,
  145
mask, 2, 27, 48, 94, 127, 142
melodrama, 42, 113, 118, 128
Miller, Arthur, 1, 3, 6, 42, 52–4, 55, 60,
  131, 133
Milton, John, 17, 116

naturalism, 33, 35, 114–15
  see also realism
New Attic Comedy, 127
new historicist critics, 3, 22, 23
Nietzsche, Friedrich, 4, 5, 35, 40, 57, 88,
  92–5, 98, 126–7, 142–4
novel, 5, 39, 40, 51, 89, 116, 117–23, 142,
  146
Nuttall, A. D., 4–5, 96, 98, 101–2, 105

O'Neill, Eugene, 19, 39, 90
orchestra, 26, 27, 38

Paulin, Tom, 137
peripeteia, 7, 104, 120
pharmakos, 10, 11–13, 14
  see also scapegoat
Plato, 29, 93, 96, 97
pleasure, 4–5, 69, 93–4, 95, 96–100,
  104–5, 109, 110
  see also catharsis
polis, 3, 4, 29, 37, 75, 76, 77, 84–5, 92,
  109
Purgatory, 16, 22, 23, 24

Racine, Jean, 6, 33, 113, 115, 126
rank, 3, 49, 53, 60, 123
  see also class, social
realism, 20, 115, 122, 127
  see also naturalism
revenge, 23, 24, 137
ritual, 2, 3, 6, 7–14, 22, 23, 24, 37, 62, 72,
  77, 94–5, 101, 105, 124, 129, 134,
  137, 142–3

sacrifice, 2, 4, 7, 10–13, 14, 20, 24, 57, 64,
  70, 72, 108
scapegoat, 10, 11, 12, 13, 14, 24, 72, 104
  see also pharmakos
Schiller, Friedrich, 3, 33–4, 35, 40, 43, 99,
  114, 115
Schlegel, August von Wilhelm, 3, 34–6,
  40, 111, 114–15, 122
science, 4, 125–6, 127, 130, 147
Segal, Charles, 8, 10–11, 44, 46, 81, 94–5,
  105

INDEX 177

Seneca, 6, 24, 36, 43, 44, 47, 48, 58
   Hercules, 58
   Medea, 47
Shakespeare, William, 2, 3, 4, 5, 6, 8, 13–14, 19, 20, 21–2, 36, 41–2, 47–8, 49–50, 54, 55, 59, 60, 61, 63, 64–9, 80, 86–9, 95, 105, 112, 117, 119, 125, 126, 128, 134, 135–6, 147, 148
   Antony and Cleopatra, 41, 47, 65–6, 67, 105, 136
      Antony, 44, 49, 65, 136
      Cleopatra, 65–6, 136
   Coriolanus, 67, 105
      Coriolanus, 49
      Volumnia, 66
   Cymbeline, 19, 55
   Hamlet, 24, 45, 54, 67–9, 86–7, 88–9, 105
      Hamlet, 8, 24, 44, 67, 69 87
      Ophelia, 67–9
   Henry V, 36
   Julius Caesar, 88–9, 105
   King Lear, 12, 17, 19, 20–2, 49, 67, 86, 87
      Cordelia, 20, 68
      Lear, 8, 44, 52, 65
   Macbeth, 41, 67, 86, 87, 124–5
      Lady Macbeth, 66
      Macbeth, 8, 65, 115, 124
   Othello, 64–5, 67, 86, 87, 88, 136, 148
      Desdemona, 64–5, 68, 87, 88
      Othello, 47–8, 64–5, 87, 88
   Richard II, 14
   Romeo and Juliet, 14, 36, 41, 49, 105
      Juliet, 14, 65, 68
   Titus Andronicus, 88, 136
   Troilus and Cressida, 86
   The Winter's Tale, 19, 55, 162
Sidney, Philip, 3, 5, 49, 97, 112–13
sin, 19, 20, 22, 56, 57, 89
   see also hamartia
soliloquy, 3, 46–7, 48
Sophocles, 42–3, 126
   Ajax, 26–7, 31
      Ajax, 11, 27
   Antigone, 4, 16, 30, 51, 73–80, 81, 83, 84, 92, 95, 120, 135, 137, 139–40
      Antigone, 8, 57, 59, 62, 71, 73–80, 92, 140
   Oedipus Rex, 101
      see also Oedipus Tyrannus
   Oedipus Tyrannus, 47, 59, 116
      Oedipus, 11, 20, 53, 54, 57, 58–9, 79, 103, 108
      Oidipous (Oedipus), 8
      see also Oedipus complex; *Oedipus Rex*
   Philoctetes, 47
      Philoctetes, 59
   Trachiniae, 47
soul, 16, 22–3, 53, 65, 71, 101, 105, 130, 138, 143
Soyinka, Wole, 6, 8, 14–15, 134–5, 142–4
Steiner, George, 2, 4, 6, 17, 19, 26, 28, 33, 36, 37, 48, 51, 57, 58, 60, 73, 74–5, 83, 115, 117–18, 124, 126, 128–30, 133, 148
Stoicism, 47, 97
Strindberg, August, 90–1, 95
sublime, the, 43, 82

Taplin, Oliver, 9
Theatre of Extremes, 5, 107–9
tragicomedy, 113
Trauerspiel, 51
Trilling, Lionel, 100, 109
Troubles, the, 137

the unities, 5, 103, 111–12, 113, 114, 115, 122, 128
unity, 35, 45, 82, 91, 93

Vernant, Jean-Pierre, 3, 9, 29, 30, 39, 44, 81

Wagner, Richard, 128
Watson, Robert, 3, 22, 23
Webster, John, 46, 64, 71
Williams, Raymond, 2, 6, 15, 19, 44, 52, 81, 124, 129–31, 133, 147

Yeats, W. B., 137–8
Yoruba drama, *see* Soyinka, Wole

Zeitlin, Froma, 3, 63–4, 71, 85, 95